TORTURING TERRORISTS

This book considers the theoretical, policy and empirical arguments relevant to the debate concerning the legalisation of interrogational torture. *Torturing Terrorists* examines, as part of a consequentialist analysis, the nature and impact of torture and the implications of its legal regulation on individuals, institutions and wider society. In making an argument against the use of torture, the book engages in a wide-ranging interdisciplinary analysis of the arguments and claims that are put forward by the proponents and opponents of legalised torture.

This book examines the ticking bomb hypothetical and explains how the component parts of the hypothetical are expansively interpreted in theory and practice. It also considers the effectiveness of torture in producing 'ticking bomb' and 'infrastructure' intelligence and examines the use of interrogational torture and coercion by state officials in Northern Ireland, Algeria, Israel and as part of the CIA's 'High Value Detainee' interrogation programme. As part of an empirical slippery slope argument, this book examines the difficulties in drafting the text of a torture statute; the difficulties of controlling the use of interrogational torture; and problems such a law could create for state officials and wider society. Finally, it critically evaluates suggestions that debating the legalisation of torture is dangerous and should be avoided.

The book will be of interest to students and academics of criminology, law, sociology and philosophy, as well as the general reader.

Philip N.S. Rumney is Professor of Criminal Justice at Bristol Law School, UWE. He has written a number of articles on the debate over the legalisation of inter-rogational torture, including a detailed analysis of the effectiveness (or otherwise) of torture as a means of producing accurate and timely intelligence disclosures. He has also authored work that examines the way in which interrogational torture can serve to undermine counter-terrorism strategies by provoking retaliation or hardening the resolve of terrorist groups and their supporters. Amongst his various research interests Philip engages in research concerning rape and freedom of expression. This work has been cited in various government reports, reviews and parliamentary debates. He is actively engaged in several empirical and developmental projects concerning sexual violence, including a school-based sexual violence myth-busting project; a domestic and sexual violence bystander intervention project; an evalua-tion of a specialis   titudes towards people charged w

'It is an unfortunate truth that the issue of torture continues to be a matter of debate, particularly in regard to "wars on terror" and, therefore, terrorists. The strength of Professor Rumney's valuable book lies not only in the insight of a sharp critical intelligence, but also in his skill at presenting and assessing such empirical information that is relevant to considering the claims about the actual consequences of resorting to torture as a matter of public policy. It would make a wonderful assignment in any course on the subject, though it should also be read and discussed by policymakers as well who may be tempted to believe that "torture works".'

Sanford Levinson, W. St. John Garwood and W. St. John Garwood, Jr. Centennial Chair and Professor of Government, The University of Texas at Austin, USA

'There is a general consensus in the public debate that the state should never use torture as a means of interrogating terrorists and that the use of torture as a tool of interrogation is so clearly contrary to democratic values that even the discussion of his topic has become virtually taboo. Phil Rumney, in this courageous and pathbreaking study, challenges the view that the issues surrounding the use of torture have been finally settled and cannot be discussed. Instead, he makes a compelling case that without confronting the moral dilemmas presented by the use of torture in the face of the threats posed by international terrorism the absolute prohibition of the use of torture may not be sustainable. This book makes an invaluable and original contribution to a controversial, but important, public debate.'

Christoph Bluth, Professor of International Relations and Security, University of Bradford, UK

TORTURING TERRORISTS

Exploring the limits of law, human rights and academic freedom

Philip N.S. Rumney

Routledge
Taylor & Francis Group

LONDON AND NEW YORK

First published 2015
by Routledge
2 Park Square, Milton Park, Abingdon, Oxon OX14 4RN

and by Routledge
711 Third Avenue, New York, NY 10017

Routledge is an imprint of the Taylor & Francis Group, an informa business

British Library Cataloguing in Publication Data
A catalogue record for this book is available from the British Library

Library of Congress Cataloging in Publication Data
Rumney, Philip N. S., author.
Torturing terrorists : exploring the limits of law, human rights, and academic freedom / Philip NS Rumney.
1. Torture (International law) 2. Torture victims--Legal status, laws, etc.
3. Detention of persons. 4. Terrorism--Prevention--Law and legislation.
5. Military interrogation. 6. Human rights. I. Title.
KZ7170.R86 2014
344.05'254--dc23
2014012536

ISBN: 978-0-415-67162-0 (hbk)
ISBN: 978-0-415-67163-7 (pbk)
ISBN: 978-0-203-08334-5 (ebk)

Typeset in Bembo
by Taylor & Francis Books

MIX
Paper from
responsible sources
FSC
www.fsc.org   FSC® C013604

Printed and bound by CPI Group (UK) Ltd, Croydon, CR0 4YY

For Mum,
Sam Burton and Martin O'Boyle

CONTENTS

ACKNOWLEDGEMENTS

It is customary for book authors to claim that their work would not have been possible without the support of friends, family and colleagues. This book is no different. I want to thank Heidi Lee of Routledge, who has shown enormous patience when deadlines have slipped. Special thanks go to my mum for her love and support. Without her I may have given up on education altogether. My colleagues and friends have also been an invaluable source of distraction and advice, including Steve Riley, Rachel Fenton, Dean Rhodes, Mark O'Brien, Lauren Rees and Ed Cape. Thanks go to Tove Oliver, who provided much support and encouragement when I received rejection letters from several publishers. I also want to say a huge thank you to my two closest friends, Sam Burton and Martin O'Boyle. Their friendship has provided a welcome distraction from the writing of this book while we have discussed and debated anything and everything related to work, politics and combat sports. Mandy Ingram has shown great patience, love, humour and support, plus coffee, cake and a keen eye for detail. Archie Ingram has provided the welcome distraction of cowboy gunfights. Huge thanks to my personal trainers and boxing coach, Gavin Brown, Trevor Scott and Dan Sarkozi. Over the last few years they have helped me work off the chocolate and made the pain of training worthwhile with their friendship.

During the writing of much of this book I have had to deal with the challenge of worsening health. In April 2013, I was fortunate to be the recipient of a double organ transplant at the Churchill Hospital Transplant Centre in Oxford. The love and support of my family and friends helped enormously in dealing with the challenges and aftermath of the operation, along with some of the other difficulties thrown up by life in the last five years. Special thanks must go to the extraordinary consultants, surgeons and nurses at the Churchill Hospital, Southmead Hospital and the Bristol Royal Infirmary.

I would like to thank Adrian Vermeule of Harvard Law School for his encouragement of this project. Despite our disagreements on many matters of substance, he has always shown me civility and a willingness to engage in dialogue. I wish to express my appreciation to Michael Welsh of Rutgers University, who has been supportive. I would also like to thank the anonymous external reviewers who commented on chapter drafts. They provided invaluable feedback with a mixture of praise and blistering criticism. I hope I have made sufficient revisions to address their concerns. I would specifically like to acknowledge an anonymous reviewer who recommended against this book being given a contract on the grounds that the book proposal was 'cast in terms of evidence and debate'. S/he apparently could see a 'strong sub text' that could 'legitimate' torture and was reason to reject the proposal: 'This book is concerned with raising an argument which might legitimate torture and I have an in principle position against supporting or providing platforms for those who wish to legalise (however that legaisation [sic] is couched) what is a vile and corrosive crime.' Without this attempt to silence me I may never have completed this book. The reviewer provided the motivation for me to finish. For that, I offer my thanks.

There are short passages in Chapter 3 that originally appeared in P. Rumney, 'The Torture Debate: A Perspective from the United Kingdom' in J. Moran and M. Phythian (eds.), *Intelligence, Security and Policing Post-9/11: the UK's Response to the 'War on Terror'* (London: Palgrave Macmillan, 2008). Thanks go to Palgrave for allowing me to re-use these passages in this book.

INTRODUCTION

Beatings, threats, mock executions, stress positions, murder, sexual assault and humiliation, drowning, punching, slapping, dragging and kicking. These are just some of the interrogation techniques officially authorised, permitted on an *ad hoc* basis or practised by Western intelligence agencies, military forces or close allies who 'softened up' or interrogated detainees as part of the War on Terror. For over a decade we have witnessed the publication of a large number of articles, books, inquiry reports and news stories concerning the use of these, and other techniques. In addition, scholars, journalists and government officials have debated the moral legitimacy and legality of interrogational torture as a means of gaining intelligence from terrorist suspects. There is, of course, a social and historic background to these events. The use of interrogational torture to gain information attracts significant public support[1] and is a long-standing feature of popular culture, including its portrayal in films such as *Dirty Harry* and television drama and comedy series such as *American Dad!*, *NYPD Blue* and *24*.[2]

More important, however, was that following 9/11 it was suggested that a security environment had emerged in which 'the U.S. had entered an age of terror'[3] and this had 'changed everything'.[4] Scholars have suggested that there had been a change in the terrorist threat and society faced a 'new terrorism' more deadly than that perpetrated by terrorist groups such as the Irish Republican Army (IRA).[5] While such claims have been challenged,[6] empirical evidence suggests that jihadist-motivated terrorism associated with the like of al Qaeda and its allies appears to be significantly more deadly than terrorism carried out by other groups[7] and suggests a commitment to mass-casualty terrorism.[8] In the last decade a number of democracies have sought to sidestep or reconfigure the absolute legal prohibition against torture as part of their counter-terrorism strategies.[9] As such, the discussion of torture has slipped from a 'theoretical provocation' to a 'doctrinal debate' fuelled by terrorism and other criminal acts.[10] In this debate it is argued that in times of emergency, security considerations must take primacy over the legal rights of terror suspects not to be tortured when they refuse to disclose life-saving information.

Recourse to torture as a means of responding to crises has a long history in democracies.[11] As such, discussion concerning the utility of interrogational torture is not simply a product of a post-9/11 panic. Some opponents of torture have described the use or legalisation of torture as a previously 'undiscussable' topic.[12] This is simply untrue. Discussions and debates concerning the desirability, or otherwise, of using interrogational torture have existed in the realms of law, theology and philosophy for many centuries.[13] Indeed, prior to 9/11, the endorsement of interrogational torture and coercion in extreme cases was evident amongst legal scholars and judges.[14] However, the post-9/11 response to al Qaeda is perhaps exceptional in the sense of the open and prolonged endorsement of torture, or other highly coercive interrogational techniques, by governments and within the scholarly community.[15] The underpinnings of the torture debate can be found in earlier emergencies and conflicts. Rejali notes that: '[a]s a matter of historical record, torture has characterised democratic as well as authoritarian states.'[16] Further, recourse to torture and other forms of coercion appears to be justified as part of 'historic narratives'[17] suggesting torture works in producing reliable intelligence and is therefore necessary.[18] Indeed, two days after 9/11 President George W. Bush discussed how he would turn uncooperative detainees over to the Saudi government.[19] This brief discussion of recent events is illustrative of the way in which 'so terrible a power'[20] can be seen to have utility by scholars, and more importantly, by states that profess a commitment to human rights.

1. The argument

Given the existing literature, it is reasonable to question whether this book can say anything new about interrogational torture and the debate over its legalisation. In the view of this author, there is still something important to be said on the topic.[21] The argument set out in this book can be simply put. The use of legalised interrogational torture against terrorist suspects would involve the adoption of an inherently expansive power. The case for legalised torture is that such a system can operate in a controlled, effective and timely manner in order to deal with grave, time-limited circumstances. As part of a consequentialist analysis it will be argued that these claims are incorrect and that legalised torture would bestow on the state an ill-defined, expansive power that may actually serve to undermine the counter-terrorist strategies of the state. This expansive power derives from various factors, including the consequentialist underpinnings used to justify legalised torture, the vagaries of language and the various mechanisms that lead to slippage and unintended consequences. In order to illustrate the problems described, this book will critically examine the three most commonly cited arguments in the torture debate: the ticking bomb hypothetical as a circumstance where torture could be legitimately used, torture as an effective interrogation tool and legalised torture as a controlled and targeted state power.

This consequentialist argument is viewed through the lens of the debate concerning the legalisation of interrogational torture. As such, the book is not primarily concerned with setting out a moral argument, although use will be made of moral theory when appropriate. The main focus will be on using evidence in order to provide an empirically-based argument against the legalisation of interrogational torture. The argument set out in the book is cumulative and involves a convergence of evidence. There is no single empirical-based argument or theory that can stand alone in rejecting the case for legalised torture. Instead, the case against legalisation rests on a series of inter-related arguments based on empirical evidence and consequentialist reasoning. It is this approach that supports the idea that there are certain actions perpetrated by the state that should never be tolerated in law, including torturing a terrorist suspect and thereby treating him as a means to an end. This book, however, does not set out a one-directional approach, it critically analyses arguments put forward on both sides of the debate.[22] It acknowledges that weak ideas exist on both sides, although it is the case for legalisation that is particularly flawed.[23] On this basis it is argued that the absolute prohibition should be retained.

Chapter 1 argues that the case against legalised torture can best be made through the use of a wide-ranging examination of consequences that will bolster deontological claims that there are certain ways of treating people that are unacceptable in all circumstances. It will be argued that the absolute legal prohibition on torture is a high status right that should not be balanced with security interests in the development of legal policy. The chapter will use utilitarian theory espoused by Bentham and Mill to support the case against legalisation by suggesting that the use of interrogational torture may be self-defeating, in that it could provoke counter-violence and reduce community co-operation with state officials. It acknowledges that there are empirical uncertainties in this area and as such the case against legalisation requires a broad analysis of consequences. Finally, it will be acknowledged that the argument that torture is worse than other forms of regulated state power and so should never be tolerated is not entirely convincing. Instead, the case against legalisation has to be based on additional grounds.

As part of this consequentialist argument, Chapter 2 explains the way in which the ticking bomb hypothetical is used to bolster the case for legalised interrogational torture. It examines each component part of the hypothetical and explains that in theory and practice it is applicable to a wide variety of situations and is not limited, as proponents of legalisation claim, to grave or catastrophic cases. These arguments often slip from ticking bomb cases to those involving much more imprecise and distant threats that could be prevented by means other than interrogational torture. They are also used to justify torture outside of time-limited circumstances and against those who are not terrorists. This chapter points out that proponents of legalised torture simply fail to engage with the empirical literature in this regard. However, so do the opponents of legalisation. They argue that the hypothetical is a fraud and unreal. They generally fail to test these claims and, as a result, make flawed arguments. The chapter concludes by arguing that a better approach is to acknowledge that ticking bomb-type events do sometimes occur, but the component parts of the hypothetical are expansively defined in theory and practice so as to undermine any notion of a tightly controlled state power.

Chapter 3 examines the question of whether interrogational torture works as a means of obtaining timely and reliable intelligence that can help prevent imminent terrorist attacks. It examines a number of factors that undermine the effectiveness of interrogational torture such as the use of cell structures by terrorist groups which limit the damage to a group if a cell member discloses information. A key part of the chapter is the division of intelligence into 'ticking bomb' and 'infrastructure' intelligence. Only the former will lead to the location of a ticking bomb, while the latter may disrupt the longer term activities of a group. The subsequent discussion considers a wide body of evidence which suggests that there is a very little evidence that torture can or will prevent imminent terrorist attacks, but there is a larger body of evidence which suggests that it may produce infrastructure intelligence. However, it is argued that this latter body of evidence, assuming it is reliable, does not lend support to the legalisation of interrogational torture. If a torture law were drafted so as to allow for the use of torture in infrastructure cases then it would lead to the torturing of potentially all suspected terrorists because such knowledge is widely held. If, however, a narrowly drafted law were introduced that only allows for the use of torture in true ticking bomb-type cases then such a change in legal policy would be based on an extremely limited body of empirical evidence. The first approach would lead to the regular use of torture; the second would result in a torture law replete with uncertainties about its future utility. This chapter concludes by arguing that this is not a basis on which to overturn the absolute prohibition.

Chapter 4 sets out two approaches to the legalisation of interrogational torture. One is a standards-based approach and the other involves the wording of an actual torture law which sets out an exception to the absolute prohibition. The purpose of this analysis is to critically examine the claim of proponents that torture can be successfully regulated without the risk of unintended consequences. It explains the different ways in which such laws could be expansively interpreted and suggests that slippage would not be prevented by either regulatory approach. It is also noted that the logic of the consequentialist argument put forward by proponents of legalisation means that interrogational torture would be unlikely to be limited to rare cases. Indeed, some proponents extend their case for legislation to include its use within the criminal justice system. The chapter utilises theoretical work that has been done on so-called slippery slope arguments and identifies a wide range of examples of slippage in the use of interrogational torture. It also explores the various mechanisms that lead to slippage, including stress, error, lack of accountability and leadership failures. The chapter concludes by pointing out that proponents of legalisation have failed to explain how such examples of slippage could be prevented or at least minimised.

Chapter 5 explains why discussing and debating the legalisation of interrogational torture is important. It challenges arguments that legalisation should be undiscussable and that it is dangerous to debate the topic. This chapter makes the case that the failure to discuss the topic may pose dangers for the absolute prohibition. Discussion allows for the development of stronger ideas to defend the absolute prohibition and also enables the arguments of the proponents of legalised torture to be fully analysed. The chapter also challenges those who have endeavoured to silence discussion of this topic and have engaged in personal vilification in response to dissenting opinions; it rejects such efforts as unscholarly and argues that they pose a risk to the prohibition. It is not so much debate or discussion that is problematic or dangerous; it is a failure to address the arguments for legalisation and to develop counter-arguments based on the wider empirical literature.

2. The need for factual analysis

Darius Rejali, who is arguably the leading contemporary writer on democracies and torture, has noted that in some widely cited texts in the torture debate: '[i]t is as if no one knows or has the time to research the huge range of institutional and social factors that would be necessary to answer the key empirical questions on which the torture debate turns.'[24] He also describes some commonly cited arguments for and against the use of interrogational torture as 'lame'.[25] Similarly, Matthews argues that amongst proponents of the use of torture there is an 'absence of [the] careful empiricism' that is required to answer key questions regarding the nature and consequences of torture.[26] In reality, much of the scholarly work in the torture debate suffers from a failure to engage in a critical examination of evidence. This is a problem that characterises counter-terrorism policy generally: 'recommendations for action ... [often] ... have little empirical grounding.'[27] What is needed then is a careful reading of the existing empirical literature and analysis of this material in order to identify reliable claims, error and gaps in our understanding.[28]

If a consequentialist argument in the torture debate is to be taken seriously, then the factual claims and evidence that underpin such an approach must be carefully considered. Many of those participating in the torture debate have exhibited a decidedly mixed approach to the use of evidence and certain trends are apparent in the manner by which scholars argue their respective positions. Assertions of fact are sometimes made with no solid, empirical grounding. Elsewhere, claims are attributed to source material that is unreliable or limited. There is a further problem and that is a failure to consider counter-evidence or argument. Hexter argued that scholars ' ... need to look for vulnerabilities in that thesis and to contrive means of testing them. Then, depending on what he finds, he can support the thesis, strengthen its weak points, or modify it to eliminate its weaknesses.'[29] Such an approach is likely to provide a more compelling argument than a one-directional approach to evidence. The case for retaining the absolute prohibition cannot be based on wishful thinking, false assertions of fact and or an unwillingness to consider theory, evidence or arguments that may serve to challenge current legal norms. It is just as important to identify weaknesses in the case for the prohibition, as it is to identify weaknesses in the case for legalisation. This does not mean that there exists some moral or evidential equivalence. Instead, identifying unsound arguments can assist in producing a more compelling case for the prohibition. Of course, subjecting the case against legalisation to the 'light of reason'[30] may not be welcomed by some scholars. As Berlin has noted, attacks on the 'central principles of the Enlightenment', including ideas of reason, rationality and objectivity have 'occurred in various forms, conservative or liberal, reactionary or revolutionary, depending on which systematic order was being attacked'.[31] If the absolute prohibition is to be effectively defended from calls for the legalisation of torture, arguments on both sides require critical evaluation.

The available evidence takes many forms, including carefully conducted empirical studies, court judgments,[32] hearing records, interviews with interrogators, terrorists and those suspected of involvement in terrorism, investigations by journalists and anecdotal evidence. It cannot be assumed that every data source is necessarily accurate, as state officials,[33] terrorists and others[34] may have reason to lie or exaggerate. Indeed, training provided to some terrorist groups stipulates that members should lie about being tortured.[35] Allegations of torture are often difficult to verify[36] and are often contested.[37] Medical evidence, however, may provide powerful evidence of abuse.[38] Some factual claims have strong corroborative support, others less so or none at all. Consequently, some degree of caution should be observed when using uncorroborated factual claims. However, caution should be even-handed. This has not always been evident within the torture debate. For example, Brecher dismisses examples of where it has been claimed that imminent terrorist attacks have been thwarted by the use of interrogational torture on the following basis: 'the only evidence available about real ticking bomb cases is anecdotal and thus inconclusive.'[39] However, Brecher accepts human rights reports, which also contain much anecdotal testimony, as reliable and supportive of his thesis.[40] If anecdotal evidence should be labelled as 'inconclusive' by an author in one instance, then all similar evidence should be treated in the same manner irrespective of whether or not it appears to support a view favoured by the author.

Anecdotal evidence should always be read with a degree of caution bearing in mind the potential for self-serving arguments or claims. Likewise, accounts of involvement in torture which utilise personal attacks and conversations with unnamed third parties, also have to be treated with caution.[41] A consistent approach to evidence should be adopted. The fact that evidence is uncorroborated or anecdotal does not make it untrue, particularly if there is some acknowledgement of torture by state officials. Indeed, Mann and Shatz argue that in determining the state use of torture it is possible to use the public statements of officials which may suggest that certain forms of torture are tolerated.[42] It is sometimes suggested that the use of interrogational torture has prevented terrorist attacks. Some dismiss such claims out-of-hand simply on the basis that they are made by state officials who have a vested interest in portraying their conduct in a favourable light.[43] Such evidence should, undoubtedly, attract a careful reading, but cannot be dismissed outright without good reason. Further, distinctions should be made between cases where a source is recounting first-hand involvement and those where someone is recounting a story they have been told.[44] First-hand accounts might offer compelling evidence where it includes claims that can be corroborated by other available sources. These accounts might have particular strength when the disclosure places the person recounting the event in an unfavourable light.[45]

3. A note on terminology

The title of this book is Torturing *Terrorists*. It is not Torturing *Suspected* Terrorists. This should not lead any reader to assume that this distinction is not properly recognised in the text. The book, in fact, engages in a detailed examination of this issue and points to the difficulties of identifying terrorists, and in particular, those with the knowledge sought in ticking bomb cases. Distinguishing between terrorists and terrorist *suspects* is a core concern when analysing the consequences of legalising interrogational torture. The book also makes repeated reference to the *proponents* of legalised interrogational torture and *opponents* of legalisation. The author makes careful use of these terms to ensure that it is clear who is proposing or opposing what. Within the literature, it is sometimes less clear whether those who argue that torture is morally justified in certain situations would favour its legalisation. Wherever this is unclear the author has endeavoured to focus on the arguments made and how they could be used to support or oppose legalisation.

Within the current torture debate reference is made to torture, inhuman and degrading treatment, coercive interrogation and many other words or phrases to describe interrogation practices that are either illegal or arguably so. A discussion of the meaning of torture is outside the scope of this book. Instead, this book makes a case against the legalisation of interrogational torture, irrespective of what legal meaning attaches to the word. Efforts to manipulate or restrict the meaning of torture are viewed by the author as unacceptable but discussion of this issue does not fall within the remit of this book. Occasionally reference is made to coercive interrogation or coercion to denote a broad range of techniques that might be classed as inhuman or degrading treatment. In the literature, the names of persons, such as Khalid Sheikh Mohammed, or organisations such as al Qaeda are spelled in several different ways, depending on the source. This book will adopt single spelling, with the exception of quotations.

Finally, this book is primarily concerned with state responses to violent non-state actors who engage in terrorist activity. This is not meant to deny that states sometimes sponsor terrorism, as the Taliban did al Qaeda, or that states do not engage in activities that are similar and sometimes far worse than the acts of terrorism which they condemn in other contexts.[46] Neither does this book suggest that Western liberal democracies and their close allies do not engage in terrorism.[47] However, this book is not concerned with a general analysis of state terrorism. It is concerned with the debate over the legalisation of interrogational torture in the context of counter-terrorism policy and practice.

Notes

1 P. Gronke *et al*, 'U.S. Public Opinion on Torture, 2001–9', (2010) 43 *PS: Political Science & Politics* 437 (arguing that support for torture amongst Americans is not as strong as has been claimed by politicians and by media commentators); J. Bean *et al*, 'Medical students' attitudes toward torture', (2008) 18 *Quarterly Journal on Rehabilitation of Torture Victims and Prevention of Torture* 99 (in a survey of medical students it was found 35% thought torture could sometimes be condoned and 27% thought it not unethical); C.S. Crandall *et al*, 'Status quo framing increases support for torture', (2009) 4 *Social Influence* 1 (describing torture as an accepted practice increases support for its use).

2 For discussion, see: S. Keslowitz, 'The Trial of Jack Bauer: The Televised Trial of America's Favorite Fictional Hero and its Influence on the Current Debate on Torture', (2010) 31 *Cardozo L. Rev.* 1125.

3 S. Talbott and N. Chanda (ed.), *The Age of Terror: America and the World after September 11* (2001) xiv.

4 L. O'Carroll, 'Tony Blair Knew Immediately that 9/11 Terror Attacks "Changed Everything"', www.guardian.co.uk 10 September 2011.

5 P. Neumann, *Old & New Terrorism: Late Modernity, Globalization and the Transformation of Political Violence* (2009); W. Laqueur, *The New Terrorism: Fanaticism and the Arms of Mass Destruction* (2000).

6 Frank Furedi argues '[v]irtually every characteristic that is associated with this new breed of destructive behaviour has been linked with terrorism in the past': *Invitation to Terror: The Expanding Empire of the Unknown* (2007) 42.

7 J.A. Piazza, 'Is Islamist Terrorism More Dangerous? An Empirical Study of Group Ideology, Organization, and Goal Structure', (2009) 21 *Terrorism and Political Violence* 62.

8 J.W. Foxell Jnr., 'The Debate on the Potential for Mass-Casualty Terrorism: The Challenge to US Security', (1999) 11 *Terrorism and Political Violence* 94.

9 For discussion of this phenomenon in the United States of America, see: J.T. Parry, *Understanding Torture: Law, Violence, and Political Identity* (2010) ch. 7.

10 G. Frankenberg, 'Torture and Taboo: An Essay Comparing Paradigms of Organized Cruelty', (2008) 56 *Am. J. Comp. L.* 403, 405–6.

11 Human Rights Watch, 'Australia: Prime Minister Should Retract Torture Remarks', 25 November 2013 (quoting the Australian Prime Minister appearing to condone the use of torture by Sri Lankan authorities).

12 A. O'Rourke *et al*, 'Torture, Slippery Slopes, Intellectual Apologists, and Ticking Bombs: An Australian Response to Bagaric and Clarke', (2005–6) 40 *U.S.F.L. Rev* 85.

13 See, for example, J.H. Langbein, *Torture and the Law of Proof: Europe and England in the Ancien Régime* (2006); Bentham, *infra* n. 20; *The Malleus Maleficarum* (1971).

14 See, for example, Lord Parker of Waddington, *Report of the Committee of Privy Counsellors appointed to consider authorised procedures for the interrogation of persons suspected of terrorism* (1972) paras. 27–42; M.S. Moore, 'Torture and the Balance of Evils', (1989) 23 *Isr. L.R.* 280; *infra* n. 32.

15 E.A. Posner and A. Vermeule, 'Should Coercive Interrogation be Legal?', (2006) 104 *Mich. L. Rev.* 671, 673.

16 D. Rejali, *Torture and Democracy* (2007) 45.

17 S. Newbery, 'Intelligence and Controversial British Interrogation Techniques: The Northern Ireland Case, 1971–72,' (2009) 20 *Irish Studies in International Affairs* 103, 106.

18 J. Yoo, *War by Other Means: An Insider's Account of the War on Terror* (New York: Atlantic Monthly Press, 2006) ch. 7.

19 B. Woodward, *State of Denial: Bush at War, Part III* (2006) 80.

20 W.L. Twining and P.E. Twining, 'Bentham on Torture', (1973) 24 *N.I.L.Q.* 305, 315.

21 It is of course for the reader to determine whether this book is a useful addition to the existing literature.

22 There are many views expressed within the torture debate but for the sake of clarity it is assumed here that these views can be divided between two sides.

23 J.L. Falvey, Jnr. and B.D. Eck engage in a similar approach when they argue that opponents of torture should focus less on brutal methods and more on the 'fundamental nature of coercion': 'Holding the High Ground, the Operational Calculus of Torture and Coercive Interrogation', (2010) 32 *Campbell L. Rev.* 561, 592.

24 D. Rejali, 'American Torture Debates', (2008) 9 *Hum. Rights Rev.* 393, 398.

25 *Id.*

26 R. Matthews, *The Absolute Violation: Why Torture Must be Prohibited* (2008) 10.

27 C. Campbell and I. Connolly, 'A Deadly Complexity: Law, Social Movements and Political Violence', (2007) 16 *Minn. J. Int'l L.* 265, 267.

28 The need to examine a range of evidence when testing claims has long been recognised: J. Milton, *Areopagitica* (1644) 19–20.

29 R.J. Evans, *Telling Lies about Hitler: The Holocaust, History and the David Irving Trial* (2002) 256 (quoting J.H. Hexter's comments regarding historians).

30 J. Le Rond D'Alembert, 'The Human Mind Emerged from Barbarism', in I. Kramnick (ed.), *The Portable Enlightenment Reader* (1995) 16.

31 I. Berlin, *Against the Current: Essays in the History of Ideas* (1979) 19–20.

32 *Public Committee Against Torture in Israel* v. *The State of Israel* (1999) 38 ILM 1471.

33 For example, an inquiry into abuses carried out at the Abu Ghraib prison by US military personnel found a basis to doubt the veracity of evidence provided by commanders to the inquiry: Major General Antonio M. Taguba, *Article 15–6 Investigation of the 800th Military Police Brigade* (2004) 24, 26, 43.

34 In *Ireland* v *United Kingdom* (1978) 2 EHRR 25, para. 93 the European Court of Human Rights (ECtHR) noted that neither the security forces, nor the alleged victims of abuse, had given 'accurate and complete accounts of what had happened'. See also: K. Zernike, 'Cited as Symbol of Abu Ghraib, Man Admits He is Not in Photo', *The New York Times* 18 March 2006.

35 *The al Qaeda Manual* (undated). This manual was seized by police in Manchester in 2005. It can be accessed via the US Department of Justice web site: www.justice.gov/ag/manualpart1_1.pdf (last accessed 1 February 2014).

36 In the context of Israel, see L. Hajjar, *Courting Conflict: The Israeli Military Court System in the West Bank and Gaza* (2005) 69.

37 The courts have long developed rules in order to deal with such factual disputes. For the approach of the ECtHR in regards allegations invoking Article 3, see: *El-Masri* v *Former Yugoslav Republic of Macedonia* Application no. 39630/09 (2012) paras. 151–3.

38 See, for example, P. Taylor, *Beating the Terrorists? Interrogation in Omagh, Gough and Castlereagh* (1980) and C. Grossman *et al*, 'Forensic Evidence in the Fight Against Torture', (2012) 19 *Human Rights Brief* 1. Medics, however, can also be complicit in torture and fail to accurately record the abuse of detainees.

39 B. Brecher, *Torture and the Ticking Bomb* (2007) 26.

40 *Id.* 53.

41 J.A. Rodriguez Jr. and B. Harlow, *Hard Measures: How Aggressive CIA Actions After 9/11 Saved American Lives* (2012).

42 I. Mann and O. Shatz, 'The Necessity Procedure: Laws of Torture in Israel and Beyond, 1987–2009', (2010) 59 *Unbound: Harvard Journal of the Legal Left* 59, 65.

43 For example, some scholars have suggested that the claims of Israeli interrogators that coercive interrogation methods have produced useful intelligence 'must be discounted': M.E. O'Connell, 'Affirming the Ban on Harsh Interrogation', (2005) 66 *Ohio St. L.J.* 1231, 1257.

44 An example of the latter is a story told to Bruce Hoffman by a Sri Lankan security official who claimed to have shot a terrorist suspect dead in order to get his co-conspirators to disclosure the location of a bomb that was later disarmed: 'A Nasty Business', *The Atlantic Monthly* 2002.

45 There are a number of accounts by US military personnel disclosing personal involvement in detainee abuse. See, for example, J. Sharrock, *Tortured: When Good Soldiers Do*

Bad Things (2010); Human Rights Watch, *Leadership Failure: Firsthand Accounts of Torture of Iraqi Detainees by the U.S. Army's 82nd Airborne Division* (2005).

46 E. Herman, *The Real Terror Network: Terrorism in Fact and Propaganda* (1982).

47 For discussion, see: A. George (ed.), *Western State Terrorism* (1991); N. Chomsky, *Pirates and Emperors, Old and New: International Terrorism in the Real World* (2003).

1

TORTURE, CONSEQUENCES AND THE PERILS OF LEGALISATION

The debate over the legalisation of interrogational torture has often left key empirical questions unanswered. This includes an understanding of how core arguments cited by the proponents of legalisation favour the existence of an expansive torture power. In order to address this concern, this chapter will set out a framework of analysis that will examine relevant theory and evidence to explain why allowing the lawful use of interrogational torture will lead to a range of negative consequences. It will begin a critical evaluation of the claim that the benefits of regulating interrogational torture outweigh the costs. The chapter will argue that deontological moral theory, which emphasises the violation of dignity and humanity inherent within torture, is an inadequate basis on which to oppose legalisation, and that in order to make a compelling case, consequences matter.[1] The use of utilitarian theory inevitably involves some consideration of the costs and benefits of legalisation. Despite the potential 'blunt calculations' involved in such an approach,[2] it is a means of producing socially useful information.[3] In so doing, it will be argued that proponents of legalisation have failed to consider a wide range of negative consequences in their case for legalised interrogational torture and that a careful examination of key arguments in favour of legalisation must lead to its rejection.

The chapter recognises that consequentialism, as with the precautionary principle,[4] could pose dangers for the absolute prohibition if it can be shown that the consequences of legalisation produce greater benefits compared to costs. This book, however, argues that an empirically-based consequentialist analysis strongly favours the retention of the absolute prohibition, while recognising that a commitment to the absolute prohibition also has potential costs.[5] Further, utilitarianism contains several limiting principles which support the case *against* legalisation.[6] This provides a framework in which empirical evidence can be considered along with an acknowledgement that the social and legal consequences inherent in legal reform are uncertain. This argument does not assume a simplistic notion of choosing between competing theories. Instead, it argues that theoretical approaches can be combined. In this case, consequentialism can be used as a means of bolstering deontological reasoning and the idea that a person should never be tortured and treated as a means to an end. The chapter will also consider the nature of torture compared with other serious harms, including death resulting from the use of lethal force by state officials. It will question justifications for the existence of the absolute prohibition based on the idea that being tortured is worse than being killed. The chapter will begin by examining the meaning of the absolute prohibition and underlying principles. It will then proceed to critically examine deontological and con-sequentialist theory and its application to the case for legalised interrogational torture. The argument presented in this chapter is not an end in itself; it is the beginning of a cumulative argument against legalisation.

1. The absolute prohibition and interest balancing: the law

Ashworth argues that rights should be placed in a hierarchy, along with 'patterns of reasoning that allow security considerations to play a different role in respect of rights of different weights'.[7] As a matter of law, it is evident that the absolute prohibition against the use of torture is highly placed in any hierarchy of rights. The high status of the prohibition can be evidenced by its standing in the international legal order. Torture is prohibited in all circumstances under numerous international conventions and customary rules of international law.[8] It is also subject to an ongoing process of monitoring by international and regional organisations and non-governmental organisations (NGOs).[9] The United Nations Convention Against Torture and Other Cruel, Inhuman or Degrading Treatment or Punishment (1984) states that: 'No exceptional circumstances whatsoever, whether a state of war or a threat of war, internal political instability or any other public emergency, may be invoked as a justification of torture.'[10] Similarly, Article 3 of the European Convention on Human Rights and Fundamental Freedoms (ECHR) does not provide for any circumstances in which torture, inhuman or degrading treatment can be permitted.[11] A derogation from Article 3 is impermissible under Article 15 of the ECHR, even where the life of a nation is threatened.[12]

The absolute prohibition enshrined in Article 3 is illustrative of deontological moral theory which 'appl[ies] to everyone: [and is] mandatory and may not be given up ... '[13] This requires an examination of actions in determining their moral acceptability:

> We must always examine the nature of our actions, to ensure that they address the humanity of every person our action affects. Only persons are ends in themselves, and we must never sacrifice them, never use a human being as a mere pawn, a means of production – not even the mass production – of good, happiness, or any other end.[14]

The absolute prohibition emphasises the humanity and dignity of the torture victim,[15] and the impact of torture on his body and mind.[16] The use of interrogational torture as a counter-terrorism strategy is a classic example of the ends (preventing an act of terrorism) justifying the means (torture).[17] The prohibition, by contrast, reflects the view 'that there are ways of treating a man that are inconsistent with recognizing him as a full member of the human community, and holds that such treatment is profoundly unjust'.[18]

In contrast to Article 3, many of the rights enumerated in the ECHR are not 'founded on a notion of liberal individualism ... [rather] [t]he structure of the Convention and each of its rights requires a balance between the interests of the community and the interests of individuals conceived of as members of the community ... .'[19] It is evident that the ECHR acknowledges some degree of tradeoff between liberty and security in the drafting of many Convention rights.[20] For example, a state can restrict the right of freedom of expression under Article 10 when such restrictions are 'prescribed by law and are necessary in a democratic society' for such purposes as the 'prevention of disorder and crime'.[21] The balancing of freedom of expression as 'one of the essential foundations of a democratic society'[22] with the interests of the community illustrates the fact that liberty and security[23] exist in tension. Wilson notes:

> liberty and power sit in an uneasy relationship ... British civil liberties existed because of the extraordinary combination of opposites and reconciliation of interests; republicanism and monarchy, authority and liberty; commerce and public service, religion and toleration; selfishness and duty; reason and passion ... All the good things in society came from a collision of interests and the heat generated by competition.[24]

The debate over the legalisation of interrogational torture highlights a contemporary tension between competing interests. The tension exists because torture is sometimes seen by state officials as a means of minimising the costs of terrorist violence by producing intelligence that can prevent a terrorist attack. Further, preventing acts of terrorism involves the protection of the right to life which Ashworth describes as fundamental 'since without life there is nothing to which to attach any human right'.[25] Waldron points out that it may be costly for the law to stipulate there is a right to live life free of torture because it prevents the state from torturing in order to gain life-saving intelligence. Thus, the legal prohibition is potentially costly[26] as it requires us to accept that terrorist attacks may take place that could have been prevented.[27] As such, some scholars propose that the prohibition should be balanced with security interests so as to allow for the use of torture in catastrophic cases in order to prevent acts of terrorism. However, the harms such scholars seek to prevent are not one-directional. The use of legalised torture may have unintended consequences, and will involve the infliction of direct harm on those who are tortured. Harm may also spread to wider society and institutions.[28] Thus, the absolute prohibition performs the important role of making it more difficult for the state to torture and less likely that negative consequences will occur.[29]

The European Court of Human Rights (ECtHR) has repeatedly reiterated the absolute nature of the prohibition.[30] It has done so in recent cases involving terrorism and other forms of criminality. In *Gäfgen* v. *Germany*[31] the Grand Chamber (GC) considered a case in which a police officer threatened a kidnap suspect with torture if he did not disclose the location of a child whom he had kidnapped. In holding that the threat constituted inhuman treatment, the court stated:

> The Court reiterates that Article 3 of the Convention enshrines one of the most fundamental values of democratic societies. Unlike most of the substantive clauses of the Convention, Article 3 makes no provision for exceptions and no derogation from it is permissible under Article 15 § 2 even in the event of a public emergency threatening the life of the nation ... The Court has confirmed that even in the most difficult circumstances, such as the fight against terrorism and organised crime, the Convention prohibits in absolute terms torture and inhuman or degrading treatment or punishment, irrespective of the conduct of the person concerned ... [32]

Evans and Morgan note that during the drafting of the ECHR, the content of Article 3 'provoked little controversy' and reflected a strong view that torture could never be justified. As noted by a UK representative participating in these discussions, protecting the life of a state, child or wife does not justify torture and that a state should 'perish' if torture is required 'in order to survive'.[33] Similarly, the GC in *Gäfgen* made clear that issuing a threat of torture was not viewed as acceptable even when done for the purpose of saving a child's life:

> ... the Court accepts the motivation for the police officers' conduct and that they acted in an attempt to save a child's life. However, it is necessary to underline that, having regard to the provision of Article 3 and to its long-established case-law ... the prohibition on ill-treatment of a person applies irrespective of the conduct of the victim or the motivation of the authorities. Torture, inhuman or degrading treatment cannot be inflicted even in circumstances where the life of an individual is at risk. No derogation is allowed even in the event of a public emergency threatening the life of the nation ... The philosophical basis underpinning the absolute nature of the right ... does not allow for any exceptions or justifying factors or balancing of interests, irrespective of the conduct of the person concerned and the nature of the offence at issue.[34]

It is clear that the court rejected any suggestion that the actions of a suspect provide a basis upon which to allow otherwise illegal treatment.[35] The language used here is uncompromising and suggests that any attempt to balance security and liberty in the context of Article 3 in cases involving terrorism is unlikely to succeed.[36] In *A* v. *Netherlands*[37] the GC considered whether diplomatic assurances that a person would not be tortured were sufficient to enable a state to forcibly expel a foreign national to his country of origin where it was claimed there was a real risk that the person would be tortured. The GC held that such assurances did not discharge obligations under Article 3, noting that the 'rigidity' of Article 3 had 'caused many difficulties for the Contracting States by preventing them in practice from enforcing expulsion measures':[38]

> The Court wishes to stress once more that it is acutely conscious of the difficulties faced by States in protecting their populations from terrorist violence and that this makes it all the more important to underline that Article 3 enshrines one of the most fundamental values of democratic societies. Unlike most of the substantive clauses of the Convention … Article 3 makes no provision for exceptions and no derogation from it is permissible under Article 15 § 2 notwithstanding the existence of a public emergency threatening the life of the nation. Even in the most difficult of circumstances, such as the fight against terrorism, and irrespective of the conduct of the person concerned, the Convention prohibits in absolute terms torture and inhuman or degrading treatment and punishment.[39]

In the earlier decision of *Saadi* v. *Italy* the GC noted that 'States face immense difficulties in modern times in protecting their communities from terrorist violence … It cannot therefore underestimate the scale of the danger of terrorism today and the threat it presents to the community. That must not, however, call into question the absolute nature of Article 3.'[40] The GC held that Article 3 did not allow for a balancing of the 'risk' of torture faced by the individual if deported with the 'danger' posed by that person to the community:

> The Court considers that the argument based on the balancing of the risk of harm if the person is sent back against the dangerousness he or she represents to the community if not sent back is misconceived. The concepts of 'risk' and 'dangerousness' in this context do not lend themselves to a balancing test because they are notions that can only be assessed independently of each other.[41]

It seems unlikely, given the strong reassertion of the absolute nature of the Article 3 prohibition in cases such as *Gäfgen*, *A* and *Saadi* that the court would ever permit the use of torture in ticking bomb cases. Thus, in this restatement of the absolute prohibition it is evident that torture falls within a class of human rights violation which Michael Ignatieff argues 'remind[s] us that there are some abuses that are genuinely intolerable … .'[42] As such, the ECtHR has rejected any 'balancing' between liberty and security in the context of interrogational torture, while recognising the potential conflict between the two.[43] Such a restatement of the absolute nature of Article 3, however, does not address the legal policy question as to whether interrogational torture *should* be permitted in exceptional cases. It is to this issue that the remainder of this book will now turn.

2. Moral theory and some empirical considerations

A democratic state cannot exist without liberty *and* security: '[o]nly a strong, safe, and stable democracy may afford and protect human rights, and only a democracy built on the foundations of human rights can exist with security.'[44] Such a formulation, however, leaves little room for absolutes and tends to underestimate the problematic consequences of increasing state power in order to promote security interests.[45] This is particularly the case in versions of the balancing argument which promote a strong tradeoff between security and liberty in response to emergency situations. For example, Posner and Vermeule have proposed what they refer to as a 'tradeoff thesis' in which they argue that during emergencies 'government should and will reduce civil liberties in order to enhance security in those domains where the two must be traded off'.[46] This type of tradeoff involves granting wide discretion to the executive and requires the judiciary to show deference where the executive claims that security risks necessitate the use of interrogational torture.[47]

Such a proposal can be objected to on a number of grounds. The first relates to the notion of balancing itself. If competing interests are to be balanced they must be identified, but many proponents of legalisation make little effort to properly engage in such an analysis.[48] There is little agreement as to what weight should be given to the various interests to be balanced or what interests should be included as part of such an approach.[49] Tradeoff between competing interests is also a complex matter because 'harsh' counter-terrorism strategies do not necessarily improve security and measures that comply with human rights norms may provide benefit.[50] Further, if key interests are excluded from the balancing process then any resulting conclusion will be flawed. Some interests are likely to be viewed as more important than others and so a basis for distinguishing between interests must be considered. In the context of torture, this is important given its standing in the international legal order. Further, the act of torture itself requires the interests of the torture victim to be considered as weighty. The matter is further complicated by the 'interwoven nature of rights'.[51] If a terror suspect is tortured, it is not only his right to be free from torture that is being violated; his detention involves the denial of other liberties, including his freedom of movement and family life.

Such interwoven rights, however, are not one-directional. In an excellent analysis of the *Gäfgen* case, Greer argues that the German state had an obligation to protect the rights of the kidnapped child, of which there were a number under German law and the ECHR, including the right to life.[52] He rightly observes that the court justified an absolute prohibition on the infliction of inhuman treatment, but in this case the murdered child who was kidnaped also had rights. Further, in certain circumstances, the state can lawfully kill a kidnapper without violating Article 2, but cannot threaten the same person while alive if it amounts to a violation of Article 3.[53] Such an approach, Greer argues requires moral justification. The point is equally applicable where a terrorist suspect threatens the lives of many more people after planting a bomb and refuses to disclose its location. There seems to be no easy resolution to these issues, because as Greer notes: '[t]here is no ideal solution ... since every alternative suffers from moral problems.'[54] Suffice to say this moral dilemma is not the primary focus of this book, but it cannot be denied that the exclusion of the victims of terrorist violence is often a gap in the moral reasoning of those who defend the absolute prohibition.

Balancing is thus a highly complex matter viewed by some scholars as a 'mysterious task' which requires a 'rigorous scrutiny' of the case for balance.[55] Indeed, the balancing of liberty and security based on a fear of consequences carries with it the attendant danger that it could result in 'moral anarchy'[56] and lead 'to implications it is difficult to accept'.[57] On consequentialist grounds one could justify almost any state use of torture, however widespread, if the greater interest of public safety is served.[58] This is, of course, the logic of consequentialist reasoning and will be discussed in more detail later in this chapter. It has been observed that 'it does not follow that sacrificing liberties will always or even generally, promote security' and that 'there is little evidence that curtailing civil liberties will do more good than harm'.[59] Indeed, the risks associated with terrorism are difficult to quantify or predict,[60] as is the effect of repressive counter-terrorism measures. As a result of these uncertainties, there are long-recognised problems in the assessment of future costs and benefits which are, by their very nature, speculative.[61] The strong version of balancing as represented by the tradeoff thesis also assumes a simplistic relationship in which restricting liberty will increase security. However, there is evidence that harsh counter-terrorism strategies, rather than countering terrorism, can actually assist terrorist groups in recruitment and reaffirm the commitment to violence.[62] It may also be difficult to judge the extent to which interrogational torture, *specifically*, has increased security as its use is normally accompanied by other counter-terrorism strategies. In addition, the successful use of torture depends on the apprehension of terrorists who possess relevant information and requires the production of accurate and timely intelligence.[63] This leaves significant room for a tradeoff failure that decreases liberty without a benefit to security. It has been argued that the proponents of tradeoff and wide executive discretion underestimate the tendency of state officials to make rash decisions which are based on poor data and give effect to fear, rather than involving a considered analysis of potential policy responses.[64]

Even if one were to argue that liberty and security should be balanced in some way, this does not necessarily lead to the conclusion that interrogational torture should be permitted. Here, there are two issues that require attention. The first relates to the nature of the harm caused by a potential terrorist attack. Zamir makes the point that the notion of national security is a 'broad concept comprising a host of interests, some of which are more important and some less so'.[65] This argument views security through the lens of surrounding circumstances.[66] It draws a distinction between times of war or where the state faces a catastrophic attack and instances where a lesser threat to national security exists. Few, if any, single acts of terrorism could be placed in the first category.[67] Indeed, Wilkinson notes that many European democracies have experienced terrorism but none have been destroyed as a result of terrorist violence.[68] As such, an argument for legalisation that features a nation-destroying event does not provide a compelling argument on the grounds that it is so unrealistic that it should not be used as a basis for determining legal policy. Instead, a range of conventional security, law enforcement and political measures have resulted in the end of terrorist plots and campaigns in Europe and elsewhere.[69] The emergency normally portrayed by the supporters of legalised torture involves a ticking bomb which would generally not constitute a threat to the existence of the state.[70] As a result, in cases where there is a lesser threat to national security it is reasonable to insist on a much greater respect for rights, particularly for any right that is deemed to have high standing in a hierarchy of rights.

The second issue to be addressed concerns the likelihood that interrogational torture will prevent harm. The question is *not* simply whether interrogational torture promotes security. It is whether it can be justified as a means of promoting security in a *time-limited emergency*. That is, in a ticking bomb-type situation where the torture power should only be used in exceptional cases, within a tight system of control which recognises 'a stopgap mechanism for extraordinary cases'.[71] In judging the consequences of legalisation, account must be taken of the likelihood that such an exceptional power will ever be needed.[72] It can be argued that the more exceptional the power, the less likely it is that a benefit will be derived. Indeed, the existence of a terrorist attack which threatens the existence of a nation is so unlikely that institutionalising a power to use interrogational torture in this specific content appears entirely unnecessary. Terrorist attacks involving lesser forms of harm are more likely, but so too are the potential negative consequences of legalisation. Further, during 'lesser' emergencies there might be pressures to torture that do not exist in non-emergency situations and this may lead to abuse and greater use of the torture power than originally intended.[73] In this way, the use of torture may create more harm than it prevents.

There is little doubt that the concept of interest balancing poses particular dangers for the absolute prohibition. As soon as one interest is balanced against another, the prohibition loses its potency and it is possible to create exceptions where the interests of potential terrorist victims are seen to outweigh those of terrorist suspects. The absolute prohibition has been criticised on the basis that it is 'admirably conscientious about the rights of prisoners, [but] studiedly indifferent to the fate of the terrorist's victims'.[74] There is no doubt that the victims of terrorist violence confront a wide variety of psychological and physical traumas, including loss of life.[75] Furthermore, the nature of certain forms of terrorism suggests an intention to maximise the number of victims and thereby the sum of human suffering.[76] Thus, it can be argued that the potential victims of terrorism have to be taken into account when considering counter-terrorism policy. However, this is a far from straightforward exercise because it cannot be assumed that torturing a terrorist suspect will necessarily prevent a terrorist attack. Indeed, the proponents of legalisation often ignore the many other ways the state can and does lawfully prevent terrorist attacks. The focus on torture, however, may partly result from a sense of panic that leads to actions to avert terrorist acts that are seen as 'senseless' and in Cohen's words 'affirm the value of utilitarian, rational action'.[77] Notions of cost/benefit, balancing and consequentialism in the torture debate fit well within this description.

Some proponents of legalisation argue that states have an obligation to torture in order to protect citizens from harm as failing to act is morally indefensible.[78] Others suggest that the state doing an act that violates a fundamental right is different from not doing an act that *might* prevent a harmful outcome,[79] and that the 'state cannot be morally liable for an omission if the thing that it omitted to do was morally impermissible'.[80] If it is to be argued that the state is obliged to torture in order to prevent acts of terrorism then the logic of consequentialism dictates that any act, however outrageous, would be justified, were the harm to be prevented large enough. On this basis it may become difficult to morally differentiate between an act of terrorism and an act of torture intended to prevent terrorism. While upholding a prohibition on torture might be characterised as 'indifferent' to the interests of the victims of terrorist violence,[81] it is the terrorist and not the state that has created the threat and should bear responsibility for the harm caused.[82] Empowering the state to engage in what otherwise would be a violation of a high status right steeped in uncertainty as to whether it will prevent the anticipated harm is not a basis for sound policy making. Further, the proponents of interrogational torture often fail to take account of the act of torture itself in their moral calculus,[83] as well as other detainee and institutional costs.[84] Even if one ignores, for the moment, the wider social impacts of torture, we know that torture causes physical and psychological trauma[85] and it involves the infliction of suffering on a defenceless victim who is not given a choice other than to comply with the wishes of his interrogator(s) or face further torment.[86]

A strict adherent to deontological theory has little choice but to ignore the interests of the victims of terrorist violence. Nagel acknowledges such a possibility when noting that '[t]hese conceptions still have to be understood, even if they will eventually be rejected'.[87] He argues that the strength of deontological arguments rest on them not producing 'disastrous results in the long run' and if they cease to have 'social utility ... those rules would lose much of their moral attractiveness'.[88] Reflecting this view, some deontologists such as Harel and Sharon argue that maintaining an absolutist deontological position potentially 'entails unreasonable consequences'.[89] They make a threshold deontology argument in which they favour the retention of the absolute prohibition until torture is 'performed *as an exception* grounded in a practical necessity rather than as a rule-governed principle or norm. In such cases, we maintain, torture is performed out of direct responsiveness to the sheer necessity dictated by the circumstances.'[90] They suggest that the absolute prohibition is retained and the actions of the torturer, which remains illegal, might be subject to some form of *ex-post* ratification.[91]

This argument clearly introduces into deontology a strong element of consequentialism: '[t]o be morally commendable, torture must be performed out of sheer necessity to save lives ... '[92] The strength of the argument is that it avoids falling into a category of moral reasoning that Charles Fried describes as 'fanatical'.[93] That is, retaining a moral absolute no matter what the consequences. The trouble however, lies in the specifics of Harel and Sharon's proposal. They are only concerned with a very narrow conception of consequences, the prevention of a terrorist attack, and have no regard for the individual or societal consequences of their proposal or the (in)ability of law to constrain or deter what is a clear endorsement of torture in circumstances of supposed necessity.[94] Further, Fried and Fried point out that this is a type of argument trying to have it both ways.[95] They wish to retain a deontological defence of the absolute prohibition and then argue that beyond a certain threshold of harm, torture can be used out of a concern for consequences.

The proponents of legalised interrogational torture rely on some form of consequentialist theory, in particular, utilitarianism to justify the regulation of torture rather than prohibition.[96] For example, Bagaric and Clarke make clear their desire to 'redeem utilitarianism'.[97] Utilitarianism is defined by Mill as a form of reasoning in which: 'actions are right in proportion as they tend to promote happiness ... pleasure, and the absence of pain'.[98] Few proponents have sought out the writings of utilitarians such as Bentham and Mill to examine whether they provide some grounds for caution when using consequentialism as a moral theory to support the case for legalisation.[99] The contours of utilitarianism in this regard reflect a point noted by Mill: 'there is every imaginable degree of rigidity and of laxity in the application of [this] standard.'[100]

There can be no limitations on state action if the *only* concern is on end results. As such, this may lead to actions such as the use of torture that involve the 'flouting of ... civilized norms' similar to the actions of terrorists.[101] Dershowitz has argued that some limits must be observed on the use of interrogational torture and that children should not be tortured for fear of hurtling down a slippery slope.[102] The logic of consequentialism suggests that such a distinction is unconvincing as it is entirely arbitrary,[103] although it must also be acknowledged there is nothing preventing legislators from introducing such a restriction. If the focus is on consequences and the prevention of catastrophe then it would not appear to matter who is tortured, whether it be a terrorist suspect, his wife and children[104] or a hospital ward full of babies,[105] as the concern is with the consequences of a terrorist attack. A deontologist, on the other hand, would reject such actions on the grounds that they are 'inherently barbaric, not because of anything to do with broader consequences'.[106] To put it another way, it is objectionable in all cases to torture persons who did not or could not have caused the harm to be prevented.[107]

3. Limiting principles and some implications

It is evident that utilitarian theory does contain potential limiting principles in the sense of recognising that certain acts which may appear, on face value, to have utility are in fact impermissible. Mill's writing contains a line of reasoning that might support the absolute prohibition. He referred to a situation in which 'it would be unworthy of an intelligent agent not to be consciously aware that [his] action is of a class which, if practised generally, would be generally injurious, and that this is the ground of the obligation to abstain from it'.[108] In many respects this is the application of utilitarian theory, but not one recognised by proponents of legalisation. There are few acts that would be more 'generally injurious' than the use of torture if it were 'practised generally'. Mill went on to state that all moral systems 'enjoin to abstain from whatever is manifestly pernicious to society'.[109] It might be countered that the use of interrogational torture is supposed to be an exceptional power and will not be 'practiced generally'.[110] However, there is evidence that torture can become institutionalised and difficult to control.[111]

Bentham provided another potential limiting principle in the utilitarian defence of torture. He argued that if an act is not useful to the community, but is mis-chievous, 'it is your *duty* at least to abstain from it: and more than that, if it is what lies in your power, and can be done without too great a sacrifice, to endeavour to prevent it' (emphasis in original).[112] Interestingly, such insights did not prevent Bentham from advocating the use of torture to gain information from criminal suspects.[113] He did this by 'glossing over' the regulatory problems and uncertainties associated with legalisation.[114] In his writings on torture, Bentham appeared to assume uncertainty as to motivation or benefit could be satisfactorily minimised under a regulatory framework. The problem is that many of the uncertainties associated with interrogational torture are factual, not legal. To take one example, Bentham refers to the notion of utility as a tendency to 'produce benefit, advan-tage ... ' or 'prevent the happening of mischief, pain, evil ... .'[115] In the context of interrogational torture this clearly raises the issue of how effective torture is as a means of gaining accurate, timely intelligence. Since Bentham's formulation requires a prediction of utility it is simply not possible to know what benefit, if any, will be derived from the use of interrogational torture in any particular case.

At this point it is important to consider whether there is an empirical basis for claiming that the legalisation of interrogational torture could be 'manifestly pernicious' which would then lead to significant uncertainty as to the benefit to be derived. There are two distinct arguments discussed in this book that suggest legalised torture would have an effect on society beyond the infliction of torture on indi-vidual terrorist suspects. The first is a slippery slope argument which suggests that torture would be difficult to control within a legal framework. This issue will be discussed in detail in Chapter 4. The second argument concerns the empirical evidence that there is a link between state repression and 'collective protest action'.[116] This is not the only possible 'pathway' to terrorist activity,[117] but has important implications for the torture debate. So-called 'hard repression', including the use of interrogational torture, may *inter alia* harden attitudes, increase recruit-ment for terrorist groups and create anger and a desire for revenge.[118] Thus, repression may serve to undermine the counter-terrorism strategies of the state rather than enhance them. There is evidence from numerous counter-terrorism campaigns in places such as Northern Ireland,[119] Egypt,[120] France,[121] Nepal,[122] Columbia,[123] Iraq and Afghanistan[124] that repression, including abuse and torture can assist in terrorist mobilisation.[125] That is not to say that there is necessarily a simple cause and effect between the two. In their study of terrorist mobilisation, Campbell and Connolly rejected a simple cause–effect relationship between repression and mobilisation. They interviewed sixteen people imprisoned for offences related to involvement with the IRA and found that 'a more nuanced picture was painted, of personal experience of lower levels of repression; of identification with the detainees from whom the abuse claims emanated; and of identification with the cause and the victims of the Bloody Sunday protest ... '.[126]

Evidence suggests that people may involve themselves in terrorist-related activity as a result of personal experiences of state violence or perceived injustice, a desire for revenge and 'sense of being part of a larger community'.[127] Richardson notes that revenge is the 'most powerful theme in any conversation with terrorists past or present ... a desire for revenge is ubiquitous among them'.[128] Similar patterns of repression, anger and a desire for revenge have been found to result from state repression in Egypt,[129] European responses to Anarchist terrorism a century ago,[130] and amongst failed Palestinian suicide bombers.[131] A serious examination of consequences also requires a recognition that terrorist groups sometimes wish to 'provoke the government to retaliate forcefully' in order to gain support and recruits.[132] Indeed, Richardson refers to a leader of the Basque separatist group ETA who 'complained that the Spanish authorities were becoming too professional and discriminating in their responses to ETA action'.[133] The link between repression and recruitment is also supported by the work of Campbell and Connolly.[134] They identified two 'big clusters of IRA recruitment' in Northern Ireland which occurred in 1972–73 and 1981–83. They note from their interviews that both mobilisations involved 'perceptions of prisoner ill-treatment, and multiple deaths for which respondents blamed the state'.[135]

Repressive counter-terrorism measures can fail on multiple levels. The targeting of the innocent by the state is clearly a serious matter which may lead to anger and a greater willingness to support or engage in terrorist activity. It may also lead to a sense of alienation and destruction of mutual respect[136] that destroys the trust necessary for people to disclose meaningful intelligence to state authorities. In an interview with Ian Cobain, Tommy McKearney, a former member of the IRA, argued that while the use of illegal interrogation methods may have short-term benefits: 'in the long term it is destructive to the aims of those who are using it, because it thoroughly alienates those against whom it is perpetrated ... their communities feel the pain as well, families, neighbours and friends. It drives people to greater excesses than they might have originally contemplated.'[137] Drawing on empirical data from South Africa, the West Bank and Northern Ireland, Campbell has argued that there exist 'links rather than simple correlations between some repressive techniques (particularly if indiscriminate or egregious) and increased collective protest action'.[138]

The use of interrogational torture, as part of a repressive counter-terrorism strategy, may contribute to the unwillingness of people living within particular communities to co-operate with state authorities.[139] Peter Taylor interviewed an army Lieutenant-Colonel who observed that: '[Internment in Northern Ireland] was a complete disaster. It turned a large number of the nationalist population ... against us ... It also meant that what little information we were getting at that time just totally dried up.'[140] A similar point was made by Lord Gardiner when arguing against the regulation of 'ill treatment by the police, for the purpose of obtaining information' in his minority report as part of the Parker Inquiry into the use of the 'five techniques' in Northern Ireland.[141] He noted that security forces rely heavily on the 'sympathy of the local population' and if this is lost then 'the difficulties of the forces of law and order are increased'.[142]

The unwillingness of community members to co-operate with state authorities might be partly explained by the fact that: '[r]epression … appear[s] to have … the effect of reinforcing a sense of self as a member of an out-group, leading to *identification with* victims of harsh repression'[143] (emphasis in original). Similarly, the use of interrogational torture not only impacts on the person who is tortured, but it also has a negative impact on family, friends and the wider community. Matthews argues that '[t]o attack individual human beings through torture entails assaulting their social attachments as well … it assaults the humanity of entire communities along gender, cultural, ethnic, familial, occupational, and generational lines'.[144] Indeed, empirical evidence shows that the 'psychological effects of torture can … have an impact on family members of the victim'. Studies of families which include a member who is a torture victim suggest high levels of divorce, 'familial discord', as well as children suffering psychological and developmental problems.[145] In this way, it can be argued that the use of interrogational torture is not a limited or socially isolated act and may reaffirm the idea that victims, relatives and the community are members of a victimised 'out-group'. Terrorist groups also engage in 'entrepreneurship' by which they exploit state repression[146] in order to build support by suggesting that community members should take action to defend themselves, their lands or beliefs from attack.[147]

The argument that the use of torture has wider social consequences is important because it tends to strengthen consequentialist arguments against legalisation.[148] Proponents of torture tend to balance the interests of an individual terrorist suspect with the interests of the wider community that the state is obliged to protect from harm.[149] At the same time, these proponents tend to either ignore[150] or deny that the problem of terrorism might be worsened by repression.[151] Even if one accepts, for a moment, that balancing is a legitimate endeavour in the context of inter-rogational torture, then as part of a consequentialist analysis it is inappropriate to ignore the potential harm that may be done in terms of terrorist mobilisation, damage to social attachments and the possibility that its use will inhibit the ability of law enforcement to gain co-operation and intelligence from the community. Bentham's duty to abstain from mischievous acts that harm the community means that those who wish to challenge the absolute prohibition need to explain why the potential harms caused by interrogational torture are outweighed by any benefit as part of the consequentialist calculus.[152] Any responsible analysis of the costs of interrogational torture requires an acknowledgement of this issue.

There is another problem of complexity and uncertainty here. State repression does not always lead to a violent counter-reaction or other forms of resistance.[153] This emphasises the difficulties of engaging in a consequentialist analysis. If there is a strong connection between torture and terrorist mobilisation then there is a stronger argument against its use on consequentialist grounds. If it is unclear whether torture will result in abuse of mobilisation, and any judgment will be clouded by uncertainty, then this may fall within Mill's argument in that it could generally be harmful to the community. Any act, of course, can be said to have uncertain outcomes. However, there is something particularly problematic about the state use of legalised torture, because of its propaganda value to terrorist groups and the potential revulsion, media attention and counter-reaction it may provoke that could undermine the whole purpose of using torture in the first place.

While a consequentialist argument against the use of torture can be made it should be acknowledged that it carries with it, certain risks. If clear benefits can be seen to derive from the use of interrogational torture, with limited costs, then of course, this would tend to support the case for legalisation. This may help to explain the reluctance of some to enter into this debate. A deontologist may simply avoid these risks by reaffirming the argument that torture is intrinsically wrong in all circumstances. When faced with an affirmative statement such as this, someone may respond with the question 'why is it always wrong?' At this point it may become harder to avoid consequentialism. The argument that we should not treat a person as a means to an end or the notion that torture is a form of barbarity,[154] may not convince a person seeking more grounded answers. As a result, what is needed is an approach advocated by Hart, who in his discussion of the death penalty, noted that the utilitarian position 'commits one, as the absolute positions do not, to a factual inquiry as to the effects upon society of the use of the death penalty'.[155] Hart pointed to the fact that opposition to the death penalty as a purely moral wrong is done without reference to 'fact or evidence'[156] and in order to address key questions a 'factual inquiry' is necessary.[157] This factual inquiry continues in the next section.

4. Comparing torture and death

The proponents of legalisation have attacked the absolute prohibition by arguing that torture is no different from other evils that are legally regulated by the state.[158] In so doing, Posner and Vermeule make reference to the legal regulation of 'deadly force' used by police officers.[159] Bagaric and Clarke make a similar point in terms of utilitarianism, arguing that the state often sacrifices the lives of some 'for the good of the whole' in situations such as war.[160] Under domestic and international law the state use of deadly force is permitted,[161] while torture is impermissible in all circumstances. On its face, this may appear inconsistent as the use of deadly force and torture can both save innocent lives. This leads proponents to the conclusion that they should be treated similarly in moral and legal constructs. However, the moral theory of consequentialism also necessitates an examination of the impact of torture on those subjected to these techniques. Mill asked: '[w]hat is there to decide whether a particular pleasure is worth purchasing at the cost of a particular pain, except the feelings and judgement of the experienced?'[162] This cannot be achieved by either minimising or ignoring harms that are central to the debate over legalisation, whether those are harms caused to terrorist suspects[163] or to the victims of terrorist violence. While proponents of legalisation tend to be concerned with the prevention of terrorist attacks and the potential victims of such attacks, they have no concern for the terrorist suspects who might be tortured. In making the case for torture on the basis that the state can use lethal force requires careful comparative analysis; no proponent has engaged in such an examination of empirical evidence. Indeed, Posner and Vermeule note that compared to the use of lethal force by police officers 'the merits and demerits of coercive interrogation are much more poorly understood than the merits and demerits of deadly force'.[164] The acknowledgement of an evidential gap undermines their case because if there is factual uncertainty then on what reliable basis can they make a solid empirical claim that the use of torture is similar to the use of lethal force? Comparative analysis involving the police's use of lethal force or death during wartime requires careful and detailed examination.[165] The proponents have failed to do this. As such, they engage in a speculative assessment which is not a sound basis upon which to develop legal policy and overturn the absolute prohibition.

Scholars who oppose the use of interrogational torture have attempted to find various ways of distinguishing death and torture in order to emphasise the unacceptability of torture. At an abstract level, none of these arguments are entirely convincing. Shue argues that torture is an attack on the defenceless and, as such, the 'manner in which torture is conducted is morally more reprehensible than the manner in which killing would occur if the laws of war were honoured'.[166] Indeed, one of the characteristics of torture is that the terrorist suspect does not have his most basic rights respected, is defenceless and under the complete control of his captors.[167] However, Shue's reference to the laws of war ignores the fact that battlefield deaths, like torture, can be slow and agonising and the laws of war provide only limited protection to combatants and non-combatants alike.[168] Wisnewski and Emerick suggest that torture is in fact worse than death.[169] They base their argument on the psychological aftermath and physical reality of torture which they characterise as a 'kind of death, but one that draws out one's pain and suffering indefinitely'.[170] This might be true, but it neglects a crucial difference between the consequences of death and torture, that is, the possibility of recovery. Death does not offer any possibility of physical or psychological recovery.

Torture and death are very serious harms to inflict on an individual. Scarry draws comparisons between the two when noting the 'kinship between pain and death, both of which are radical and absolute ... Each only happens because of the body. In each, the contents of consciousness are destroyed. The two are the most intense forms of negation ... physical pain always mimes death and the infliction of physical pain is always a mock execution.'[171] There are also linkages between torture and death that go beyond the infliction of pain.[172] In her interviews with victims of torture by the Argentine army during its 'Dirty War' in the 1970s and early 1980s, Feitlowitz found that fear of death was common and in some instances the desire to die in order to escape torture was in evidence.[173] Here, the torture itself raised the prospect of death or made it seem preferable to continued abuse. One victim recounted: '[f]rom the moment I was kidnapped I believed I was condemned to die ... '[174] A 16-year-old, pregnant victim said she desired death in order to escape her torment: 'I wanted to die, but they wouldn't let me. They "saved" me only so they could go on torturing me.'[175] Another detainee attempted to kill herself.[176] This was a particular reality of the Algerian repression where the French authorities murdered thousands of prisoners after they had been tortured. Alleg, who was tortured by the French authorities in Algeria, recounts in his memoir that he was aware at the time of his arrest that other prisoners had been killed: 'I lived like this for a space of a month, with the prospect of death always in front of me. It might happen that evening, it might be the next day at dawn.'[177] Further, the mental torment of torture was inescapable: 'psychic torture was infinitely worse. ... because it was constant. I want to be very clear on this point ... torture was constant and inescapable ... '[178]

The empirical literature also points to fear generated by torture. For example, waterboarding has been described as 'an utterly terrifying event ... Psychologically this can result in significant long-term post traumatic stress, and produce anxiety and depression.'[179] Abu Zubaydeh, who was interrogated by the CIA told the International Committee for the Red Cross that during his experience of waterboarding: 'I thought I was going to die. I lost control of my urine. Since then I still lose control of my urine when under stress.'[180] Khalid Sheikh Mohammed stated 'injuries to my ankles and wrists also occurred during the water-boarding as I struggled in panic of not being able to breath'.[181] Repeated use of waterboarding is seen as particularly traumatic: 'The acute suffering produced during the immediate infliction of *submarino* is superseded by the often unbearable fear of repeating the experience. In the aftermath, it may lead to horrific memories that persist in the form of recurrent "drowning nightmares."'[182] Indeed, one victim of waterboarding under the Pinochet dictatorship in Chile stated: 'Even today I wake up because of having nightmares of dying from drowning.'[183] Correa has discussed the findings of the Valech Commission which interviewed more than 28,000 victims of 'political imprisonment and torture' in Chile during the rule of the dictatorship headed by Augusto Pinochet.[184] According to Correa the Commission found that waterboarding results in similar negative effects to other forms of torture: 'torture provoked a near-death experience that made victims feel helpless. Most victims reported feeling deep humiliation and that their lives were entirely at the mercy of their torturers.'[185] The Commission reported that victims were still experiencing trauma thirty years after the torture: '[m]ost victims reported having some or all of the symptoms of post traumatic stress disorder, including feelings of insecurity or fear, humiliation, worthlessness, shame, guilt, depression, anxiety, and hopelessness.'[186]

This evidence points to experience that involves a level of intensity that is inescapable. Death may sometimes be slow, but the use of lethal force by police officers cannot normally be seen as approaching this intensity because it does not involve the deliberate infliction of sustained suffering. Torture is by its nature inflicted to a point at which the suspect can no longer resist. In fact, the lawful use of lethal force is intended to be a quick and effective means of eliminating a threat – anything else will mean the a continuation of that threat.[187] This type of argument may provide a basis for distinguishing between the use of lethal force and torture,[188] but is not entirely satisfactory given that death is an end, and while torture inflects terrible harms, recovery, to some degree, is possible.

Conclusion

This chapter has set out the beginnings of a consequentialist analysis. The purpose of the analysis is to combine consequentialism and empirical evidence in order to address a legal policy question.[189] While recognising that a consequentialist approach could pose risks to the absolute prohibition, this chapter has demonstrated that an examination of consequences is crucial to the case against the legalisation of interrogational torture. However, it does not have to fit within a narrow utilitarian conception of 'morality by numbers'[190] as it is a crude measure and endangers minorities who are sometimes unjustly targeted by the state in times of crisis.[191] Instead, consequentialism provides a means of supporting the deontological claim that it is wrong to torture and use a person as a means to an end in all cases. This reinforces the idea that torture is always impermissible and that there are no circumstances where it should be legally permitted.[192] Such an approach may not please purists, but it does provide a strong, empirically sound basis on which to critically analyse the case for legalised torture and is not inconsistent with either theory, given the flexible ways in which both are often interpreted.

While the absolute prohibition against the use of torture is upheld by the ECtHR, it does so on narrow legalistic grounds. While the court has referred to the difficulties the prohibition can cause for states, it does not allow concern for the victims of terrorist violence to impact on its decisions in terrorism cases. This chapter argues for the retention of the prohibition, and that the interests of those who may be killed or injured by terrorists must be acknowledged. The reason for not allowing such interests to guide legal policy is that the consequences of legalisation would likely cause much greater harm than torture could ever prevent. This case can only be made by an examination of consequences. A persistent re-affirmation of the absolute prohibition fails to address key concerns, including the costs of the absolute prohibition.[193] This chapter has also drawn attention to the often-ignored limiting principles that exist within consequentialism, without which there would be few moral or legal constraints on the use of interrogational torture. While consequentialism could pose a risk to the prohibition if the benefits of torture are seen to outweigh the costs, its use is intended to posit a strong argument against legalisation using the very foundational theory upon which the proponents of legalisation rely. In this way, it is possible to build an empirically-based argument that torture is wrong as a matter of theory, legal doctrine and practice. The next chapter continues to build the cumulative case against legalisation by arguing that the commonly cited ticking bomb argument provides for an expansive state torture power.

Notes

1 Matthews argues that '[s]ince everyone accepts that torture is evil, and since everyone agrees that all human beings have a *prima facie* right not to be tortured, the debate has to be handled on consequentialist grounds': R. Matthews, *The Absolute Violation: Why Torture Must be Prohibited* (2008) 204–5.

2 M.L. Gross, *Moral Dilemmas of Modern War: Torture, Assassination, and Blackmail in an Age of Asymmetric Conflict* (2010) 136.
3 For advocacy of what the author refers to as benefit/cost analysis, see D.C. Hubin, 'The Moral Justification of Benefit/Cost Analysis', (1994) 10 *Economics and Philosophy* 169.
4 Counter-terrorism policy is sometimes discussed on the basis of a precautionary principle: D. Runciman, 'The Precautionary Principle', *London Review of Books* vol. 26, 1 April 2004. This approach can lead to various results depending on whether the precautionary focus is on liberty or security. Further, increasing the power of the state to use coercive means to gain intelligence as a precaution in order to prevent harm from acts of terrorism may shut down other avenues of intelligence gathering. It might also create a violent backlash. In this way, the application of the precautionary principle in favour of security could be self-defeating.
5 For a wide-ranging analysis examining the costs and benefits of a variety of counter-terrorism strategies, see G. Blum and P.B. Heymann, *Laws, Outlaws, and Terrorists: Lessons from the War on Terrorism* (2010).
6 While this book makes a number of references to utilitarianism, particularly when discussing the work of Bentham and Mill, it will generally refer to consequentialism.
7 A. Ashworth, 'Security, Terrorism and the Value of Human Rights', in B.J. Goold and L. Lazarus, *Security and Human Rights* (2007) 225.
8 In *Filartiga* v. *Pena-Irala* 630 F.2d 876, para. 54 (1980) it was noted: 'the international community has come to recognize the common danger posed by the flagrant disregard of basic human rights and particularly the right to be free of torture ... civilized nations have banded together to prescribe acceptable norms of international behavior ... Among the rights universally proclaimed by all nations ... is the right to be free of physical torture ... the torturer has become like the pirate and slave trader before him *hostis humani generis*, an enemy of all mankind.'
9 In relation to the role of the United Nations, see: 'On Negotiating with Torturers', in K. Roth *et al* (ed.), *Torture: Does It Make Us Safer? Is It Ever OK? A Human Rights Perspective* (2005) ch. 8 (featuring an interview with Sir Nigel Rodley, former UN Special Rapporteur on Torture). For a critical review of the work and impact of the UN Committee Against Torture, see: R. McQuigg, 'How effective is the United Nations Committee Against Torture?' (2011) 22 *E.J.I.L.* 813.
10 Article 2(2). The nature of this prohibition was recently reaffirmed by the UN Committee Against Torture, thus: 'The Committee recalls that the prohibition against torture is absolute and non-derogable and that *no exceptional circumstances whatsoever* may be invoked by a State Party to justify acts of torture.' (emphasis in original) *Decision of the Committee against Torture under article 22 of the Convention against Torture and Other Cruel, Inhuman or Degrading Treatment or Punishment (forty-seventh session)* Communication No. 428/2010 (2011) para. 15.5. It was suggested that this absolute prohibition may not extend to cruel, inhuman and degrading treatment. In Commission of Human Rights discussions as part of the drafting process of the United Nations Convention Against Torture, the United States made the following assertion: 'The United States believes that "cruel, inhuman or degrading treatment or punishment" is a more relative term; international standards are more difficult to achieve and what might constitute cruel treatment in times of peace might not rise to that level during emergency conditions.' Commission of Human Rights, *Question of the human rights of all persons subjected to any form of detention or imprisonment, in particular: torture and other cruel, inhuman or degrading treatment or punishment*. Summary prepared by Secretary-General in accordance with Commission Resolution 18 (XXXIV) E/CN.4/1314, 19 December 1978, para. 53. In their book on the United Nations Convention Against Torture, Manfred Nowak and Elizabeth McArthur note that 'the US position seemed to have been accepted by the drafters without much opposition.' M. Nowak and E. McArthur, *The United Nations Convention Against Torture: A Commentary* (2005) 118. A similar claim was made in a Central Intelligence Agency, Office of General Counsel memo, thus:

'The [Torture] Convention permits the use of [cruel and inhuman treatment or treatment that "shocks the conscience"] in exigent circumstances, such as a national emergency or war': CIA-OGC, *Legal Principles Applicable to CIA Detention and Interrogation of Captured Al-Qa'ida Personnel* (undated).

11 Article 3 states: 'No one shall be subjected to torture or to inhuman or degrading treatment or punishment'.

12 Article 15(1) states: 'In time of war or other public emergency threatening the life of the nation any High Contracting Party may take measures derogating from its obligations under this Convention to the extent strictly required by the exigencies of the situation ... ' Article 15(2) prohibits derogation from Article 3.

13 T. Nagel, 'Agent-Relativity and Deontology', in S. Darwall (ed.), *Deontology* (2003) 104.

14 Y. Ginbar, *Why Not Torture Terrorists? Moral, Practical, and Legal Aspects of the 'Ticking Bomb' Justification for Torture* (2008) 19.

15 Amnesty International, *Human Dignity Denied: Torture and Accountability in the 'War on Terror'* (2004) (noting *inter alia*: '[r]espect for human dignity [is] ... the heart of international human rights and humanitarian law').

16 For an excellent discussion, see J. Conroy, *Unspeakable Acts, Ordinary People: The Dynamics of Torture* (1999).

17 Similar reasoning can be applied to the actions of terrorists themselves who use their victims as a means to pursue their ideological or other motivational ends.

18 R. Dworkin, *Taking Rights Seriously* (1977) 198.

19 D. Feldman, *Civil Liberties and Human Rights in England and Wales* 2nd edn. (2002) 110.

20 Of course, increasing security does not necessarily reduce the costs of terrorism. Didier Bigo and Elspeth Guild argue that 'the effect [of increasing security] is often far from giving more protection to individuals' and that '[i]f securitisation means coercion without effective protection, then desecuritisation is a necessary step': D. Bigo and E. Guild, 'The Worst-case Scenario and the Man on the Clapham Omnibus', in Goold and Lazarus, *supra* n. 7, 112.

21 Article 10(2).

22 *Jersild v. Denmark* (1995) 19 EHRR 1, para. 31.

23 Jeremy Waldron has noted that the notion of security is a 'vague and ambiguous concept': 'Safety and Security', (2006) 85 *Nebraska L. Rev.* 454, 456. For the purpose of this book security simply means a state of affairs where citizens live their everyday lives without undue fear of being a victim of a terrorist act. This does not mean total, guaranteed security in all circumstances. No-one can ever expect to live in a completely secure world.

24 B. Wilson, *What Price Liberty? How Freedom Was Won and is Being Lost* (2009) 85.

25 Ashworth, *supra* n. 7, 213. Some of the proponents of legalisation argue that states are under a moral duty to torture in order to save innocent life: M. Bagaric and J. Clarke, *Torture: When the Unthinkable is Morally Permissible* (2007) 72–3.

26 M. Ignateff, 'Moral Prohibition at a Price', in Roth, *supra* n. 9, 26 (defenders of an absolute prohibition against torture 'should be honest enough to admit that moral prohibition comes at a price').

27 J. Waldron, *The Law* (1990) 95.

28 Of course, the Article 3 prohibition can be defended on utilitarian grounds as it inhibits the spread of torture from 'ticking bomb' cases, to everyday circumstances.

29 Dworkin, *supra* n. 18, ch. 7 (discussing *inter alia* the purpose and potential cost of rights).

30 For the most recent example at the time of writing, see: *Novoselov v. Russia* Application no. 33954/05 (2013).

31 Application no. 22978/05 (2010).

32 *Id* para. 87. The Grand Chamber recently invoked similar reasoning in the context of a case involving the torture of a German citizen subject to 'rendition' by the Central Intelligence Agency: *El-Masri v. The Former Yugoslav Republic of Macedonia* Application no. 39630/09 (2012), para. 195.

33 M.D. Evans and R. Morgan, *Preventing Torture: A Study of the European Convention for the Prevention of Torture and Inhuman or Degrading Treatment or Punishment* (1998) 70–1.
34 *Supra* n. 31, para. 107.
35 By contrast some scholars maintain that the actions of terrorists mean 'that the balancing of their pain against the well-bring of others' is morally permissible: T. Meisels, *The Trouble with Terror: Liberty, Security, and the Response to Terrorism* (2008) 188.
36 The question has arisen in relation to other criminal acts. In *Jalloh* v. *Germany* Application no. 54810/00 (2006) the Grand Chamber was prepared to judge the existence of inhuman or degrading treatment in light of the seriousness of the criminal acts a suspect was believed to have committed. However, the unambiguous endorsement of the absolute prohibition in *Gäfgen*, and its rejection of any balancing approach taking into account the conduct of the victim of an Article 3 violation would suggest that the approach in *Jalloh* is not applicable to torture. The Grand Chamber has also recently held that the slapping of suspects by police offices during questioning was not a violation of Article 3: *Bouyid* v. *Belgium* Application No. 23380/09 (2013).
37 *A* v. *Netherlands* Application no. 4900/06 (2010).
38 *Id.* para. 25.
39 *Id.* para. 143.
40 Application no. 37201/06, §§ 139–40 (2008), para. 137.
41 *Id.* para. 139.
42 M. Ignatieff, *Human Rights as Politics and Idolatry* (2001) 22. See also M. Ignatieff, *The Lesser Evil: Political Ethics in an Age of Terror* (2004) 135–44 (arguing that lesser forms of coercion that do not amount to torture may be justified in response to the greater evil of terrorist violence).
43 In *A* v. *The Netherlands* the ECtHR noted: '[t]errorism seriously endangered the right to life, which was the necessary precondition for enjoyment of all other fundamental rights': *supra* n. 37, para. 127.
44 A. Barak, 'Human Rights in Times of Terror – a Judicial Point of View', (2008) 28 *Legal Studies* 493, 497.
45 For a detailed analysis of the problems associated with the use of state power and the benefits of security, see I. Loader and N. Walker, *Civilizing Security* (2007).
46 E.A. Posner and A. Vermeule, *Terror in the Balance: Security, Liberty, and the Courts* (2007) 5.
47 *Id* 207–8.
48 Unlike most proponents of legalisation, Posner and Vermeule have identified a wide range of interests, although some are absent: *id* ch. 6.
49 For a critical view of balancing, see L. Zedner, *Security* (2009) 134–7.
50 K. Roach, 'Must we Trade Rights for Security? The Choice Between Smart, Harsh, or Proportionate Security Strategies in Canada and Britain', (2006) 27 *Cardozo L. Rev.* 2151, 2153–5.
51 L.K. Donohue, *The Cost of Counterterrorism: Power, Politics and Liberty* (2008) 116.
52 S. Greer, 'Should Police Threats to Torture Suspects Always be Severely Punished? Reflections on the *Gäfgen* Case' (2011) 11 *Human Rights Law Review* 67, 80–2.
53 *Id.* 83.
54 *Id.* 88.
55 D. Bigo and E. Guild, 'The World-case Scenario and the Man on the Clapham Omnibus', in Goold and Lazarus, *supra* n. 7, 114.
56 C.A. Gearty, 'Terrorism and Human Rights', [2007] *E.H.R.L.R.* 1, 3. Indeed, lessons might be learned from the judiciary whose use of the balancing metaphor suggests it has been used with little evidence of consistency or principle: T.A. Aleinikoff, 'Constitutional Law in the Age of Balancing', (1987) 96 *Yale L.J.* 943.
57 R.B. Brandt, 'Towards a Credible Form of Utilitarianism', in S. Darwall (ed.), *Consequentialism* (2008) 208.
58 A recent example makes the point. Charles Fuqua, a 2012 Republican candidate for the Arkansas State House of Representatives, argued, on the basis of Biblical and

consequentialist reasoning, that 'rebellious children' should be executed as a deterrent to others in order to maintain 'civil order'. He stipulates that such executions should only take place after appropriate legal proceedings and would be used 'rarely': J. Celock, 'Charlie Fuqua, Arkansas Legislative Candidate, Endorses Death Penalty For Rebellious Children In Book', *HuffPost Politics* 8 October 2012.

59 D. Cole and J.X. Dempsey, *Terrorism and the Constitution: Sacrificing Civil Liberties in the Name of National Security* (2006) 240, 242.

60 H.H. Willis *et al*, *Estimating Terrorism Risk* (Santa Monica: RAND Corporation, 2005) 14–5. Nate Silver argues that it is important to makes forecasts of possible future terrorist threats and that problems can occur when there is a failure to forecast particular risks: *The Signal and the Noise: The Art and Science of Prediction* (2013) 421.

61 For discussion, see S.O. Hansson, 'Philosophical Problems in Cost-benefit Analysis', (2007) 23 *Economics and Philosophy* 163, 171–2.

62 For discussion, see C. Campbell and I. Connolly, 'Making War on Terror? Global Lessons from Northern Ireland', (2006) 69 *MLR* 935.

63 A.N. Guiora, 'Transnational Comparative Analysis of Balancing Competing Interests in Counter-Terrorism', (2006) 20 *Temp. Int'l & Comp. L.J.* 363, 376 (arguing that failed counter-terrorism strategies are 'imbalanced').

64 These issues will be considered in more detail in Chapter 4, but for an excellent overview in relation to the use of interrogational torture, see S. Holmes, 'In Case of Emergency: Misunderstanding Tradeoffs in the War on Terror', (2009) 97 *Cal. L. Rev.* 301, 337–47.

65 I. Zamir, 'Human Rights and National Security', (1989) 23 *Isr. L. Rev.* 375, 380.

66 Posner and Vermeule engage in a similar contextual analysis when they argue that in 'normal times' the benefits of the absolute prohibition outweigh the harm, '[d]uring emergencies, the moral harms from coercive interrogation remain constant while the potential benefits rise': *supra* n. 46, 215. However, they may be underestimating the cost of legalisation by ignoring harms that occur, or are more likely to occur, in times of emergency such as a growth in the use of interrogational torture and slippage.

67 *Id.* Exceptional cases might include acts of terrorism that involve the detonation of a nuclear weapon or use of other types of weapons of mass destruction. Some have argued that the specific threat posed by terrorism challenges the 'effective sovereignty' of the modern state and requires a (temporary) rebalancing of liberty and security through the use of an 'emergency constitution': B. Ackerman, *Before the Next Attack: Preserving Civil Liberties in an Age of Terrorism* (2006). Conor Gearty has noted that despite Ackerman's denial, his proposed emergency powers could be invoked in a range of potential circumstances in order to provide powers to deal with criminals and others who supposedly cannot be dealt with by the criminal justice process: 'The Superpatriotic Fervour of the Moment', (2008) 28 *O.J.L.S.* 183, 187–90 (discussion of the examples of the mafia and Communism).

68 P. Wilkinson, *Terrorism Versus Democracy: The Liberal State Response* (2002) 220.

69 *Id.* A.K. Cronin, *How Terrorism Ends: Understanding the Decline and Demise of Terrorist Campaigns* (2009).

70 Although some scholars have dismissed the threat of nuclear terrorism, there is a literature which suggests that such fears are credible. For contrasting work on this topic, see F. Furedi, *Invitation to Terror: The Expanding Empire of the Unknown* (2007) ch. 2 (largely dismisses the threat of nuclear terrorism); M. Flood, 'Nuclear Sabotage', (1976-June) *Bulletin of the Atomic Scientists* 29 (discussing sabotage and attacks on nuclear facilities); J. Penkrot, 'Cowering in Fear', (1977-January) *Bulletin of the Atomic Scientists* 6 (disputing some of Flood's factual claims); M. Willrich and T.B. Taylor, *Nuclear Theft: Risks and Safeguards* (1977); G. Allison, *Nuclear Terrorism: The Ultimate Preventable Catastrophe* (2005); D. Nelson, 'Pakistan's nuclear bases targeted by al-Qaeda' www. telegraph.co.uk 11 August 2009 (discussing repeated armed attacks on Pakistan's nuclear facilities).

71 B. Wittes, *Law and the Long War: The Future of Justice in the Age of Terror* (2008) 209.

72 Wittes argues that in the United States of America terrorist attacks are 'infrequent' and therefore a ticking bomb-type situation is 'exceptionally unlikely,' *id.* 189.

73 For consideration of this argument, see Chapter 4.

74 P. Bobbitt, *Terror and Consent: The Wars for the Twenty-First Century* (2008) 387.

75 A. Silke (ed.), *Terrorists, Victims and Society: Psychological Perspectives on Terrorism and Its Consequences* (2003) chs. 7–10 (discussing a range of impacts on children, as well as the effects of isolated and protracted acts of terrorism).

76 See, for example, G. Meotti, *A New Shoah: The Untold Story of Israel's Victims of Terrorism* (2010); D. Filkins, *The Forever War: Dispatches from the War on Terror* (2009) Ch. 10 (discussing *inter alia* tactics by terrorists intended to maximise casualties such as the use of multiple suicide bombers and car bombs to attack single targets).

77 S. Cohen, *Folks Devils and Moral Panics* 3rd edn. (2002) 57. For discussion of moral panic in the context of post-9/11 responses to terrorism, see D. Rothe and S.L. Muzzatti, 'Enemies Everywhere: Terrorism, Moral Panic, and US Civil Society', (2004) 12 *Critical Criminology* 327.

78 Bagaric and Clarke, *supra* n. 25, 72.

79 T. Nagel, 'War and Massacre', in S. Scheffler (ed.), *Consequentialism and Its Critics* (1988).

80 B. Juratowitch, 'Torture is Always Wrong', (2008) 22 *Public Affairs* 81, 83.

81 P. Bobbitt, *Terror and Consent: The Wars for the Twenty-First Century* (2008) 387.

82 Juratowitch, *supra* n. 80, 83.

83 J.C.C. Smart and B. Williams, *Utilitarianism: For and Against* (1991) 14. This description is in the context of act utilitarianism which includes the examination of actions as part of the utilitarian calculus. It would appear that there is no reason not to consider the nature of the act (torture) as part of the formulation adopted in this book given that it has immediate and longer-lasting consequences.

84 For discussion, see J.M. Arrigo, 'A Utilitarian Argument Against Torture Interrogation of Terrorists', (2004) 10 *Science and Engineering Ethics* 543.

85 The literature is extensive, but see, for example, M. Başoğlu *et al*, 'Torture vs Other Cruel, Inhuman, and Degrading Treatment: Is the Distinction Real or Apparent?' (2007) 64 *Arch. Gen. Psychiatry* 277; T.A. Campbell, 'Psychological Assessment, Diagnosis, and Treatment of Torture Survivors: A Review', (2007) 27 *Clinical Psychology Rev.* 628; A.E. Ojeda (ed.), *The Trauma of Psychological Torture* (2008).

86 Juratowitch, *supra* n. 80, 87.

87 Nagel, *supra* n. 79, 103.

88 *Id* 103.

89 A. Harel and A. Sharon, 'What is Really Wrong with Torture?' [2008] *J.I.C.J.* 241.

90 *Id* 251. Similarly, in his writings on lying which are generally seen as an advocacy of a deontological perspective, Immanuel Kant also uses a consequentialist (slippery-slope) argument: I. Kant, *The Metaphysics of Morals* in Darwall, *supra* n. 13, 24.

91 Harrel and Sharon, *supra* n. 89, 259.

92 *Id* 250.

93 C. Fried, *Right and Wrong* (1978) 10. However, see Fried's recent co-authored work on torture: *infra* n. 95, 30–1.

94 For similar problems, see A. Sen, 'Utilitarianism and Welfarism', in Darwall, *supra* n. 57, 268–71. The narrow approach to the question of consequences is illustrated by the work of Bagaric and Clarke, *supra* n. 25, and can be contrasted with the broader discussion of issues by Posner and Vermeule: *supra* n. 46, ch. 6.

95 C. Fried and G. Fried, *Because it is Wrong: Torture, Privacy and Presidential Power in the Age of Terrorism* (2010) 29.

96 See, for example, Bagaric and Clarke, *supra* n. 25, ch. 3; A.M. Dershowitz, *Why Terrorism Works: Understanding the Threat, Responding to the Challenge* (2003) ch. 4.

97 Bagaric and Clarke, *supra* n. 25, 33.

98 A. Ryan (ed.), *John Stuart Mill and Jeremy Bentham: Utilitarianism and Other Essays* (1987) 278.
99 For example, Bagaric and Clarke, who make explicit use of utilitarian theory, make only brief reference to the work of Bentham and Mill: *supra* n. 25, 29.
100 Ryan, *supra* n. 98, 293.
101 S. Holmes, 'Is Defiance of Law a Proof of Success? Magical Thinking in the War on Terror', in K.J. Greenberg (e.d.), *The Torture Debate in America* (2005) 133.
102 Dershowitz, *supra* n. 96, 146.
103 See, for example, Juratowitch, supra n. 80, 83–5; Fried and Fried, *supra* n. 95, 30.
104 Fried and Fried, *id.*
105 Juratowitch, *supra* n. 80, 84.
106 *Id.*
107 S.F. Colb, 'Why is Torture "Different" and how "Different" is it?' (2009) 30 *Cardozo L. Rev.* 1411, 1441–6 (comparing interrogational torture with self-defence).
108 Ryan, *supra* n. 98, 291.
109 *Id.*
110 Bagaric and Clarke argue that a torture power can be controlled and its legalisation will not result in its widespread use: *supra* n. 25, Ch. 4.
111 B. Brecher, *Torture and the Ticking Bomb* (2008) 57–74. See also Chapter 4.
112 Ryan, *supra* n. 98, 82.
113 W.L. Twining and P.E. Twining, 'Bentham *on* Torture', (1973) 24 *N.I.L.Q.* 305, 321.
114 R. Morgan, 'The Utilitarian Justification of Torture: Denial, Desert and Disinformation', (2000) 2 *Punishment & Society* 181, 188. Bentham's Introduction to the *Principles of Morals and Legislation* was written 'some time before 1780': *supra* n. 98, 9. He authored his work on torture between 1777 and 1779. It is therefore entirely possible that Bentham's insights concerning benefit or purpose could have been more fully explored in his work on torture.
115 Ryan, *supra* n. 98, 66.
116 C. Campbell, 'Beyond Radicalization-Towards an Integrated Anti-Violence Rule of Law Strategy', in A.M. Salinas de Frías *et al*, (eds), *Counter-Terrorism: International Law and Practice* (2012) 270.
117 C. McCauley and S. Moskalenko, 'Mechanisms of Political Radicalization: Pathways Toward Terrorism', (2008) 20 *Terrorism and Political Violence* 415.
118 State repression can take many forms and falls along a continuum. Some scholars have made a distinction between 'hard' and 'soft' repression. The use of interrogational torture undoubtedly falls within the 'hard repression' category: C. Davenport *et al*, (eds), *Repression and Mobilization* (2005) xxvii, 3–4.
119 Campbell, *supra* n. 116.
120 For discussion, see F.A. Gerges, *Journey of the Jihadist: Inside Muslim Militancy* (2007) 57–8; G. Kepel, and J-P. Milelli, *Al Qaeda in its Own Words* (2008) 150–4.
121 J. Merriman, *The Dynamite Club: How a Bombing in Fin-de-Siècle Paris Ignited the Age of Modern Terror* (2009).
122 P.K. Davis *et al*, *Understanding and Influencing Public Support for Insurgency and Terrorism* (2012) 127.
123 M. Florez-Morris, 'Why Some Columbian Guerrilla Members Stayed in the Movement Until Demobilization: A Micro-Sociological Case Study of Factors the Influenced Members' Commitment to Three Former Rebel Organizations: M-19, EPL, and CRS', (2010) 22 *Terrorism and Political Violence* 216, 224–5.
124 See, for example, Report of the Committee on Armed Services United State Senate, *Inquiry into the Treatment of Detainees in US Custody* (2008) xii.
125 For a detailed discussion, see P. Rumney, 'Making Things Worse? Interrogational Torture and Counter-terrorism Policy', (2013) 12 *Contemporary Issues in Law* 339.
126 Campbell and Connolly, *supra* n. 62, 949.
127 L. Richardson, *What Terrorists Want: Understanding the Enemy, Containing the Threat* (2006) 74. See also R. Fields, 'Terrorised into Terrorist: "Pete the Para" Strikes Again',

in: Y. Alexander and A. O'Day, *Ireland's Terrorist Trauma: Interdisciplinary Perspectives* (1989).

128 Richardson, *id* 88.

129 F.A. Gerges, *The Far Enemy: Why Jihad Went Global* (2007) 9.

130 R.B. Jensen, 'The International Campaign Against Anarchist Terrorism, 1880–1930s', (2009) 21 *Terrorism and Political Violence* 89, 99, 101, 105.

131 A series of interviews with would-be Palestinian terrorists suggests that revenge is one of a number of different motivations: A. Merari *et al*, 'Making Palestinian "Martyrdom Operations"/"Suicide Attacks": Interviews with Would-Be Perpetrators and Organizers', (2010) 22 *Terrorism and Political Violence* 102, 109–10.

132 Richardson, *supra* n. 127, 78–9.

133 *Id* 79.

134 Campbell and Connolly, *supra* n. 62, 947–50.

135 *Id* at 950. Campbell and Connolly cite research in which 'the picture suggested in the survey was of rebel leaders manipulating experiences and perceptions of repression to build their organisation' (at 950). See also T.P. Coogan, *The IRA* (1989) 436.

136 C. Douzinas, *The End of Human Rights: Critical Legal Thought at the Turn of the Century* (2000) 293.

137 I. Cobain, *Cruel Britannia: A Secret History of Torture* (2012) 203. This offers support to the work of Matthews in terms of how torture on one individual can impact a wider social circle.

138 Campbell, *supra* n. 116, 270.

139 This point has also been made in the context of other counter-terrorism strategies, including state surveillance: S. Macdonald, 'Why We Should Abandon the Balance Metaphor: A New Approach to Counterterrorism Policy', (2008) 15 *ILSA Journal of International & Comparative Law* 95, 118–9.

140 P. Taylor, *Brits: The War Against the IRA* (2001) 67.

141 For discussion of these techniques, see Chapters 3 and 4.

142 Lord Parker of Waddington, *Report of the Committee of Privy Counsellors appointed to consider authorised procedures for the interrogation of persons suspected of terrorism* (1972) para. 15.

143 *Id.*

144 Matthews, *supra* n. 1, 54, 58.

145 T.A. Campbell, 'Psychological assessment, diagnosis, and treatment of torture survivors: A review', (2007) 25 *Clinical Psychology Review* 628, 634.

146 Campbell, *supra* n. 116, 258.

147 For discussion of this tactic by jihadists, see D. Cook, *Understanding Jihad* (2005); G. Kepel, and J-P. Milelli, *Al Qaeda in its Own Words* (2008); M. Haybeck, *Knowing the Enemy: Jihadist Ideology and the War on Terror* (2006).

148 V. Bufacchi and J.M. Arrigo, 'Torture, Terrorism and the State: A Refutation of the Ticking-Bomb Argument', (2006) 23 *Journal of Applied Philosophy* 355.

149 For perhaps the most pronounced defence of utilitarian moral theory as a means of justifying the use of interrogational torture, see Bagaric and Clarke, *supra* n. 25, Ch. 3.

150 It is rare for any proponent of interrogational torture to acknowledge any wider social impact of its use. Posner and Vermeule make the argument that the use of interrogational torture would have a positive impact on Muslim perception of the United States by demonstrating 'strength' and a willingness to do what is necessary to protect citizens: *supra* n. 46, 206.

151 For an example of denial, see J. Yoo, *War by Other Means: An Insider's Account of the War on Terror* (2006) 192–3.

152 It might be argued, for example, that the isolated use of interrogational torture would not have these impacts. But that of course assumes that torture would be used in isolated instances.

153 Campbell and Connolly, *supra* n. 62, 941.

154 Juratowitch, *supra* n. 80.

155 H.L.A. Hart, *Punishment and Responsibility* (1968) 73.

156 *Id.*
157 *Id.* 71–3.
158 Posner and Vermeule, *supra* n. 46, 215.
159 *Id.* ch. 6.
160 Bagaric and Clarke, *supra* n. 25, 31–2.
161 For example, Article 2(1) of the ECHR states that 'Everyone's right to life shall be protected by law … ' Article 2(1)(a) states *inter alia* 'Deprivation of life shall not be regarded as inflicted in contravention of this article when it results from the use of force which is no more than absolutely necessary: (a) in defence of any person from unlawful violence'.
162 Ryan, *supra* n. 98, 282.
163 In a 1955 report that examined the use of torture by the authorities in Algeria, the Civil Inspector-General in Algeria noted that he had been assured by the police a water pipe interrogation method, that involved forcing water into the stomach of detainees, involved 'no risk to the health of the victim': Office of the Governor-General, Civil Inspectorate-General in Algeria, Algiers, 2 March 1955, cited in P. Vidal-Naquet, *Torture: Cancer of Democracy: France and Algeria 1954–62* (1963) 177. See also: S. Harris, *The End of Faith: Religion, Terror, and the Future of Reason* (2006) 194 ('Torture need not even impose a significant risk of death or permanent injury on its victims … ').
164 Posner and Vermeule, *supra* n. 46, 213. For a similar point comparing the efficacy of various degrees of coercion on recalcitrant suspects, see: R.A. Posner, *Not a Suicide Pact: The Constitution in a Time of National Emergency* (2006) 82.
165 There are some issues that could never be properly addressed. For example, police officers can achieve a very high degree of expertise in using firearms with practice; but interrogators cannot practice torturing unwilling and highly motivated subjects. Again, this might suggest another difference between the two harms, although state authorities would undoubtedly draw on the expertise of agencies such as the CIA.
166 H. Shue, 'Torture', in S. Levinson (ed.), *Torture: A Collection* (2004) 51.
167 E. Scarry, *The Body in Pain: The Making and Unmaking of the World* (1985) 34–5.
168 See, for example, C. af Jochnick and R. Normand, 'The Legitimization of Violence: A Critical History of the Laws of War' (1994) 35 *Harv. Int'l L.J. 49*; R. Normand and C. af Jochnick, 'The Legitimation of Violence: A Critical Analysis of the Gulf War', (1994) 35 *Harv. Int'l L.J.* 387. Here, it is argued that humanitarian concerns are only of secondary importance to the permissibility of violence in the laws of war.
169 J. Jeremy Wisnewski and R.D. Emerick, *The Ethics of Torture* (2009) 63.
170 *Id.*
171 Scarry, *supra* n. 167, 31.
172 Proponents of legalisation rarely acknowledge the reality of torture or its linkage with death. This reflects a general approach to legalisation that underestimates the costs of legalisation by ignoring the harm caused to the victims of interrogational torture.
173 M. Feitlowitz, *A Lexicon of Terror: Argentina and the Legacies of Torture* (1998).
174 *Id.* 81.
175 *Id.* 51.
176 *Id.* 59.
177 H. Alleg, *The Question* (1958) 93.
178 Feitlowitz, *supra* n. 173, 76.
179 A. Keller, Director of the Bellevue/New York University School of Medicine Program for Survivors of Torture, cited in B Walsh, 'Waterboarding: A Mental and Physical Trauma,' www.Time.com 20 April 2009.
180 International Committee of the Red Cross, *ICRC Report on the Treatment of Fourteen 'High Value Detainees' in CIA Custody* (2007) 30.
181 *Id* 36. The report notes that scars were visible on Khalid Sheikh Mohammed's wrists and ankles. This may also have been caused by shackling which forced KSM to stand for extended periods, *id.* 35.

182 H. Reyes, 'The Worst Scars are in the Mind: Psychological Torture', (2007) 89 *International Review of the Red Cross* 591, 603–4.
183 C. Correa, 'Waterboarding Prisoners and Justifying Torture: Lessons for the U.S. from the Chilean Experience', (2007) 14 *Hum. Rts. Brief* 21, 22.
184 *Id.* 21.
185 *Id.* 22.
186 *Id.*
187 For discussion of the law and practice of the police use of firearms and lethal force, see M. Punch, *Shoot to Kill: Police Accountability, Firearms and Fatal Force* (2011).
188 A distinction has also been made on the basis of the effectiveness of torture and lethal force, but is inevitably speculative: P. Rumney, 'Is Coercive Interrogation of Terrorist Suspects Effective? A Response to Bagaric and Clarke', (2006) 40 *U.S.F.L. Rev.* 479, 482–5.
189 Wisnewski and Emerick, *supra* n. 169, 33.
190 Dershowitz, *supra* n. 96, 146.
191 For discussion, see D. Cole, *Enemy Aliens: Double Standards and Constitutional Freedoms in the War on Terrorism* (2005) Ch. 3.
192 Juratowitch, *supra* n. 80, 89.
193 U. Steinhoff, 'Torture-The Case for Dirty Harry and Against Alan Dershowitz', in D. Rodin, *War, Torture & Terrorism: Ethics and War in the 21st Century* (2007) 105.

2

THE TICKING BOMB ARGUMENT

Critical perspectives

'For the U.S., most cases for permitting harsh treatment of detainees on moral grounds begin with variants of the "ticking time-bomb" scenario.'[1]

'[A]rtificial cases make bad ethics.'[2]

In 2008, Associate Justice of the United States Supreme Court, Antonin Scalia, stated in an interview with the British Broadcasting Corporation (BBC) that in the context of interrogating a suspected terrorist: 'Is it really so easy to determine that smacking someone in the face to determine where he has hidden the bomb that is about to blow up Los Angeles is prohibited in the constitution? It would be absurd to say you couldn't do that. And once you acknowledge that, we're into a different game. How close does the threat have to be? And how severe can the infliction of pain be?'[3] The scenario sketched out by Justice Scalia lies at the core of arguments for the legalisation of interrogational torture. The so-called 'ticking bomb' hypothetical or argument mentioned in the first quote above is used to illustrate a situation where there is a threat to innocent life from a ticking bomb or some other threat, time is of the essence and the state is faced with the dilemma of what to do in order to extract life-saving intelligence from an uncooperative suspect. Virtually every scholar who has argued for the use or legalisation of interrogational torture uses this hypothetical, or something similar to it.[4] In this way, the hypothetical is a tool used to illustrate a scenario that is said to warrant the use of torture.[5]

Given its prominence in the torture debate, this chapter will examine the history of the ticking bomb hypothetical and its use by judges, politicians and scholars from a consequentialist perspective, and will consider an important distinction in its usage. First, there is the hypothetical that is used to posit a *what if?* question which sometimes forms part of an argument for the use of interrogational torture. Second, the chapter will analyse how the ticking bomb hypothetical has been considered in real world decision-making. The chapter will also carefully analyse the component parts of the hypothetical and how they are interpreted by scholars and state officials. It will note the problems created by the fluid meanings which attach to notions of imminence, threat and identity. In other words, these notions are often interpreted expansively to enable torture and coercion to be permitted. This is deeply problematic for law as a means of controlling state power. The chapter will argue that the hypothetical as a foundational argument in the case for legalisation does not provide a sound basis upon which to legislate.

Finally, the chapter will test what will be referred to as the unreality thesis. Opponents of torture and its legalisation have claimed that the hypothetical is a 'horribly misinformed' thought experiment[6] and not a realistic basis upon which to make decisions regarding ethics and legal policy. Typical criticisms echo that of the second quote at the start of the chapter and include claims that it is 'empirically impossible',[7] 'completely divorced from reality'[8] and has 'affinities with science fiction'.[9] These criticisms are often accompanied by a claim that the combination of events depicted in the hypothetical have never occurred in real life and, indeed, could never occur. In examining the unreality thesis, as well as other factual claims made by those participating in the torture debate, this analysis will take account of a wide range of contemporary and historic evidence. In so doing, it becomes readily apparent that the proponents fail to recognise the expansive nature of the components that comprise the ticking bomb hypothetical. This chapter will conclude by arguing that the hypothetical does have use in some contexts, but does not offer a sound basis upon which to base sound counter-terrorism law making.

1. A brief history of the ticking bomb hypothetical

The ticking bomb hypothetical is the modern version of a moral dilemma examined by philosophers, lawyers, journalists and novelists, over many centuries. While the modern manifestation of the hypothetical concerns a terrorist attack, historically, other dangers have also been highlighted. In the eighteenth century, Jeremy Bentham discussed a hypothetical involving two men who were apprehended on suspicion of committing arson.[10] One of the men escaped from custody and his accomplice refused to disclose the escapee's true identity. The imminent threat was that the escapee may have wished to pursue his criminal acts of arson.[11] The purpose of torture in such circumstances would be to 'put a stop to such actions of the like kind ... as either the delinquent himself or others might be disposed to commit on (any) future occasions that might arise.'[12] In these circumstances, Bentham suggests that the question as to whether the prisoner has the information being sought 'seems a point as easy to judge of as any other'[13] and argues that there is 'no more danger in trusting a Judge to decide upon this question, whether it is in the power of the prisoner to give such or such a piece of information, than in trusting him to decide upon any other question.'[14] Finally, he notes that the use of torture may not even be necessary as '[i]n general Cases [sic] a man's knowing that it may be applied will be sufficient'.[15] These statements contain faulty assumptions relating to identity and effectiveness that will be explored in more detail later in this book. Suffice to say his formulation is hardly unique in this regard.

In more recent times, the threat of arson featured in Bentham's hypothetical has morphed into an imminent terrorist attack.[16] An early example of this can be found in Jean Lartéguy's *Les Centurions*[17] in which the threat takes the form of a terrorist who has planted bombs in shops. He discloses the location of the bombs under torture and as a result, the attack is foiled.[18] Since then, the hypothetical has been used by scholars,[19] members of the judiciary[20] and government lawyers in arguments relating to appropriate legal and policy responses to imminent threats posed by terrorists and others suspected of involvement in criminal activity.[21] The watershed moment for the hypothetical was the aftermath of the 9/11 terrorist attacks. Soon after, its use became a regular feature of scholarly and media debates about how to deal with terrorist suspects who refused to disclose potentially life-saving information pertaining to future terrorist attacks.[22] It was even used by a journalist as part of an argument to support the British government's wish to extend the length of time terrorist suspects could be held by the police without charge.[23] Of more significance was when the hypothetical was used in a US Department of Justice's Office of Legal Counsel (OLC) memorandum to provide an illustration and justification for the use of force during interrogation against a terrorist suspect under the Eighth Amendment to the US Constitution:

> The use of force must also be proportional, i.e., there should also be some relationship between the technique used and the necessity of its use. So, if officials had credible threat information that a U.S. city was to be the target of a large-scale terrorist attack a month from now and the detainee was in a position to have information that could lead to the thwarting of that attack, physical contact such as shoving or slapping the detainee clearly would not be disproportionate to the threat posed ... [24]

In the same document the hypothetical was also used to illustrate an argument that torture and other forms of coercion during interrogation would be a proportionate response to a threat of terrorist attack in the context of the defence of necessity:

> It appears to us that the necessity defence could be successfully maintained in response to an allegation of a violation of a criminal statute ... al Qaeda has other sleeper cells within the United States that may be planning similar attacks. Al Qaeda seeks to develop and deploy chemical, biological and nuclear weapons of mass destruction. Under these circumstances, a particular detainee may possess information that could enable the United States to prevent imminent attacks that could equal or surpass the September 11 attacks in their magnitude. Clearly, any harm that might occur during an

interrogation would pale to insignificance compared to the harm avoided by preventing such an attack, which could take hundreds or thousands of lives.[25]

Before progressing further, it is worth considering a particular characteristic which can be found in Bentham's version of the hypothetical, as well as in its use by OLC lawyers. The way in which the components of the hypothetical are defined appears uncertain. In the OLC memo, reference is made to torture that *could* prevent a terrorist attack, in circumstances where the detainee *may* possess intelligence about a threat which *could* take many lives. The memo indicates a significant element of uncertainty surrounding the existence and nature of the threat and whether the detainee possesses life-saving intelligence. Some constructions of the hypothetical, such as that set out by Zuckerman,[26] avoid any such uncertainties by simply depicting a situation in which torture, in a time of imminent threat, is successfully used and the threat of harm avoided. Bentham adopts both approaches when he states that the escaped detainee *might* pose a threat and assumes that torture or its threatened use *would* work to elicit information and that it is a relatively *easy* task to determine who should be subject to interrogational torture. Here, he assumes away the question of effectiveness and the problem of identifying the guilty. These various approaches to the hypothetical illustrate the fluid way in which it can be constructed. It is worth acknowledging that Bentham recognised the uncertainties in this area when stating: '[p]erfect certainty … is an advantage scarce permitted to human kind.'[27] Indeed, as this chapter develops it will become clear that the ticking bomb argument is uncertain in theory and practice.

At this point, it is worth considering whether this fluidity of construction and meaning have implications for the case against the legalisation of interrogational torture. The hypothetical may be expansively defined where it exists as a pure thought experiment. In this context it has no relevance to law. If the hypothetical is used in the context of legal rule or policy-making then it has a great deal of relevance. A critical analysis helps to explain how the consequentialist underpinnings of the hypothetical result in a fluidity of meaning that attaches to the various component parts that make up the hypothetical. The hypothetical contains several components – imminence, intelligence, harm and identity that are in theory and practice capable of an expansive meaning. Of particular importance to this analysis is the meaning that attaches to them in the context of counter-terrorism policy and practice. Here, it is evident that there are serious doubts to be raised regarding the ability of a torture law to operate in a limited, targeted and controlled manner.

2. The use of ticking bomb arguments

a. Judicial usage

As part of their professional role, judges interpret statutory and constitutional provisions in the context of emergency situations where life might be under threat. In such cases, judges occasionally make reference to the ticking bomb hypothetical.

Judges use it as a means of identifying the limits of appropriate conduct on the part of state officials, as well as defining the rights of the individual. Variations on the ticking bomb hypothetical are also in evidence. In such situations the courts have considered whether certain rights that are enjoyed by suspects in normal circumstances can be lawfully denied an individual in emergency or 'exigent' situations. Within English law, reference to the hypothetical has been extremely rare. In *A* v. *Secretary of State for the Home Department*, Lord Bingham[28] and Lord Nicholls of Birkenhead considered the issue of when, if ever, it would be appropriate for state authorities to use intelligence resulting from torture. In discussing a situation in which intelligence had been obtained as a result of torture from a detainee held in another country, Lord Nicholls stated:

> The intuitive response to these questions is that if use of such information might save lives it would be absurd to reject it. If the police were to learn of the whereabouts of a ticking bomb it would be ludicrous for them to disregard this information if it had been procured by torture. No one suggests the police should act in this way.[29]

A similar view has been expressed by the UK government. In responding to claims by former US President George W. Bush that the use of waterboarding by the CIA prevented terrorist attacks in the UK. Officials told *The Daily Telegraph* that if they received intelligence about an imminent attack which was obtained by torture 'they would have to act if it could save lives'.[30]

The use of interrogational torture has also been considered by English judges in the context of police actions during criminal investigations. These situations have seemingly not involved ticking bombs. Rather, these cases have involved attempts to gain confessions, rather than intelligence. Some of these cases have involved police tactics that have crossed a high threshold of seriousness.[31] This is illustrative of a wider trend in the historic and contemporary literature which indicates that the use of interrogational torture by police officers during investigations is often conducted with the aim of securing confessions, rather than for the purpose of eliciting information to prevent imminent harm.[32] By comparison, there are a much smaller number of cases in which police officers outside of the United Kingdom have used physical coercion during interrogation to secure potentially life-saving information,[33] sometimes in situations that are similar to the events often depicted in the ticking bomb hypothetical.[34]

The courts in the United States of America have made reference to ticking bomb-type situations to provide a means of identifying a particular class of case in which police officers, faced with a time-limited situation where life is endangered, are not required to respect all the normal legal protections offered to criminal suspects. For example, the US courts have established exceptions to the decision of the Supreme Court in *Miranda* v. *Arizona*[35] which stated that prior to questioning, a criminal suspect must be 'warned ... that he has the right to remain silent, that anything he says can be used against him in a court of law, that he has the right to the presence of an attorney, and that if he cannot afford an attorney one will be appointed for him prior to any questioning if he so desires'.[36] In *New York* v. *Quarles*[37] the US Supreme Court recognised that in certain situations there existed a 'public safety' exception to the requirement that *Miranda* warnings be given prior to questioning.[38] In his dissenting opinion, Justice Thurgood Marshall thought a public safety exception was unnecessary. He did, however, make use of the ticking bomb hypothetical:

> If a bomb is about to explode or the public is otherwise imminently imper-iled, the police are free to interrogate suspects without advising them of their constitutional rights. Such unconsented questioning may take place not only when police officers act on instinct, but also when higher faculties lead them to believe that advising a suspect of his constitutional rights might decrease the likelihood that the suspect would reveal life-saving information ... [39]

In a number of cases, there has been recognition of an exception (sometimes referred to as the rescue doctrine[40]) to the principle in *Miranda* allowing the questioning of suspects in emergency situations, such as those involving an imminent threat to life.[41] In a review of relevant decisions, the California Court of Appeals in *People* v. *Riddle*[42] stated that: '[t]he principle of exigent circumstances, although relatively rare in application, is firmly established in law.'[43] It concluded that in the context of *Miranda* 'exigent circumstances may excuse compliance with the *Miranda* rules in instances of overriding need to save human life or to rescue persons whose lives are in danger'.[44] In the earlier decision of *People* v. *Modesto*,[45] the defendant had killed one girl and attacked and abducted another. On his arrest, he was questioned by police officers regarding the location of the missing girl. The officers told Modesto that they thought she could still be alive and be saved. With the cooperation of the defendant, the girl's body was subsequently located.[46] Traynor C.J. noted that the defendant's statements to the police: ' ... were freely and voluntarily made at a time when the officers were concerned primarily with the possibility of saving [the victim's] life. The paramount interest in saving her life, if possible, clearly justified the officers in not impeding their rescue efforts by informing defendant of his rights to remain silent and to the assistance of counsel.'[47] In *State* v. *Dean* the defendant was in the midst of a kidnap plot and was detained by the FBI when he attempted to pick up the ransom he had demanded.[48] In recognising a rescue doctrine under the Fifth Amendment,[49] the court noted the reason for its existence:

> While it is sadly true that all kidnap victims are not found alive, this does not compel the conclusion that a belief rescue is possible is unreasonable. A consideration frequently will be that accomplices of the captured kidnaper may be under instruction to kill the victim if the compatriot has not returned within a specified period of time. Maybe the victim is then dying or stuffed in a vehicle trunk which might not be discovered for days or weeks. Such considerations strongly support the rescue doctrine of *Modesto*.[50]

The experience of the courts in the United States makes clear that exigent circumstances can occur in a range of factual circumstances and differing legal contexts. For example, Cynthia Lee has noted that:

> Warrantless container searches are ... permitted under what is called the exigent circumstances exception. This exception to the warrant requirement is somewhat of a catch-all, permitting police to conduct warrantless searches whenever an emergency situation exists ... generally, the police must be dealing with an emergency situation that makes obtaining a warrant impracticable and the officer conducting the search must have probable cause to believe evidence of a crime will be found in the place searched.[51]

It is evident that an example of such an emergency situation would involve a ticking bomb. Likewise, in *Florida* v. *Wells*[52] the hypothetical was cited during oral argument in the context of a case involving the searching of canisters by a police officer. Under questioning, one of the lawyers before the court used the ticking bomb hypothetical to suggest that police officers should have discretion to search where there was a 'special exigency', such as when a person possessed a suitcase containing a bomb 'because the special exigency would be a legitimate danger to the police or to the citizenry'.[53] In other cases, the ticking bomb is replaced with hostage-taking. During oral argument before the US Supreme Court in *Chavez* v. *Martinez*,[54] Justice Scalia combined a variant of the ticking bomb hypothetical with the issue of coerced confessions. He questioned counsel about when conduct by a police officer should be deemed unconstitutional under the Fifth Amendment:

> Question: Suppose you have a situation in which a felon has taken a hostage and buried the hostage somewhere, and suppose that it is possible for the police official to use a degree of coercion which would not shock the conscience. It isn't beating the person with a rubber hose, but let's say failing to give a *Miranda* warning, or using ... a sort of trickery ... that would amount to coercion, threatening perhaps, you know, if you don't confess, your brother will be prosecuted or something like that. It would be sufficient to exclude the testimony from the confession from the trial, but the policeman doesn't care about that. He wants to save the life ... of the hostage ...
>
> Mr Paz: ... I would say *Quarles* gives us the direction. When there is an immediate danger, when there's a danger to the public, then clearly there would be no constitutional violation. The Court has already made that decision. I don't think that that's really an issue that we have to struggle with.[55]

This body of case law and its reference to the ticking bomb-type situations has influenced the development of policy by federal agencies. In 2011, *The New York Times* published a previously secret memorandum that had been drafted by the US Department of Justice and the Federal Bureau of Investigation (FBI) which concerned the use of *Miranda* warnings in the interrogation of terrorist suspects.[56] The memo, dated 21 October 2010, specifically recognises the existence of exigent circumstances that would justify the FBI not giving a *Miranda* warning to a suspect. It states *inter alia*: 'Identifying and apprehending suspected terrorists, interrogating them to obtain intelligence about terrorist activities and impending terrorist attacks ... are critical to protecting the American people.' The memo reflects much of the case law on exigent circumstances when it goes on to state: 'agents should ask any and all questions that are reasonably prompted by an immediate concern for the safety of the public or the arresting agents without advising the arrestee of his *Miranda* rights ... After all applicable public safety questions have been exhausted, agents should advise the arrestee of his *Miranda* rights and seek a waiver of those rights ... '[57] A similar provision exists in the UK. In Operation GIRD, six men were arrested as part of an investigation by the Metropolitan Police into an alleged plan to attack the Pope who was visiting London.[58] The threat was believed to be imminent and the men were the subject of 'safety interviews'.[59] A subsequent report into the operation noted: 'The purpose of a safety interview (or urgent interview) is to elicit information from a suspect which may help the police to avert significant risks, including to human life.'[60] In such circumstances a person may not be reminded of his right to a lawyer[61] and may be interviewed somewhere other than a designated location for interview.[62] It is clear that the safety interview is permitted precisely for the types of situation depicted in the hypothetical or its variants.

Perhaps the most significant judicial use of the ticking bomb hypothetical in the context of interrogational torture and coercion has been by the Israeli High Court of Justice (HCJ). In *Public Committee Against Torture in Israel* v. *The State of Israel* the HCJ found that the Israeli General Security Service (GSS) did not have lawful authority to use techniques such as shaking or stress positions in order to force detainees to divulge information pertaining to imminent terrorist attacks.[63] In stark contrast to the approach of the ECtHR discussed in Chapter 1,[64] the HCJ went on to argue that a necessity defence might be available where physical coercion was used in cases involving 'ticking time bombs' where 'there exists a concrete level of imminent danger of the explosion's occurrence'.[65] On the back of this decision, Israeli-based human rights groups have argued that Israeli security forces use interrogational torture against large numbers of detainees based on the pretext of an expansively defined notion of imminent threat.[66]

In a subsequent decision, the HCJ rejected as unlawful the use of an 'early warning' procedure by which local residents who were used by the Israeli army to warn wanted persons, and innocent people with them, that they may be injured during arrest. The purpose of the procedure was to give the suspect(s) the opportunity to surrender peacefully.[67] In his judgment, Vice President M. Cheshin made use of the *PCATI* decision in drawing comparison with the competing interests presented in the case, as well as the difficulties of controlling coercive powers by the state.[68] At the beginning of his judgment, Cheshin noted that the issue to be decided was 'most difficult' and that 'No matter which solution I choose, the time will come that I will regret my choice.' He went on to note: 'there is no clear legal rule to show us the way, and I shall decide according to my own way of legal reasoning.'[69] Consequently, he sought guidance from the *PCATI* decision noting that in this type of case 'interests and values of the first degree stood opposite each other, and deciding which interests and values would prevail, and which interests would retreat, was hard – unbearably hard'.[70] He argued that there were dangers in permitting the state a power which would be interpreted in 'conditions of mortal danger', and that as a result, legal rules may not be followed in practice. He noted that there was also a problem that exceptional powers may become normalised: '[r]outine, according to its very nature, deteriorates the sensitivity and caution needed to perform the procedure, and the concern that the special and rare will become regular and routine – even bureaucratic – is great.'[71]

This is an important recognition of the potential difficulties that arise where exceptional powers are claimed by the state which place security personnel in 'conditions of mortal danger' on the basis of a ticking bomb-type argument. Cheshin recognises that there is a danger that an extension of state power may result in unintended consequences. This problem goes to the very heart of the control of state power, the nature of regulation and the difference between rules and their interpretation in practice.[72] Indeed, the experience of Israel and other states (including the United Kingdom) that have used state-sanctioned coercive interrogation has confirmed the legitimacy of this concern.[73] Given the context of Cheshin's assertion, it is evident that these problems are not unique to the use of interrogational torture, but it is the judicial acknowledgement of potential abuse that is to be welcomed.

b. The ticking bomb in the political sphere

The idea of an imminent threat of terrorist attack has influenced political responses to terrorism, as well as the legislative agenda in some jurisdictions. It has done so in three ways. First, it can operate by pressuring politicians to pursue a counter-terrorist legislative agenda. In such circumstances, legislation can be introduced quickly, particularly in situations immediately following a terrorist attack in the hope that new measures will prevent further attacks. Second, the notion of imminent threat can subdue political opposition to such measures because legislators do not want to be seen to be failing to protect the innocent from terrorist violence. In such circumstances, security is often seen as an interest more important to protect than liberty. Third, the notion of imminent threat can create genuine fear amongst legislators, as well the media and general public. As such, it may have a 'desensitizing effect, leading otherwise morally committed persons to accept harsh tactics as a "lesser evil" against more ominous risks to national security'.[74]

In response to rationalised justifications for torture, which often rest on utilitarian underpinnings,[75] it has been argued that legislating in times of imminent crisis produces poorly drafted laws; that specific terrorist attacks are sometimes used as a cover for a pre-existing political and legislative agenda[76] and that politicians sometimes exaggerate the urgency of threats when making the case for new counter-terrorist measures. Indeed, Gardner argues that government agencies 'have always under-stood that the most effective way to protect themselves is to err on the side of threat inflation'.[77] It is also argued that in such circumstances the legislative process takes insufficient account of concerns over civil liberties.[78] Further, it is claimed that legislators may have little understanding of the measures they enact. For example, Cole and Dempsey have described the enactment of the USA Patriot Act shortly after the 9/11 attacks as involving little debate or consideration by Congress, suggesting that in the Senate it was 'clear that even supporters of the legislation had not read it and did not understand its provisions'.[79] Further, they suggest that Congress passed the legislation under 'extraordinary pressure from the Attorney General, who essentially threatened Congress that the blood of the victims of future terrorist attacks would be on its hands if it did not swiftly adopt the administration's proposals'.[80]

Counter-terrorism law-making in the United Kingdom highlights issues that are relevant here. In 1974, the UK Parliament enacted the Prevention of Terrorism (Temporary Provisions) Act (PTA). This legislation was enacted following an upsurge of terrorist attacks, including a series of pub bombings in Woolwich, Guildford and Birmingham by the IRA in October and November of 1974, which killed 28 people and injured hundreds of others. The Act passed its Parliamentary stages in four days with limited Parliamentary opposition.[81] When the government introduced the counter-terrorism Bill in Parliament it did not claim that it pos-sessed specific intelligence suggesting further imminent attacks. However, there clearly existed a fear of further attack, given that the bombings in November 1974 were part of an ongoing campaign of terrorist violence.[82] The Bill included measures that were viewed by the government as 'draconian ... [and] unprecedented in peace-time',[83] including powers to criminalise the financing and membership of 'pro-scribed organisations' and to exclude people suspected of involvement in terrorism from entering various parts of the United Kingdom.[84]

In light of the recent bombings and with fear of further attacks, during the House of Commons debates, repeated references were made by Home Secretary, Roy Jenkins MP, for the need to remain 'rational and calm'.[85] Another MP stated: 'we must take great care that in the heat of the moment we do not undertake steps, which though they may seem logical and certainly emotionally justifiable at the time, would lead to a [negative] atmosphere.'[86] Despite these assertions, two key characteristics can be identified in the debates that are also in evidence in discussions concerning the ticking bomb hypothetical. The first characteristic is a sense of imminent threat. The Home Secretary argued that the counter-terrorism measures debated were only justified because there existed a 'clear and present danger'.[87] It was also described by another MP as a 'very dangerous situation',[88] with reference being made to the need for a 'speedy' passage of the Bill.[89] The second characteristic of debate was the pre-eminence of security concerns. One member of the Official Opposition, Sir Keith Joseph MP, expressed a view which was undoubtedly shared by many other MPs: '[n]ational security must, with due care for civil liberties, now take priority.'[90] While reference was certainly made to the issue of civil liberties which would be threatened by the Bill,[91] security concerns, and the need for immediate action, appeared to be of primary importance. Indeed, some MPs did appear to react in a manner which suggested irrationality and panic. For example, Ronald Bell MP asked a question of the Home Secretary, which included the following: 'does he recognise that ruthless will on one side can be successfully met only by ruthless will on the other? Does he accept that it may even be necessary, because of the vulnerability of the community to attack of this kind, to adopt whatever is the peacetime equivalent to counter-attack?'[92]

Despite the pressure to act quickly, some measures that were strongly advocated by MPs were rejected by the government. The introduction of identity cards[93] and the return of capital punishment were proposed,[94] with the suggestion that the government Bill did not 'go far enough'.[95] Neither measure was introduced following the attacks.[96] One could therefore argue that the fear of future terrorist attacks did not result in 'panic' measures so much as it accelerated the law-making process.[97] Indeed, the government had previously secretly prepared a draft Bill containing a number of key provisions which were then put before Parliament.[98]

With the benefit of hindsight, public statements by politicians that emphasise the imminent nature of a threat can appear exaggerated.[99] In this context, exaggeration can involve the inflation of the scale of a potential threat, as well as the risk and imminence of its occurrence. In 2005, the Australian Prime Minister, John Howard, issued a public statement setting out his intention to introduce emergency legislation in order to 'strengthen the capacity of law enforcement agencies to effectively respond' to a 'potential terrorist threat'. He also noted that there existed an 'assessment [by] intelligence agencies that a terrorist attack in Australia is feasible and could well occur'.[100] The legislation was introduced and passed within 48 hours with the support of the Official Opposition party whose leader and Shadow Minister for Homeland Security had been briefed on the imminent terrorist threat. Lynch notes that from a legal perspective the reforms were probably not necessary, as the powers already existed to deal with the threat of terrorism.[101] He also engages in a detailed analysis of whether changes were urgently required and notes: 'arrests did not take place immediately upon the new powers being granted … it is difficult to square an *urgent* need for new powers to prevent an attack and not using them until over a week after the announcement of the threat'.[102] However, he identifies an important contextual element in considering the urgency of the legislative response, which is also of relevance to the UK experience of counter-terrorism law making:

> [W]ith the benefit of hindsight we may conclude that the threat was not so imminent as to have required the response it received … But that does *not* amount to saying that the Government's approach was verifiably illegitimate or manipulative. It was clearly one which was open to it on the evidence of what it knew. The threat may not have been imminent but the intelligence was sufficient to warrant all precaution (emphasis in original).[103]

Explicit use of the ticking bomb hypothetical was used in the nomination hearing for a new director of the CIA before the Senate Intelligence Committee in 2009.

Nominee, Leon Panetta was asked by Senator Richard Burr whether he would ever request permission for the use of coercive interrogation techniques in a ticking bomb case. Panetta answered in the affirmative:

> If we had a ticking bomb situation and whatever was being used, I felt was not sufficient, I would not hesitate to go to the President ... and request whatever additional authority I would need ... But I think this President would do nothing that would violate the laws that were in place.[104]

By contrast, in his nomination hearing to become US Attorney General before the Senate Judiciary Committee, Eric Holder took a different approach. Senator John Cornyn asked Holder about a scenario based on the ticking bomb hypothetical:

> ... you're familiar with the ticking time bomb scenario ... Let's say as Attorney General you find out that there are terrorists that have access to chemical, biological, or nuclear weapons, and that you have a detainee who's in possession of information that, if disclosed, would prevent those weapons from being detonated in the United States and thousands, maybe tens of thousands people being killed. You would still refuse to condone aggressive interrogation techniques like waterboarding to get that information, which would, under my hypothetical, save perhaps tens of thousands of lives?[105]

Holder responded by arguing that there were alternatives to waterboarding and doubted whether its use 'is necessarily going to produce the results that we want'. He also said that: 'people will say almost anything to avoid torture. They will give you whatever information they think you want to hear.' When pressed by Senator Cornyn, Holder argued that he did not agree with the premise underlying the hypothetical: 'I'm not willing to accept ... [that waterboarding] ... is the only way that I could get ... information from those people.' Of course, this raises the question of what would happen if other non-coercive techniques were used and failed to gain compliance. The contrast between the testimony of Pandetta and Holder is clear. Holder takes an approach akin to the scholarly opponents of interrogational torture who reject the hypothetical and attack the premises underlying it, while Pandetta considered what he would be prepared to do should permitted interrogation techniques fail. Of course, these differing answers might simply result from the way in which questions were framed, but they hint at a difference of opinion as to what might be done in times of emergency. The use of the hypothetical in these two instances had utility in highlighting such differing approaches.

Unsurprisingly, terrorist attacks focus the attention of the general public and politicians on preventive measures. As noted by Sunstein: '[i]f images of the threat come easily to mind, people are far more likely to be frightened and concerned than if they do not.'[106] It is not the case that the fear of future attacks is necessarily unfounded or disproportionate. It is reasonable for governments to consider the future likelihood of terrorist violence and appropriate responses. Instead, the problem lies in the conclusions and actions that result from the belief that an imminent threat exists. Further, it is feasible that there can be an exaggerated fear of the likelihood of future attacks. Sunstein notes that in the context of the US, '[t]he vividness of the attacks of 9/11 drives people's probability judgments about terrorism'.[107] It may also be the case that vividness drives some of the more extreme suggested responses to the problem of terrorism, as suggested by the legislator in the UK Parliament who referred to the need for a 'ruthless ... counter attack' in response to IRA violence.[108] More generally, the response of the politicians discussed in this section can be characterised as involving a precautionary approach in which security interests took priority. This is not necessarily unreasonable, but of course depends on the measures being adopted. The use of ticking bomb arguments can pose particular problems for the protection of human rights as legal prohibitions are challenged by consequentialist fears. However, the utility of such arguments in certain judical and political contexts should not be denied.

c. The ticking bomb hypothetical as a trap for liberals?

Writing in 2006, Luban asked why the ticking bomb scenario has become so important to the torture debate. He suggests that it is used as a means of cornering opponents of torture so that they are forced to accept that, in certain limited circumstances, torture is an acceptable means of preventing a terrorist attack:

> The ticking time-bomb is proffered against liberals who believe in an absolute prohibition against torture. The idea is to force the liberal prohibitionist to admit, that yes, even he or even she would agree to torture in at least this one situation. Once the prohibitionist admits that, then she has conceded that her opposition to torture is not based on principle ... Dialectically, getting the prohibitionist to address the ticking time-bomb is like getting the vegetarian to eat just one little oyster because it has a nervous system. Once she does that – *gotcha!* (emphasis in original).[109]

Leaving aside Luban's speculation regarding the motivations of those who propose the use of torture, this assertion can be analysed in several ways. The ticking bomb hypothetical serves the purpose of illustrating a consequentialist case for the use of torture. But it does so by ignoring a range of issues that require consideration before it is possible to properly address the dilemma posed. The trap, if there is one, is to engage with the hypothetical and not insist on a greater depth of analysis. Luban claims it asks what an *individual* would do in a ticking bomb case. This is problematic because the key issue is not a question of individual choice. Rather, it concerns what the *state* should be able to do in the circumstances depicted in the hypothetical. Further, it is no more a trap for liberals than any other argument, such as the premise contained within the hypothetical that torture can or will work as an intelligence gathering tool. Finally, Luban's argument carries with it an air of pessimism. To assume that the ticking bomb hypothetical has the effect of undermining the case against the legalisation of interrogational torture makes unwarranted assumptions regarding the persuasive force of the hypothetical. A better approach in dealing with the hypothetical is to develop a response which includes an explanation as to why it provides a weak basis upon which to abandon the absolute prohibition. This chapter begins this process by next detailing the expansive nature of the hypothetical.

3. The component parts of the ticking bomb hypothetical

The ticking bomb hypothetical is comprised of a number of component parts or conditions that should exist in order to provide a case for the use of interrogational torture. Allhoff observes: 'the [hypothetical] should be read as providing *sufficient* conditions for the application of torture', but only if the various conditions explicit and implicit within the hypothetical exist (emphasis in original).[110] He also argues that 'since the conditions are meant to be sufficient, rather than necessary, we have *no information* (yet) as to whether torture is permissible in the real world when one or more of the conditions is not met' (emphasis in original).[111] Other scholars have claimed that if the conditions of the hypothetical are met this will then mean that torture is 'morally obligated'.[112] Of course, even if this were true, whatever is morally obligated does not require its introduction as a matter of legal policy. If one were to favour the regulation of interrogational torture, then the preferable view is that the conditions be seen as *necessary* for the use of interrogational torture. The conditions are of central importance as they would form part of a legal regulatory framework that would authorise the infliction of torture. There is also another reason why these conditions are important and therefore necessary. If taken seriously, they would operate to control the use of legalised torture.

The ticking bomb hypothetical is much-used and for good reason. It is a useful tool to illustrate time-limited situations in the context of judicial decision-making and testing the resolve of government officials who might be tempted to seek torture powers. However, while the hypothetical has some use, problems begin to emerge where it is used as part of an argument favouring the legalisation or use of interrogational torture. If such an approach is adopted as part of a law-based regulatory regime, then it is likely to lead to an expansive torture power.[113] If the power were tightly drafted, interpreted and controlled its use should be extremely rare. However, it would appear pointless to create a state torture power, undermine the absolute prohibition and risk creating various negative consequences if it were to be used so rarely. As will become apparent in the next section, theoretical and real world use of interrogational torture suggests the existence of an expansive torture power. It would appear that the fear of consequences (the threat of terrorist violence) has a significant influence on the way these conditions are interpreted. In the next section four components that are commonly cited as being part of the hypothetical will be considered: imminence, intelligence, nature of the imminent threat and identifying those who would be subject to torture. Some scholars argue that the hypothetical includes a number of hidden conditions and assumptions.[114] For example, it is suggested that a condition of the hypothetical is that the use of interrogational torture be successful. Given its importance, the question of effectiveness will be briefly discussed here, and in more detail in Chapter 3.

a. Imminence

A key condition of the ticking bomb hypothetical is that state institutions or its citizenry face an imminent terrorist threat. While some commentators construct the hypothetical so the bomb will explode in a matter of minutes or a few short hours,[115] others depict the bomb as exploding days or even weeks ahead. Indeed, one of the key characteristics of the hypothetical is that imminence is defined expansively. In the OLC memorandum discussed earlier there is reference to an attack taking place in 'one month'.[116] Dershowitz considers the potential use of torture in response to 'dire circumstances', 'imminent attacks', 'plans' and the use of torture to gain 'information about terrorist "sleeper cells" and future targets'.[117] In Israel, the Landau Commission argued that where the bomb is ticking 'what difference does it make, in terms of the necessity to act, whether the charge is certain to be detonated in five minutes or five days?'.[118] This is a perspective dominated by a concern with end results. The Commission also made clear that the issue of necessity should be viewed in light of the 'flexible test' of 'the concept of the lesser evil'[119] and that '[e]verything depends on weighing the two evils against each other'.[120] This, of course, rests heavily on the weight given to each evil and is hardly straightforward.[121]

In the *PCATI* decision, the Israeli HCJ held that the question of immediacy pertains to the need to act, rather than the threat being immediate, though the two are clearly related – a need to act with immediacy clearly implies a threat that demands action.[122] The decision endeavours to link imminence with a vague evidential standard in the description of a ticking time bomb where 'there exists a concrete level of imminent danger of the explosion's occurrence'.[123] Like the Landau Commission, President A. Barak defined immediacy in an expansive manner: 'the imminence criteria is satisfied even if the bomb is set to explode in a few days, or perhaps even after a few weeks, provided the danger is certain to materialize and there is no alternative means of preventing its materialization.'[124] It is worth noting that if a bomb is set to explode in several weeks' time it would seem more appropriate to use conventional policing methods to find it; it is unclear how interrogators or intelligence analysts could know that the danger was 'certain to materialize'. The formulation offered by Landau and Barak appear to offer the Israel state license to continue using techniques that were already engrained as part of its counter-terrorism strategy.

Matthews criticises the use of the hypothetical precisely because it involves a time-limited situation. He argues that interrogators will often have to focus their attention on the preparation of a terrorist-attack because once a bomb is ticking there is little time left for state authorities to discover its location before it explodes.[125] He argues 'political actors [sic] favour quick actions because these increase the chance of achieving desired goals' and reduce the chance of detection by state authorities.[126] While this is generally true, there are examples in the literature of bombs that tick for significant periods of time. For example, on 12 October 1984 a bomb exploded at the Grand Hotel in Brighton in an attempt by the IRA to assassinate UK Prime Minister Margaret Thatcher and members of her cabinet. The bomb killed five people and injured 34. The man responsible, Patrick Magee, had planted the bomb twenty-four days earlier while staying at the hotel.[127] But what implications does such an occurrence have for analysis of the ticking bomb hypothetical and the legalisation of torture? This set of facts reminds us that the 'ticking bomb', both in terms of the hypothetical and real world decision-making, is an elastic concept. The factual scenario found in many descriptions of the ticking bomb argument recognises this. However, if torture were to be permitted several weeks before a terrorist attack was due to take place, it would grant state authorities a wide torture power which would likely increase the number of suspects who could face coercion and torture.

The expansive way in which imminence is interpreted in counter-terrorism policy is evidenced by a US Department of Justice White Paper which sets out the circumstances in which legal force can be used against a US citizen in another country who is a 'senior operational leader' of al Qaeda or an associated group.[128] The document sets out a three-part test that must be satisfied for a US citizen to be targeted abroad, including where it has been determined that the 'targeted individual poses an imminent threat of violent attack against the United States'.[129] The document goes on to explain what is meant by imminent in this context. The document states that there is no requirement that the US have evidence that a specific attack 'will take place in the immediate future' because it 'would not allow the United States sufficient time to defend itself'.[130] The document refers to the organisational structure of al Qaeda and the ability of its members to quickly disperse and points out that there would be 'only a limited window of opportunity within which to defend Americans'.[131] As a result of these factors the document argues that '[b]y its nature ... the threat posed by al-Qa'ida and its associated forces demands a broader concept of imminence in judging when a person continually planning terror attacks presents an imminent threat, making the use of force appropriate'.[132] For the purpose of this book, the important issue is that this document and its broader conception of imminence expands to fit with a desire to achieve consequentialist goals.

There is some empirical data concerning how the notion of imminence is interpreted in the real world of interrogational torture. The Israeli-based human rights group B'Tselem has claimed that most cases in which coercive methods have been justified before the Israeli courts as involving the threat of a ticking bomb, have proved 'totally unsubstantiated'.[133] It has cited examples where the use of coercion was justified against three detainees on the grounds that they possessed information that would prevent terrorist attacks. In one case the authorities claimed to have evidence from six witnesses to support the allegation that a detainee was 'active in a military organization'. All three detainees were subsequently released without charge.[134] B'Tselem also noted that some interrogations only occurred during weekdays,[135] stating: "'[i]ntensive interrogation", then, is rather peculiar. The lethal bomb ticks away during the week, ceases, miraculously, on the weekend, and begins to tick again when the interrogators return from their day of rest.'[136] Elsewhere, it has been claimed that there are long delays between arrest and interrogation which raises a question regarding the urgency of the threat that led to the arrest.[137]

So while there is some evidence that imminence appears to be defined broadly in practice, it is worth acknowledging that imminence is not a word that possesses a meaning denoting an exact measure of time. A dictionary definition of 'imminent', for example, includes reference to 'impending', 'approaching', 'forthcoming', 'looming' and 'threatening'.[138] These meanings support the suggestion that imminence has a flexible meaning. Further, it can be argued that the meaning of imminence partly depends on surrounding circumstances. For example, if a terrorist group acquired a nuclear weapon then this would be seen as an imminent threat irrespective of when or if the group planned to detonate it. This is because so long as the group possesses the weapon they have the ability to cause catastrophic harm. The group may plan to threaten to use the weapon in an attempt to coerce the state to meet their demands. Alternatively, they may have no intention of using the weapon given that its use could result in loss of support.[139] However, plans change and the state is not going to know the true intentions of the terrorists. Consequently, one can argue that the *danger* is immediate and so too the need to recover the weapon. But this fluidity of meaning is undoubtedly problematic.

It might be argued that the more distant the threat, the more opportunity there is to use conventional intelligence and policing techniques. This, however, assumes that state officials possess a threat timeline. On the other hand, even under the *PCATI* model of regulation, state officials can never truly know that there are 'no alternative means' of prevention.[140] The fact that coercion appears to be commonly used by the GSS suggests that these words have little meaning as a rule of last resort. Matthews argues that any time limit imposed on the meaning of imminence will be 'arbitrary' and that any rules will have 'grey zones' and that the setting of a time limit 'may prevent the achievement of intelligence goals'.[141] This also has implications for the legalisation of interrogational torture as it would exist within a framework of rules. As a consequence, immediacy would have to be given a legal meaning otherwise state authorities, as suggested by the Israel example, would be free to use torture or coercion expansively under a vague notion of imminence.

b. Intelligence

In the debate over the legalisation of interrogational torture, reference is inevitably made to the intelligence needed to avert an imminent terrorist attack. By contrast, relatively little is said about the nature of intelligence that state authorities seek. For the purpose of this discussion two types of intelligence can be identified. The first type of intelligence is that needed to prevent an imminent terrorist attack, such as that depicted in the typical ticking bomb hypothetical and shall be referred to as *ticking bomb intelligence*. The second type of intelligence will be referred to as *infrastructure intelligence* and concerns such things as information relating to group organisation, cell membership, expertise, financiers and recruiters, arms dumps, trainers, safe houses, ideology, as well as plans for future terrorist attacks. Both types of intelligence can prevent future attacks, as well as undermine the ability of terrorist groups to function effectively. Thus, both ticking bomb and infrastructure intelligence can save lives. However, there are clear differences; while ticking bomb intelligence may frustrate an imminent attack, the disclosure of infrastructure intelligence will assist authorities in undermining the ability of terrorist groups to recruit, finance their activities and generally operate in the longer term. Clearly, not all intelligence can be so neatly divided in this way, but this division allows us to do several things. First, it allows us to judge more accurately the extent to which interrogational torture 'works' as an intelligence gathering tool. Second, torture that has been used to elicit ticking bomb intelligence can be properly distinguished from torture used to gather infrastructure intelligence. Indeed, some of the most prominent examples of supposed successful interrogational torture leading to the disclosure of intelligence appear to involve the disclosure of confessions or infrastructure intelligence[142] and proponents also merge ticking bomb and infrastructure intelligence in their case for legalisation.[143] In reality, there is only very limited evidence suggesting interrogational torture can produce ticking bomb intelligence.[144] On this ground alone the necessity of legalising interrogational torture is open to serious doubt.

c. Nature of the imminent threat

In the typical ticking bomb hypothetical the imminent threat involves a terrorist attack that threatens loss of life. The nature of harm depicted within the hypothetical is described in a variety of ways. Zedner argues that the hypothetical requires a threat which is 'sufficiently grave' in the sense that the 'measure must be proportionate to the putative harm', which would prevent measures being introduced on the basis of 'generalized fear or insecurity, or by some unspecified threat'.[145] Some scholars have attempted to quantify the harm that is required before special interrogation procedures for suspected terrorists would be permitted. Radsan has suggested that such procedures should only be invoked in relation to terrorist attacks 'that have caused or reasonably may cause the deaths of three or more United States citizens'.[146] Given the unpredictable nature of terrorist attacks, making such a stipulation is largely pointless. Indeed, given the inherent uncertainties, it seems very likely that most, if not all, future terrorist attacks could be assumed to risk the life of at least three people or be viewed as 'sufficiently grave'. Thus, the promise of limiting state power in this way may be illusory.

In making judgements that involve predicting the harm that would trigger the use of interrogational torture there are contextual issues regarding the scale of the terrorist threat that require consideration. The suggestion of a threshold level beyond which torture would be permissible assumes that intelligence is available to identify the threat and the nature of that threat. Following the 9/11 attacks, we have become more accustomed to hearing of single attacks that involve the deaths of dozens or even hundreds of individuals. Such acts of so-called mass casualty terrorism are not a recent phenomenon,[147] but only some terrorist groups seek to kill large numbers of people in single strikes. For example, between 1969 and 2001 the IRA murdered more than 1,700 people. However, Neumann notes that of these attacks 'there were just seven incidents in which the IRA killed ten or more people'.[148] By contrast, jihadist groups, which are the prime source of terrorism facing the United Kingdom at this time,[149] pose a greater threat in terms of the toll of individual attacks. Many plots and failed attacks that have taken place in the United Kingdom were intended to cause mass casualties. Indeed, the level of harm posed by such terrorists has been the subject of empirical analysis. Piazza has examined the worldwide casualty rates from differing types of terrorist groups in the period 1998–2005. Islamist groups associated with al Qaeda killed an average of 36.1 people per attack, Islamist groups not associated with al Qaeda killed 9.4 people per attack and leftist and rightist terrorist groups 3.3 and 5.1 people per attack, respectively.[150]

Irrespective of whether one characterises the potential future harm as being 'grave' or one stipulates a minimal number of potential victims, such assessments would rely heavily on analysis of available intelligence. This is complicated by the fact that terrorist groups often engage in a range of illegal activity such as bombings, kidnappings, thefts and robberies. All of these activities cause harm, but it cannot always be assumed that an individual terrorist possesses information about an imminent *attack* which will result in loss of life. It is evident that in some jurisdictions, distinctions are not made between different types of serious criminality. In a United Nations Special Rapporteur report concerning Israel and the Palestinian territories, it was noted:

> the Special Rapporteur was shocked by the unconvincing and vague illustrations by the Israeli Security Agency of when a 'ticking bomb' scenario may be applicable. One such example given concerned the apprehension of a person found in possession of a small laboratory for manufacturing explosives and items capable of being used to perpetrate a kidnapping. Based upon information that the person had previously attempted a kidnapping, although not prosecuted for it, the Israeli Security Agency advised that it took these facts as amounting to a 'ticking bomb' scenario, although special interrogation techniques were not actually used.[151]

Indeed, if interrogational torture were to be introduced with the primary aim of preventing an expansive range of imminent harms including kidnapping, then it is apparent that interrogational torture could also be justified in kidnap cases such as *Modesto* and *Dean* which were discussed earlier.[152] Indeed, Poser and Vermeule have suggested, on the basis of a cost-benefit analysis, that interrogational torture might be justified in cases involving 'kidnappers with a violent history who ... refuse to disclose the location of the kidnapping victim'.[153] Again, the focus on consequences leads to the extension of coercive powers beyond acts of terrorism and related criminality, to kidnapping and could feasibly go even further. Consequentialist reasoning appears to offer no limiting principle to prevent such slippage[154] and provides further evidence of the way in which the conditions of the hypothetical, when applied in real world situations, expand to address particular security needs.

d. Identifying those who would be subject to torture

It is a self-evident part of the ticking bomb argument that it requires state authorities to detain a person with the knowledge that could lead to the prevention of an imminent terrorist attack. There are two issues that arise. First is who should be subject to interrogational torture and second is the extent to which the authorities can accurately identify terrorists who possess life-saving information. Both of these questions have implications for the legal regulation of interrogational torture. In a review of the scholarly and wider literature it is evident that there is considerable disagreement as to the identity of those who, it is argued, could be legitimately subjected to interrogational torture. On the one hand, there is the commonly expressed view that it is a terrorist in possession of life-saving information who is the legitimate subject of torture. On the other, some scholars and commentators have argued that the class of potential torture victims could be much wider. For example, in their argument in favour of a legally regulated system of interrogational torture, Bagaric and Clarke have argued that:

> As a general rule, torture should normally be confined to people that are responsible in some way for the threatened harm. However, this is not invariably the case. People who are simply aware of the threatened harm, that is, 'innocent people,' may in some circumstances also be subjected to torture.[155]

In arguing for a regulatory framework for torture, Bagaric and Clarke identify five variables that they claim are 'relevant in determining whether torture is permissible'.[156] One of the variables is the 'probability' of the detainee's guilt or possession of relevant information.[157] They admit that 'it will be rare that conclusive proof is available that an individual does, in fact, possess the required knowledge [and] potential torturees will not have been through a trial process in which their guilt has been established'. They claim that this is not a 'decisive objection ... to the use of torture' because trials do 'not seem to be a particularly effective process'.[158] Radsan takes a more restrictive approach, arguing that it is better to hold fewer people in 'special detention' and include only those with a connection to 'the most significant terrorist plots'.[159] By contrast, in Israel, where interrogators are permitted to use the necessary defence in the context of some coercive methods, a United Nations Special Rapporteur expressed concern regarding an 'admission by the Israeli Security Agency officials that, in principle, there was no distinction, in the use of the "ticking bomb" scenario, between a terrorist suspect and a person otherwise holding information about a terrorist incident'.[160] Of course, if the prevention of terrorist attacks is the primary concern such distinctions are of little importance and an expansive definition is inevitable.

Some go even further. In an op-ed piece in *The Independent*, Bruce Anderson suggested that the family members of terrorists, including children, could be legitimately tortured: '[a]fter much agonising, I have come to the conclusion that there is only one answer ... Torture the wife and children. It is a disgusting idea. It is almost a tragedy that we even have to discuss it, let alone think of acting upon it. But there is nothing to be gained from refusing to face facts.'[161] This goes even further than Bagaric and Clarke's view that innocents with knowledge of an attack could be tortured. In Anderson's proposal, family members are merely tools to be used to ratchet up the pressure on a suspected terrorist. Further, the argument that innocents, particularly those with no possible knowledge of a life-saving nature can be legitimately tortured provides one of the clearest examples of consequentialist reasoning in the torture debate.[162] It is also a classic example, from the point of view of deontological reasoning, of using a person purely as a means to an end. It might be argued that torturing children in order to prevent the killing of a greater number is the lesser of two evils. In this way, the use of interrogational torture to prevent acts of terrorism can be seen to serve a higher moral purpose. The problem is that it involves a grotesque act, violating the most basic notions of decency. Even if one accepts that torture can be legitimately practiced against adults,[163] it abandons any notion of a limiting principle for it to be applied to children. Further, to torture the innocent appears to entail a contradiction. The protection of innocent life is a valuable and important duty of government. However, any government that wishes to torture a child in order to force its father (or mother) to disclose the location of a ticking bomb violates this duty.[164] Of course, adults who possess intelligence about future attacks may have a moral duty to divulge this information to the authorities[165] and it might be argued that the criminal law should require the reporting of an imminent terrorist attack.[166] But widening the class of potential torture victims who are, in fact, innocent of any involvement in the creation of an imminent terrorist threat significantly widens the scope of a torture law. This appears to set consequences and the minimisation of harm as the sole basis upon which a decision to use torture is to be judged and there appears to be no limit to the use of such powers.

e. A note on the question of effectiveness

The first four conditions that have been discussed in this section are core parts of the ticking bomb hypothetical. The question of effectiveness is somewhat different in that opponents of legalisation argue that the hypothetical assumes torture will work in eliciting life-saving intelligence, but that such an assumption 'is both over-simplistic and over-optimistic'[167] and that torture is ineffective.[168] However, the hypothetical makes no specific claims as to the effectiveness of torture. That is because it is often used simply as an illustration of the conditions that should be met if torture is to be viewed as permissible. It does not require that the torture be successful. The opponents of legislation frame the hypothetical in such a way as to require that the use of torture be successful. For example, Rodley states:

> The reality is that the usual sort of circumstances that is given – for example, the nuclear bomb that is going to go off in twenty minutes – is a load of rubbish. First of all, the individual will know the bomb is going to go off in twenty minutes and can last twenty minutes. Second of all, all he has to do is send the person somewhere else for that twenty minutes until the bomb goes off.[169]

Wisnewski and Emerick make a similar argument when they attack the hypothetical on the ground that torture is an ineffective means of obtaining life-saving information in emergency situations: 'Everything hangs on the immediacy of the impending bomb. It is this immediacy however, that makes the [hypothetical] incoherent: there is no such thing as effective interrogational torture that lasts only 30 seconds … any method of coercion will require substantial time to be effective.'[170] This point can be queried in two ways. The first is empirical. They provide no evidence to support this claim. Indeed, there is evidence that interrogational torture does sometimes produce timely and reliable results in circumstances where false or misleading information could have been provided instead.[171] Second, this criticism assumes that all terrorists are equally able to withstand coercion and indeed, equally committed to their cause. Brecher argues that a terrorist is 'rather more dedicated and determined than you or I'.[172] In many instances this may well be true, but cannot be assumed to always be the case. However, despite these weaknesses, there can be little doubt that where an attack is a few minutes away, interrogational torture has little to offer. This is particularly the case when terrorist groups compartmentalise knowledge in order to frustrate interrogators and train recruits to resist questioning. In a time-limited situation, interrogators are particularly vulnerable to false or misleading disclosures and lack the time to discover the device and defuse it. It is on the basis of an examination of evidence that it can be argued that the intelligence benefits to be derived from interrogational torture may, in many cases, be non-existent. But this is very different from the overstated case put forward by opponents of legalisation who rely on conjecture or assumption. It is this specific issue that the next section will address.

4. Criticism of the hypothetical: an evaluation

a. The unreality thesis

While all the arguments in favour of the legalisation of interrogational torture are forcefully rejected by opponents of legislation, the ticking bomb hypothetical is treated with particular disdain. This takes the form of two broad approaches to the hypothetical. The first approach is to deny that the hypothetical has any relevance to real life circumstances. In addition to the 'artificial case' criticism made by Shue at the start of this chapter, the hypothetical has been described in a range of disparaging ways, including: 'notorious',[173] 'intellectual fraud',[174] 'unrealistic',[175] 'silly', 'deeply corrupt',[176] a 'utopian fantasy'[177] and having 'affinities with science fiction'.[178] Human Rights Watch has criticised the hypothetical as it ' … rests on the impossible combination of perfect timing … perfect information … and absolute certainty over the outcome … '.[179] It is in this form the unreality thesis is most strongly affirmed. Perhaps surprisingly, few of these claims are substantiated.[180] Some other opponents of legalisation attempt to narrow the relevance of the hypothetical by suggesting that it is merely a thought experiment. For example, Wisnewski argues that: '[t]o call a thought-experiment used to generate and test intuitions "unrealistic" is like criticizing a dog for barking'.[181] One of the most strongly worded criticisms of the ticking bomb hypothetical is by Matthews, who describes it as 'nonsense', 'a horror fantasy', 'a logical illusion', 'empirically impossible', 'has nothing to do with the world in which human beings act', 'completely divorced from reality', '[a]hopeless conceptual mess', 'vacuous' and 'is a piece of sophistry'.[182]

In his analysis of the hypothetical, McCoy is more grounded in his criticism. He argues that the 'fundamental flaw in this fanciful scenario is its pretzel-like, ex post facto logic'. He rejects the hypothetical in part, on the basis of probability: 'It assumes an improbable, even impossible, cluster of variables' and goes on to argue that: '[s]uch an extraordinary string of coincidences probably never has and never will occur'.[183] He refers to an attempt by a *New York Times* journalist to find verification of claims that the use of interrogational torture has prevented terrorist attacks. The journalist found a source that named only one specific example – the same example that had been cited by the Israeli Justice Ministry in an earlier letter to Human Rights Watch.[184] He goes on: '[w]ith reality so uncooperative, torture advocates spin two sorts of scenarios, the fictional and the fabulous … sometimes they twist the truth into a fable, a facsimile of this implausible scenario … '[185] McCoy is correct to point out that in the construction of the hypothetical *ex post facto* logic is often applied to bolster the conclusion derived from a given set of facts. He is also correct to note the importance of empirical data to this discussion. However, his conclusion rests on an assumption that such data do not exist. If it can be shown that ticking bomb-type situations have arisen and interrogational torture has worked to prevent terrorist attacks then this is an important refutation of a central objection to the hypothetical. In their construction of the unreality thesis, opponents of legalisation sometimes merge two separate issues which must be distinguished. First, the hypothetical as a 'What if …?' question sets out a scenario which requires us to consider what could or should be done as a preventive measure in such circumstances. Second, one must consider whether the events depicted in the hypothetical have ever occurred in the real world. This is an empirical question. It is evident that in much of the highly critical work in this area, false or misleading empirical claims are made which are thought to prove that a ticking bomb–type event has never or could never occur.

Further, outright denial of the hypothetical's relevance to the real world involves an assumption regarding risk. The assumption here is that ticking bomb cases have never and will never occur and so do not require consideration in the development of counter-terrorism policy. In other words, the unreality thesis involves a claim of zero or near-zero risk.[186] This would appear to be a dangerous assumption to make without an examination of evidence. Indeed, denial of a risk can have consequences. Sunstein notes that in the United States of America, prior to 9/11 the 'risk of terrorism was foolishly neglected' and that '[t]he neglect was a product of "unavailability bias," in which the absence of readily available incidents of harm made people unreasonably indifferent to the risk'.[187] The risks associated with terrorism are, of course, uncertain. Such risks are very difficult to quantify and this difficulty allows people to minimise the likelihood of ticking bomb-type events taking place.[188] However, the denial of the hypothetical does not arise because 'readily available incidents' do not exist. On the contrary, denial results from the fact that such incidents that are located in the literature are simply not considered by opponents of legalisation.

Brecher has rightly noted the way in which some advocates of interrogational torture have constructed a version of the ticking bomb hypothetical that is 'strikingly careless'.[189] However, critics of the hypothetical are also guilty of serious failures which suggest a similar level of carelessness in failing to consider real world events. For example, Scheppele argues the hypothetical 'deviates from any conceivable real-world situation'.[190] She also makes an empirical claim that 'it has generally been impossible to learn the details of a terrorist plot with any certainty before the plot is launched'[191] and points to the 'fuzzy' nature of some claims by state authorities.[192] Such fuzziness does of course raise questions about the reliability of state claims. Other opponents of torture claim that: ' … the idea that the authorities might get a dangerous terrorist into their custody, after he has planned an attack but before he has executed it, is a utopian fantasy … To set policies on the basis of such far-fetched scenarios would be folly.'[193] There is a problem with these criticisms. They suggest a factual impossibility at the core of the hypothetical. However, it is the case that law enforcement officials regularly arrest individuals involved in plots, conspiracies or criminal attempts to carry out terrorist acts, as well as many other crimes.[194] Similarly, it is not uncommon for the police to seize bombs or other armaments prior to their use in terrorist attacks.[195] These cases show the ability of the police and security services to disrupt ongoing criminal plans before the intended attack has taken place. Such cases may not be an exact fit with the hypothetical, but they suggest a more sophisticated response is necessary than that offered by the unreality thesis.

Further, the suggestion that plots cannot be prevented ignores the reality of terrorist operations. Given that terrorist attacks can take weeks, months or even longer to prepare, this provides state authorities with potential opportunities to apprehend plotters. Indeed, one might argue that this provides opportunity for conventional policing techniques to be used. Even if one takes Holmes's point regarding a situation in which a terrorist is arrested after a bomb is planted, the literature appears to give us examples from across a range of jurisdictions.[196] In his book examining the so-called 'Battle of Algiers', *A Savage War of Peace*, Horne refers to an 'appalling moral dilemma' faced by Paul Teitgen who had responsibility for over-seeing the police. In the words of Horne: 'Fernand Yveton, the Communist had been caught red-handed placing a bomb in the gasworks where he was employed. But a second bomb had not been discovered, and if it exploded and set off the gasometers thousands of lives might be lost. Nothing would induce Yveton to reveal its whereabouts.'[197] As recounted by Horne, Teitgen refused to authorise the torture of Yveton and recounted how he 'trembled the whole afternoon', but fortunately the bomb did not explode.[198] Of course, such situations are likely to be infrequent because there would generally be a short time window for the authorities to intervene between the planting and detonation of a bomb.

Some critics of the hypothetical go further than Holmes by making explicit factual claims that are, in fact, unfounded. Richard Jackson has argued that ' … in thousands of cases of torture … from Algeria to Israel, no bomb has ever been found'.[199] The use of bombs is one tool in the arsenal possessed by terrorists. Terrorist groups engage in a range of criminal activities such as kidnapping, where something akin to ticking bomb intelligence would prove useful in order to secure the timely release of a detainee. However, if one examines Jackson's narrow claim, is it correct? In *Public Committee Against Torture in Israel* v. *The State of Israel*[200] the Israeli High Court of Justice cited, what on its face appeared to be ticking bomb and infrastructure intelligence disclosures:

> The applicant in HC 7563/97 (Abd al Rahman Ismail Ganimat) was arrested … and interrogated by the GSS … He claimed to have been tortured by his investigators (through use of the 'Shabach' position, excessive tightening of handcuffs and sleep deprivation). His interrogation revealed that he was involved in numerous terrorist activities in the course of which many Israeli citizens were killed. He was instrumental in the kidnapping and murder of [an] IDF soldier (Sharon Edry …); Additionally, he was involved in the bombing of Cafe 'Appropo' in Tel Aviv, in which three women were murdered and thirty people were injured.
>
> … A powerful explosive device, identical to the one detonated at Cafe 'Appropo' in Tel Aviv was found in the applicant's village (Tzurif) subsequent to the dismantling and interrogation of the terrorist cell to which he belonged. Uncovering this explosive device thwarted an attack similar to the one at Cafe 'Appropo.' According to GSS investigators, the applicant possessed additional crucial information which he only revealed as a result of their inter-rogation. Revealing this information immediately was essential to safeguarding state and regional security and preventing danger to human life.[201]

It is unclear to what extent a linkage can be made between the use of interroga-tional torture and the discovery of the bomb in this case. The text makes reference to the bomb being found after the dismantling and interrogation of the terrorist cell members. What is not clear is if the two events are linked, although it is implied, whether the bomb was ready for use, whether it was being stored or how long it took to find it after the initial interrogation. From a consequentialist perspective this may not matter, but from a regulatory perspective it is important because the notion of imminence surely has to have some limitation.[202] Indeed, it would appear that the interrogation of Ganimat was more akin to a fishing expedition than a focussed set of questions intended to discover a ticking bomb of which officials were already aware. The text does not claim that Ganimat identified the location of the bomb and so it might be that coercion, if the claim is accurate, provided certain clues, but it was at best an indirect means of locating the bomb. The *PCATI* decision also cites another example of torture producing intelligence:

> The applicant in H.C. 6536/96 (Hat'm Abu Zayda), was arrested ... and interrogated by GSS investigators ... His attorney complained about the interrogation methods allegedly used against his client (deprivation of sleep, shaking, beatings, and use of the 'Shabach' position) ... the applicant in question was subsequently convicted of activities in the military branch of the Hamas terrorist organization ... The convicting Court held that the applicant both recruited and constructed the Hamas' infrastructure, for the purpose of kidnapping Israeli soldiers and carrying out terrorist attacks against security forces. It has been argued before us that the information provided by the applicant during the course of his interrogation led to the thwarting of an actual plan to carry out serious terrorist attacks, including the kidnapping of soldiers.[203]

As with the previous example, the interrogation may have resulted in the disclosure of infrastructure or even ticking bomb intelligence, but the claim regarding plans is vague with no clear timescale. Further, it was a claim made without further supporting evidence. There is, however, a more concrete example. On 14 October 1994, Hamas militants abducted a 19-year-old Israeli army corporal, Nachshon Wachsman. They threatened to kill him unless 200 Hamas prisoners were immediately released by the Israeli authorities.[204] Through their investigations the authorities found the hire car shop where the vehicle used in the kidnap had been rented by Jihad Yaghmour, a Hamas operative. Yaghmour was arrested and subjected to an interrogation involving 'special means'.[205] As a result, Pedahzur notes, 'Yaghmour broke down and revealed all the details of the kidnapping, including the exact location where Wachsman was being held'.[206] In the subsequent rescue mission Wachsman was murdered by his captors. Yitzhak Rabin, the Israeli Prime Minister, acknowledged that Yaghmour had been subjected to coercive interrogation methods: 'If we'd been so careful to follow the Landau Commission [guidelines], we would never have found out where [Wachsman] was being held.'[207] This case directly challenges the assertions of opponents of legalisation who claim that torture and coercion cannot produce timely and reliable disclosures. Of course, the Israelis were unable to save Wachsman, but that is not in itself a defect of the methods used to extract the information. The most that interrogational torture can do is provide timely and reliable information. Other interceding events may, of course, undermine the usefulness of the disclosure.

While Brecher dismisses the ticking bomb hypothetical as 'fantasy', he makes a surprising admission: '[b]ut that is not to say that there can be no genuine cases where torturing one person seems the only possible way left of saving the life of one or more others and where it really is known that they have the requisite information.'[208] Here, he acknowledges a widely publicised case before the German courts, discussed earlier, in which the police threatened to torture a kidnapper if he did not divulge the location of his kidnap victim.[209] Brecher fails to explain how such a factual situation cannot occur in a terrorism case when he accepts it can occur in a kidnap case. It is one thing to argue that a ticking bomb-type situation might be rare, it is quite another to claim it is a 'fantasy' and could never occur. In reality, a hypothetical involving a ticking bomb or kidnappings involve many of the same characteristics which lessen the utility of interrogational torture. The more factual variables and uncertainties that make up such a situation, the less likely it is that the event depicted in the hypothetical will take place in real life. This is an obvious problem with using the hypothetical as a basis for public policy making. It appears to have an air of unreality. The problem with this claim, however, is that the empirical evidence suggests that events similar to the ticking bomb hypothetical do occur. As a result, alternative ways have to be used to deal with this reality.[210]

When predicting risk and determining possible responses, certain risks do not require consideration. For example, a zombie invasion of the city of Leicester would fall into this category.[211] By contrast terrorists and terrorist attacks do exist. State efforts to prevent such attacks are required. It is simply irresponsible for public officials not to address potential threats. Where officials do not consider a range of threats that have varying degrees of probability then they will fail to understand their nature and neglect preventive measures.[212] Recognising that circumstances akin to the hypothetical do occur may create some difficulties for the opponents of legalisation. This, however, will only occur if criticism of the ticking bomb hypothetical is based on a denial of reality. The claim that the events depicted in the hypothetical have never occurred in the real world is problematic because it sits uneasily with actual events. Denial is a shortcut means of avoiding the challenges posed by real world events and inhibits the development of a stronger argument against the legalisation of interrogational torture.

b. Fallacies, premises and the unreality thesis

Instead of outright denial, some opponents of legalisation offer a somewhat more sophisticated version of the unreality thesis by suggesting that there exist a series of 'deductive fallacies' within the ticking bomb hypothetical.[213] Vittorio Bufacchi and Jean Maria Arrigo argue that the '"deductive fallacy" occurs when a certain argument infers invalid conclusions from certain premises, either because the conclusions rest on a different set of premises, and/or because the premises don't support the conclusion'.[214] In order to illustrate this point they set out the following hypothetical which contains various premises (P) and conclusions (C):

(P1): Terrorist is captured.
(P2): If the terrorist is tortured, he/she will reveal information regarding the location of the primed bomb before the bomb detonates.
Therefore (C1): Terrorist ought to be tortured.
Therefore (C2): The information regarding the location of the primed bomb is retrieved.
Therefore (C3): The bomb is found and disconnected before it explodes, saving the lives of many innocent people.[215]

They rightly note that for the conclusions to follow the premises, 'other "invisible premises" must be in place'.[216] These invisible premises include an assumption that the use of torture will result in the disclosure of accurate and timely information that allows the bomb to be located and disconnected in the time available to state officials. All ticking bomb arguments contain such hidden premises which, in reality, would operate to minimise the likelihood of torture saving innocent lives in the context of an actual ticking bomb. In other words, the hypothetical requires a sequence of events which are unlikely. Indeed, Bufacchi and Arrigo argue that the 'ticking-bomb argument is so hyperbolical to have more affinities with science fiction than political science'.[217] Shue makes a similar point when he suggests that the ticking bomb hypothetical is unrealistic on two grounds. He argues that the hypothetical is misleading because it is 'idealized', in that it assumes *inter alia* that authorities have detained a terrorist with life-saving information and that there is timely disclosure of this information.[218] In addition, he argues that the hypothetical involves an 'abstraction' and is based on an unrealistic assessment of how legalised torture would work in practice, including the problem of controlling coercive powers and how torturers could be identified and trained.[219] He argues that this combination of idealisation and abstraction make the hypothetical a 'disastrously misleading analogy from which to derive conclusions about reality'.[220]

There are a number of difficulties with the analysis offered by Bufacchi, Arrigo and Shue that can be illustrated by reference to another hypothetical scenario. If their analysis holds true one would expect their reasoning to apply equally to other types of cases which have all the characteristics of the hypothetical. The following hypothetical differs from the one set out by Bufacchi and Arrigo only in that it involves a kidnapping:

(P1): Kidnapper is captured.
(P2): If the kidnapper is tortured, he/she will reveal information regarding the location of the kidnap victim and they will be saved from harm.
Therefore (C1): Kidnapper ought to be tortured.
Therefore (C2): The information regarding the location of the victim is retrieved.
Therefore (C3): The victim is found safe and well.

If one follows the approach of Bufacchi and Arrigo, then we can identify a number of 'invisible premises' in such a scenario. As with the ticking bomb hypothetical, it assumes torture will work, that the kidnapper knows the location of the kidnap victim and that that the information can be gathered in a timely manner. On this basis it could be argued that the scenario has 'affinities with science fiction'. But how resilient is this conclusion? There appears to be a fundamental flaw in the premises that gives rise to the conclusion: it is detached from empirical reality. Indeed, the kidnap hypothetical is not a hypothetical at all, it is very similar to the facts of the case of *Leon* v. *Wainwright*[221] and the Wachsman case discussed earlier. The reality is that state officials in many jurisdictions have been involved in preventing criminal activities which, taken in the abstract, might be seen as highly unlikely and containing 'invisible premises'. A further illustration can be offered in the form of the case of *R* v. *Campbell*.[222] Here, the police intervened to prevent an armed robbery of a post office. According to the Court of Appeal:

> [i]t seems that police officers had information which led them to believe that an attempt might be made at some time in the future to rob a sub post office ... They had their eye on the place for a number of days, if not more. Some of the officers keeping watch were armed. That was doubtless because they had good reason to suspect that the would-be robber would carry out an armed robbery if he were able to.[223]

If this case were described as a hypothetical then one could identify a whole range of factual variables that would give it an air of unreality. For example, the intelligence the police possessed may have been wholly inaccurate and there may be no plan to rob a post office (or anywhere else), the robber may have become ill and decided not to rob the post office that day, the intelligence might have been partly accurate, but the exact post office to be robbed might have been incorrectly identified or the would-be robber may have changed his mind or he may have spotted the police officers lying in wait and aborted his plan. The possible factual variations are endless, but as Allhoff notes: '[s]trictly speaking, *every* state of affairs is infinitely unlikely since there are a finite number of ways that state of affairs could have been realized and an infinite number of ways in which it could have failed to have been realized' (emphasis in original).[224] Consequently, it matters little how many hidden premises exist in a hypothetical if very similar events have actually taken place in the real world. Bufacchi and Arrigo's analysis is helpful in pointing out that for interrogational torture to be effective in response to a ticking bomb scenario, a range of hidden premises must also be satisfied, suggesting that the events depicted in the hypothetical are unlikely to occur regularly. However, their analysis does not provide evidence that the hypothetical is unreal, nor has 'affinities with science fiction'.

5. Conclusion

This chapter has identified the main components that comprise the ticking bomb hypothetical and the way in which they are interpreted. It is evident that the hypothetical as theorised and practised is an expansive concept. At the same time, it is an idealised scenario,[225] containing many uncertainties and assumptions that proponents of legalised interrogational torture often ignore. This results from a consequentialist focus that tends to mask uncertainty and concentrates on end results. In addition, the use of the hypothetical as part of the case for legalisation tends to avoid the discussion of limiting principles. As a result, scholarly proponents of legalisation argue for its use in an expansive range of circumstances, from attacks a few minutes or hours away, to many weeks and months and against terrorist suspects and family members. Others have advocated the torture of children and the innocent. Similar issues exist in the real world use of interrogational torture. As the evidence suggests, interrogational torture is used in a wide range of circumstances, involving an expansively defined set of circumstances using ticking bomb and infrastructure intelligence, and against terrorist suspects, family members and the completely innocent. This does not bode well for a regulatory framework in which torture is supposed to be used only in controlled, narrowly defined circumstances. A legal regulatory framework requires precision and the demands of a narrowly drafted torture statute are likely to make its real world use highly unlikely, unless these restrictions are eased.[226]

On the other side of the debate, despite repeated claims that evidence is central to their opposition to interrogational torture there are marked empirical blind spots in the analysis of those opposed to the legalisation or use of torture.[227] Many have adopted an all-too-familiar tactic in the torture debate. They make factual claims that have little regard for the historic or contemporary literature and are guilty of what Bobbitt has described as the 'blithe assuming away of the problem'.[228] Conceptually, most opponents of legalisation who deny the real world relevance of the hypothetical conflate low probability of a ticking bomb event in the real world with *no possibility* that it could occur and fail to acknowledge the credible evidence that factual situations similar to the hypothetical do occur. These scholars engage in a form of 'confirmation bias, by which people tend to seek out, and to believe, evidence that supports their own antecedent views'.[229] In this instance, opponents of torture show little evidence of seeking out contradictory evidence.

Indeed, while the hypothetical contains various premises and assumptions, none, either singularly or in combination, operate to make the hypothetical irrelevant to real world decision-making. This chapter has detailed the way in which politicians, policy makers and judges have used the hypothetical. That does not mean, of course, that *every* use of the hypothetical should be endorsed, but at the same time, its utility to the judiciary cannot be denied. It is evident from the case law surveyed here that members of the judiciary have found the ticking bomb hypothetical a useful means by which to illustrate and explore the creation of exceptions to general legal rules. Of course, it could be that any person making use of the hypothetical is adopting a form of reasoning that is deeply flawed and which should be abandoned. However, the opponents of legalisation offer no alternative tool to illustrate the appropriate formulation of policy or general legal rules with exceptions which are derived from the application of the hypothetical.

However rare the ticking bomb scenario might be in real life, it can be argued that this is hardly the point. The hypothetical is asking how the state should respond *if* the events depicted were to occur in the future. It would be irresponsible of state officials who have duties pertaining to the safety of citizens not to consider *what if?* questions when determining issues of public policy.[230] Even rare events in the context of counter-terrorism require consideration when the consequences are potentially grave. The public safety doctrine that has developed following the decision of the US Supreme Court in *Miranda* has been repeatedly utilised in recent decades. It takes little in the way of an imagination to recognise the problems that could be created for local and federal law enforcement in the United States if the judiciary abandoned the reasoning underlying the doctrine, which rests, in part on the ticking bomb hypothetical and its variants. By contrast, other uses of the hypothetical, such as in the *PCATI* decision, have led to more serious consequences for the rights of those detained by the state.

Recognising that the hypothetical does on occasion, reflect real-life events, may pose a danger for the absolute prohibition against torture and this is perhaps why the hypothetical is so aggressively attacked by its critics. However, there are two responses to this concern. First, the hypothetical poses no greater danger for the absolute prohibition than any of the other arguments cited in favour of the legalisation of interrogational torture. Second, the use of unsound or empirically flawed arguments is hardly a basis upon which to reject the hypothetical. Such an approach does nothing to bolster the case for retaining the absolute prohibition. If the ticking bomb hypothetical can be seen as a poor basis upon which to argue for the legalisation of interrogational torture, it is not because it is a fiction, unreal or a fraud. Rather, it is because it contains component parts that are ill-defined and inherently expansive in their nature when applied in real life situations. In the context of creating a law-based regulatory framework, the component parts are expansively defined in theory and practice because they are part of a consequentialist argument with no obvious limiting principles. This will not stop the hypothetical being used in the future as part of a case for the use and legalisation of interrogational torture. As such it is important that it is dealt with in a manner that does not involve false or exaggerated claims. However, it must be viewed in light of a range of other empirical issues. It is to those that this book will now turn.

Notes

1 J.R. Schlesinger *et al*, *Final Report of the Independent Panel to Review Department of Defense Detention Practices* (2004) Appendix H, 2.
2 H. Shue, 'Torture', (1978) 7 *Phil. & Pub. Aff.* 124, 141.
3 'US Judge Steps in to Torture Row', www.bbc.co.uk/news 12 February 2008.
4 However, it is also the case that interrogational torture is sometimes justified as a means of eliciting intelligence in circumstances that do not involve an imminent attack. The CIA's 'High Value Detainee' programme targeted high-ranking detainees who may have known of imminent attacks, but also those who 'has/had direct involvement in planning and preparing terrorist actions against the USA or its allies, or assisting the al-Qaeda leadership in planning and preparing such terrorist actions'. Fax for Daniel

Levin, Assistant Attorney General, Office of Legal Counsel, from [name redacted] Assistant General Counsel, CIA; January 4, 2005, cited in Office of Legal Counsel, *Re: Application of 18 U.S.C. §§ 2340–2340A to Certain Techniques That May Be Used in the Interrogation of High Value al Qaeda: Detainees* 10 May 2005, 6. Indeed, it has been argued that the use of interrogational torture can be justified on the basis that coercion is the lesser of two evils. Such reasoning clearly does not limit the use of interrogational torture to only those situations involving an imminent attack. For discussion, see M. Ignatieff, *The Lesser Evil: Political Ethics in the Age of Terror* (2004) and *Commission of Inquiry into the Methods of Investigation of the General Security Service Regarding Hostile Terrorist Activity* (1987), *infra* nn. 119–21 and accompanying text. The Commission was chaired by former Israeli Supreme Court Justice Moshe Landau and hereinafter will be referred to as the 'Landau Commission'.

5 J. Jeremy Wisnewski has suggested that the hypothetical is not 'typically' used to justify the use of torture; 'in fact', he states: 'I do not think I have *ever* seen it used this way' (emphasis in original). Instead, he claims the hypothetical is used as a device to test intuitions: 'Hearing a Still-Ticking Bomb Argument: A Reply to Bufacchi and Arrigo', (2009) 26 *Journal of Applied Philosophy* 205, 208. While the hypothetical certainly tests our moral intuitions, it is also cited, by journalists, scholars, politicians and judges, as part of an argument that the use of torture can be justified.

6 J. Jeremy Wisnewski and R.D. Emerick, *The Ethics of Torture* (2009) 97.

7 R. Matthews, *The Absolute Violation: Why Torture Must be Prohibited* (2008) 96.

8 *Id.* 207.

9 See, for example, V. Bufacchi and J.M. Arrigo, 'Torture, Terrorism and the State: a Refutation of the Ticking Bomb Argument' (2006) 23 *Journal of Applied Philosophy* 355, 358.

10 W.L. Twining and P.E. Twining, 'Bentham *on* Torture', (1973) 24 *N.I.L.Q.* 305, 316.

11 *Id.* 316–7. At the time Bentham was writing, the threat of arson was a particularly serious one given the limited means available to extinguish fires.

12 *Id.* 321. Bentham's formulation does make some reference, albeit vaguely, to the time frame in which information is being sought. He states that torture should only be used 'in cases which admit no delay' (at 313).

13 *Id.* 318.

14 *Id.* An obvious difference is that punishment follows a finding of guilt by a court in which evidence is tested. By contrast, the use of interrogational torture is likely based on a belief or assumption that the torture victim can provide the information that is being sought.

15 *Id.*

16 Similar moral dilemmas have involved a train driver, who after the brakes fail can either do nothing and kill a group of children or deliberately direct the train onto another track and kill a drunk lying on the rails: A.M. Dershowitz, *Why Terrorism Works: Understanding the Threat, Responding to the Challenge* (2002) 132. In another hypothetical, the inhabitants of a city live a perfect life because one child lives in 'abominable misery'. If the child is released the perfect life of the city dwellers will end: M.J. Sandel, *Justice: What is the Right Thing to Do?* (2009) 40–1.

17 (1960) cited in D. Rejali, *Torture and Democracy* (2007) 545–6.

18 *Id.*

19 See, for example, Zuckerman has stated: 'it is [not] impossible to envisage situations where the organs of the State may excusably resort to torture. Where it is known that a bomb has been planted in a crowded building it is perhaps justifiable to torture the suspect so that lives may be saved by discovering its location'. A. Zuckerman, 'The Right against Self-incrimination: an Obstacle to the Supervision of Interrogation', (1986) 100 *LQR* 43, n. 4. In 1989, the *Israeli Law Review* published a series of articles examining the use of torture and other coercion methods during interrogation. See, for example, M.S. Moore, 'Torture and the Balance of Evils', (1989) 23 *Isr. L.R.* 280.

20 For detailed discussion, see *infra* nn. 28–71 and accompanying text.
21 See *infra* nn. 24 and 25 and accompanying text.
22 See, for example, J. Alters, 'Time to Think about Torture', *Newsweek* 5 November 2001; M. Slackman, 'The World: A Dangerous Calculus; What's Wrong with Torturing a Qaeda Higher-Up?' *The New York Times* 16 May 2004.
23 M. d'Ancona, 'Grandstanding MPs are playing with all our lives', www.Telegraph.co. uk 9 November 2005.
24 Office of Legal Counsel, *Memorandum for William J. Haynes II, General Counsel of the Department of Defense, Re: Military Interrogation of Alien Unlawful Combatants Held Outside the United States* 14 March 2003, 61–2.
25 *Id.* 75.
26 *Supra* n. 19.
27 Twining and Twining, *supra* n. 10, 317.
28 [2006] 2 AC 221, para. 47 (noting that if a suspect were tortured and '[i]f under such torture a man revealed the whereabouts of a bomb in the Houses of Parliament, the authorities could remove the bomb and, if possible, arrest the terrorist who planted it', but the act of torture would be a 'flagrant' breach Article 3 of the ECHR).
29 *Id.* paras. 67–8.
30 D. Gardham, 'Britain "Will Act on Torture Intelligence"', *The Daily Telegraph* 10 November 2010.
31 In *R v. Twitchell* [2000] 1 Cr. App. R. 373 (appellant claimed that during his interrogation by police officers he was handcuffed and a plastic bag was placed over his head in order to convince him to confess).
32 See, for example, *Brown v. Mississippi* 297 US 278 (1936) (defendants confessed to a killing after being whipped by police officers); C. Mullen, *Error of Judgement: The Truth about the Birmingham Bombings* (1997) (discussing the brutal treatment by police officers of the 'Birmingham Six' who were believed to be IRA terrorists responsible for the Birmingham pub bombings in 1974, but who were entirely innocent); Human Rights Watch, *Confessions at any Cost: Police Torture in Russia* (1999) 1 (noting the 'rampant; ill-treatment of detainees in Russia during and following arrest'). For one of many similar cases before the ECtHR, see: *Nechiporuk and Yonkalo v. Ukraine* (2011) (application no. 42310/04) (the court held that a suspect was the victim of torture inflicted on him by police officers for the purpose of forcing him to confess to a murder).
33 See, for example, *Leon v. Wainwright* 734 F 2d 770 (11th Cir., 1984).
34 When commenting on the *Gäfgen* case discussed in Chapter 1, Eirik Bjorge notes that although it 'did not involve "terrorism"' it did possess the hallmarks of the "ticking bomb" scenario', E. Bjorge, 'Torture and "Ticking Bomb" Scenarios,' (2011) L.Q.R. 196, 199. Greer challenges the description of this case as involving a ticking bomb-type scenario: 'Should Police Threats to Torture Suspects Always be Severely Punished? Reflections on the *Gäfgen* Case' (2011) 11 *Human Rights Law Review* 67, 85. The author of this book recognises the distinctions Greer highlights, but since no two cases are identical they do not detract from the fact that ticking bomb and kidnap cases may involve the urgent need for life-saving information from an unwilling suspect in order to prevent (or reduce) harm.
35 384 US 436 (1966).
36 *Id.* 479.
37 467 US 649 (1984).
38 *Id.* 655. Justice Rehnquist, who gave the opinion of the Court stated:

> *We conclude that the need for answers to questions in a situation posing a threat to the public safety outweighs the need for the prophylactic rule protecting the Fifth Amendment's privilege against self-incrimination. We decline to place officers … in the untenable position of having to consider, often in a matter of seconds, whether it best serves society for them to ask the necessary questions without the Miranda warnings and render whatever probative evidence they uncover inadmissible, or for them to give the warnings in order to preserve the admissibility of evidence they*

might uncover but possibly damage or destroy their ability to obtain that evidence and neutralize the volatile situation confronting them.

(at 657–8)

39 *Id.* 686. Marshall noted that there was 'nothing' in the Fifth Amendment or *Miranda* which would 'proscribe this sort of emergency questioning' (at 686). A 2011 empirical study found nine cases in which *Quarles* was applied to cases involving explosive devices: J. Wright, 'Mirandizing Terrorists? An Empirical Analysis of the Public Safety Exception', (2011) 111 *Colum. L. Rev.* 1296, 1329 (also noting the application of the *Quarles* exception has been applied in cases involving firearms and other threats).
40 J.B. Zeitlin, 'Voluntariness with a Vengeance: *Miranda* and a Modern Alternative', (2001) 14 *St. Thomas L. Rev.* 109, 145.
41 In *United States* v. *Smith* 7 F.3d 1164 (1993) the Court of Appeals for the Fifth Circuit held that a *Miranda* warning was not required in cases involving alleged death threats to the US President.
42 83 Cal. App. 3d 563 (1978).
43 *Id.* 573.
44 *Id.* 573, 574.
45 62 Cal.2d 436 (1965).
46 *Id.* 444.
47 *Id.* 446.
48 39 Cal. App. 3d 875 (1974).
49 The Fifth Amendment sets out certain due process rights for criminal suspects and defendants.
50 *Dean, supra* n. 48, 883–4.
51 C. Lee, 'Package Bombs, Footlockers, and Laptops: What the Disappearing Container Doctrine Can Tell Us about the Fourth Amendment', (2010) 100 *The Journal of Criminal Law and Criminology* 1403, 1463.
52 495 US 1 (1990).
53 An audio recording of the oral argument can be heard via the following link: www. oyez.org/cases/1980–89/1989/1989_88_1835 (accessed: 1 February 2014).
54 538 US 760 (2003).
55 An audio recording of the oral argument can be heard via the following link: www. oyez.org/cases/2000–2009/2002/2002_01_1444 (accessed: 1 February 2014).
56 US Department of Justice and Federal Bureau of Investigation, *Custodial Interrogation for Public Safety and Intelligence-Gathering Purposes of Operational Terrorists Inside the United States* (2010). It appears that the memo is a restatement of existing policy: 'The Department of Justice and the FBI believe that we can maximize our ability to accomplish [our] objectives by continuing to adhere to FBI policy regarding the use of *Miranda* warnings for custodial interrogation of operational terrorists … '
57 *Id.*
58 D. Anderson Q.C., *Operation GIRD: Report Following Review* (2011).
59 See also *R* v. *Ibrahim and others* [2008] EWCA Crim 880. Here, the appellants, who were participants in the failed 21/7 terrorist attacks in London, argued that the inclusion of evidence gained during 'safety interviews' when they did not have the opportunity to consult a solicitor rendered their trial unfair. This argument was rejected by the Court of Appeal on the basis *inter alia* that they did not incriminate themselves during the safety interviews.
60 *Id.* para 48.
61 *PACE Code of Practice* (2013) Code H, para. 6.7.
62 *Id.* para 11.2.
63 *Public Committee Against Torture in Israel* v. *The State of Israel* 38 I.L.M. 1471 (1999), para. 32 (hereafter *PCATI*).
64 Chapter 1, nn. 30–43 and accompanying text.
65 *PCATI, supra* n. 63, para. 34.

66 See *infra* n. 131–4 and accompanying text. See also Chapter 4.
67 *Adalah-The Legal Center for Arab Minority Rights in Israel* v. *GOC Central Command IDF et al* 45 I.L.M. 271 (2006) 492–4.
68 *Id*. 499.
69 *Id*.
70 *Id*.
71 *Id*. 500.
72 *Id*.
73 For detailed discussion, see Chapter 4.
74 M. Welch, *Crimes of Power & States of Impunity: The U.S. Response to Terror* (2009) 76.
75 S. Cohen, *States of Denial: Knowing About Atrocities and Suffering* (2001) 110.
76 Peter Hall accused the government of hiding the 'real purpose' behind the enactment of the Prevention of Terrorism (Temporary Provisions) Act 1974 (hereinafter PTA). He argued that the Act was 'presented as the government's reaction to the Birmingham pub bombings but the reality is that the Act came off the shelf ready for use'. He suggested that the purpose behind the Act was actually *inter alia* the 'criminalisation of political opposition' and 'the exploitation of anti-Irish racism'. 'The Prevention of Terrorism Acts', in A. Jennings (ed.), *Justice Under Fire: The Abuse of Civil Liberties in Northern Ireland* (1990) 183–4. In contrast, it can be argued that a responsible government should have contingency plans in order to respond to changing circumstances.
77 D. Gardner, *Risk: The Science and Politics of Fear* (2009) 323.
78 K.D. Ewing, *Bonfire of the Liberties: New Labour, Human Rights and the Rule of Law* (2010) 221 (arguing that anti-terrorism laws 'bite deeply into constitutional principle and established civil liberty').
79 D. Cole and J.X. Dempsey, *Terrorism and the Constitution: Sacrificing Civil Liberties in the Name of National Security* (2006) 196.
80 *Id*. 195.
81 C. Walker, *The Prevention of Terrorism in British Law* 2nd ed (1992) 31–3.
82 *Id*. 32.
83 HC Hansard, col. 35, 25 November 1974.
84 *Id*. cols. 33–5.
85 HC Hansard, col. 1674, 22 November 1974. See also col. 1678 for similar remarks.
86 *Id*. col. 1673 (Mr Hooson).
87 HC Hansard, col. 635, 28 November 1974.
88 *Supra* n. 85, col. 1674 (Mr Silverman).
89 *Id*. col. 1675 (Mr Jenkins).
90 *Supra* n. 87, col. 643.
91 For example, Leo Abse MP, who when referring to the Bill, commented: 'It is the old story of hurried legislation passed in the white heat of an emotional aftermath – more haste less rights.' *Id*. col. 658.
92 *Supra* n. 85, col. 1681.
93 See, for example, *supra* n. 87, col. 652.
94 *Supra* n. 85, cols. 1679–80.
95 *Supra* n. 87, col. 652.
96 *Supra* n. 83, cols. 34–5, 37 (arguing the high financial and manpower cost of identity cards would be 'disproportionate to any results that might be achieved' and that the cards are 'eminently forgeable documents').
97 Of course, the measures can also be criticised on the grounds that they significantly restricted liberty and with hindsight, had only a limited impact on the terrorist threat: Walker, *supra* n. 81, at Ch. 11.
98 *Id*. 32.
99 Geoffrey Bennett notes that in the mid-nineteenth century politicians and senior police officers warned about the existence of a large number of armed Fenians in London. As a result, a range of counter-measures to this exaggerated threat were implemented or

considered: 'Legislative Responses to Terrorism: A View from Britain', (2005) 109 *Penn. St. L. Rev.* 947, 949.
100 John Howard, Prime Minister of Australia, 'Anti-Terrorism Bill', 2 November 2005.
101 A. Lynch, 'Legislating with Urgency – The Enactment of the Anti-Terrorism Act [No 1] 2005', (2006) 30 *Melbourne University Law Review* 747, 768.
102 *Id.* 772.
103 *Id.* 773.
104 M. Mazzetti, 'Panetta Open to Tougher Methods in Some C.I.A. Interrogation', *The New York Times* 5 February 2009.
105 'Senate Confirmation Hearings: Eric Holder, Day One', *The New York Times* 16 January 2009.
106 C.R. Sunstein, *Worst Case-Scenarios* (2007) 54.
107 *Id.* 57.
108 *Supra* n. 92 and accompanying text.
109 D. Luban, 'Liberalism, Torture, and the Ticking Bomb', in K.J. Greenberg (ed.), *The Torture Debate in America* (2006) 44.
110 F. Allhoff, 'A Defense of Torture: Separation of Cases, Ticking Time-bombs, and Moral Justification', (2005) 19 *International Journal of Applied Philosophy* 243, 246.
111 *Id.* 246.
112 Matthews, *supra* n. 7, 78.
113 The interpretation of a legal code based on the component parts of the hypothetical is equally problematic and will be considered in Chapter 4.
114 John Kleinig has argued that the hypothetical contains six assumptions: 1. That the authorities know there is a ticking bomb; 2. There is an imminent danger with a 'pressing' need to act; 3. That the threat is very serious and torture is a proportionate response; 4. Other means of getting the information will fail; 5. The person detained is responsible for the threat; 6. Torture will work. He goes on to argue that in the form he has stated them, these 'strong assumptions … are unlikely to be replicated in the real world'. He also argues that the suggestions that such a scenario could never occur in the real world 'over-reaches': J. Kleinig, 'Ticking Bombs and Torture Warrants', (2005) 10 *Deakin Law Review* 614, 616–8, 622.
115 See, for example, M. Bagaric and J. Clarke, *Torture: When the Unthinkable is Morally Permissible* (2007) 2 (featuring a scenario in which a bomb is due to explode on an unidentified aircraft within 30 minutes); Kleinig, *id.* 614 (featuring a nuclear device in an undisclosed location that will explode within one hour). See also B. Brecher, *Torture and the Ticking Bomb* (2008) 27–8 (discussing various versions of the ticking bomb hypothetical).
116 *Supra* n. 24 and accompanying text.
117 Dershowitz, *supra* n. 16, 136, 162, 143–4, 139.
118 Landau Commission, *supra* n. 4, para. 3.15.
119 Internal quotation marks removed.
120 Landau Commission, *supra* n. 4, paras. 3.12, 3.15–3.16.
121 This raises the identical problems to the notion of 'balancing' discussed I Chapter 1.
122 PCATI, *supra* n. 63, para. 34.
123 *Id.* paras. 34. The US government's National Terrorism Advisory System has an alert system designed to warn citizens or institutions of potential terrorist threats. An 'Imminent Alert' is described as warning of a 'credible, specific, and impending terrorist threat or on-going attack … that is sufficiently specific and credible to recommend … protective measures to thwart or mitigate against an attack'. Department of Homeland Security, *NTAS National Terrorism Advisory System Interim Stakeholder Information Handbook* (undated) 5.
124 *Id.* The court uses 'immediacy' and 'imminence' in the judgment. It will be assumed here that the words are interchangeable in terms of their intended meaning.
125 Matthews, *supra* n. 7, 75–6.

126 *Id.* Matthews refuses to use the word terrorist except when referred to as 'terrorist'. One of the labels he favours is 'political actor'. Some terrorist leaders have no such reluctance. In an October 2001 interview with Al-Jazeera television correspondent Tayseer Alouni, Bin Laden made reference to the 9/11 attacks as 'great on all levels' and stated: 'We practice the good terrorism which stops them from killing our children in Palestine and elsewhere': 'Transcript of Bin Laden's October interview', www. CNN.com 5 February 2002. It is worth noting that if one is to refer to 'actors', then a more appropriate label is 'violent non-state actor': P. Williams, *Violent Non-Sate Actors and National and International Security* (International Relations and Security Network, 2008).

127 'Patrick Magee: The IRA Brighton bomber', www.bbc.co.uk/news 22 June 1999.

128 Department of Justice White Paper, *Lawfulness of a Lethal Operation Directed Against a US Citizen Who is a Senior Operational Leader of Al-Qa'ida or an Associated Force* (undated).

129 *Id.* 6.

130 *Id.* 7.

131 *Id.*

132 *Id.*

133 B'Tselem, *Routine Torture: Interrogation Methods of the General Security Service* (1998) 30.

134 *Id.* 30–1.

135 *Id.* 15–6.

136 *Id.* 16. Similar findings can be found in a report by the Public Committee Against Torture in Israel which examined the testimony of 9 detainees who claimed to have been subjected to interrogational torture: *Ticking Bombs -Testimonies of Torture Victims in Israel* (2007). There are also allegations that children are targeted for abuse when questioned on suspicion of stone throwing: B'Tselem, *No Minor Matter: Violation of the Rights of Palestinian Minors Arrested by Israel on Suspicion of Stone-Throwing* (2011).

137 Public Committee Against Torture in Israel, *Back to a Routine of Torture* (2003) 58–9.

138 *Chambers Giant Paperback English Dictionary* (1992) 525.

139 Cronin cites examples of terrorist groups in Northern Ireland, Spain, Italy and Egypt losing support and suffering a popular backlash as a result of attacks on 'illegitimate' targets: A.K. Cronin, *How Terrorism Ends: Understanding the Decline and Demise of Terrorist Campaigns* (2009) 108–10.

140 *PCATI, supra* n. 124 and accompanying text.

141 Matthews, *supra* n. 7, 75.

142 Bagaric and Clarke, *supra* n. 115, ch. 6.

143 Dershowitz, *supra* n. 117 and accompanying text.

144 These issues will be discussed in detail in Chapter 3.

145 L. Zedner, 'Terrorism, the Ticking Bomb, and Criminal Justice Values', *Criminal Justice Matters* September 2003, 18.

146 J. Radsan, 'A Better Model for Interrogating High-Level Terrorists', (2006) 79 *Temple L. Rev.* 1227, 1235.

147 See, for example, F. Ferudi, *Invitation to Terror: The Expanding Empire of the Unknown* (2007) 42 (noting 'Acts of apparently indiscriminate violence have a long history').

148 P.R. Neumann, *Old & New Terrorism: Late Modernity, Globalization and the Transformation of Political Violence* (2009) 35.

149 Home Office, *Prevent Strategy* (2011) ch. 5.

150 J.A. Piazza, 'Is Islamist Terrorism More Dangerous? An Empirical Study of Group Ideology, Organization, and Goal Structure', (2009) 21 *Terrorism and Political Violence* 62.

151 Report of the Special Rapporteur on the promotion and protection of human rights and fundamental freedoms while countering terrorism, *Martin Scheinin – Mission to Israel, Including Visit to Occupied Palestinian Territory* A/HRC/6/17/Add.4, 16 October 2007, para. 20.

152 *Supra* nn. 45–50 and accompanying text.

153 They note that the costs of placing tight limitations on who can be subjected to interrogational torture might be 'too high', and violent kidnappers might be a class of

offender who should be subject of coercion: E.A. Posner and A. Vermeule, *Terror in the Balance: Security, Liberty, and the Courts* (2007) 212. This view would appear to have some support amongst survey participants who, in one study, favoured the use of various forms of coercion, including torture, against kidnappers, the accomplices of armed robbers, the family members of terrorists and terrorists themselves in ticking bomb-type situations: R.J. Homant and M.J. Witkowski, 'Support for Coercive Interrogation Among College Students: Torture and the Ticking Bomb Scenario', (2011) *6 Journal of Applied Security Research* 135.

154 For discussion, see Homant and Witkowski, *id.*

155 Bagaric and Clarke, *supra* n. 115, 36–7.

156 *Id.* 38.

157 *Id.* 38.

158 *Id.* 37. For analysis of this claim, see P. Rumney, 'Is Coercive Interrogation of Terrorist Suspects Effective? A Response to Bagaric and Clarke', (2006) 40 *U.S.F.L. Rev.* 479.

159 Radsan, *supra* n. 146, 1234.

160 *Supra* n. 151, para. 21.

161 B. Anderson, 'We not only have a right to use torture. We have a duty', *The Independent* 15 February 2010.

162 For discussion, see Chapter 1.

163 On this point, see Dershowitz, *supra* n. 16, 146.

164 S.J. Heyman, 'The First Duty of Government: Protection, Liberty and the Fourteenth Amendment', (1991) 41 *Duke L.J.* 507, 513–20 (discussing early constitutional writings regarding the duty or responsibility of the state to protract citizens).

165 In drawing on the requirement that witnesses give evidence in court (or risk imprisonment), Bagaric and Clarke argue that 'people who have information that can save many lives, if questioned, are morally required to provide the information. It would be morally wrong for them to decline to do so, for the same reasons that it is wrong for a person to refuse to save a baby drowning in a puddle', *supra* n. 115, 36–7. On the grounds of pure harm minimisation such a view might be justified. However, there are three possible objections to such a proposal. The first is that torturing innocents significantly increases the number of people who could be seen as legitimate targets for interrogational torture by the state. Second, given the often fragmented nature of intelligence, legitimising the torture of innocents could lead to friends, associates and even entire families being tortured in order to gather enough information to locate an imminent threat. Third, the identification of innocents holding life-saving information is often likely to be based on a belief or mere assumption that someone knows of information useful to the authorities in preventing an imminent attack. This potentially increases the likelihood that individuals with no knowledge will be targeted.

166 The duty to provide information to the police regarding terrorism-related offences already exists in relation to certain classes of terrorist activity. Section 19 of the Terrorism Act 2000 (as amended) places a duty on individuals to disclose to a police officer a 'belief or suspicion' that another person has committed offences that involve the financing of terrorist activities, including money laundering and fund raising.

167 Buffachi and Arrigo, *supra* n. 9, 361.

168 This of course assumes such a detainee is a person who possesses the knowledge being sought.

169 Y. Ginbar, *Why Not Torture Terrorists? Moral, Practical, and Legal Aspects of the 'Ticking Bomb' Justification for Torture* (2007) 125, n. 100.

170 Wisnewski and Emerick, *supra* n. 6, 32.

171 See Chapter 3 for a detailed discussion.

172 Brecher, *supra* n. 115, 27.

173 N. MacMaster, 'Torture: from Algiers to Abu Ghraib', (2004) 46 *Race & Class* 1, 3.

174 Luban, *supra* n. 109, 36.

175 O. Gross, 'Torture and an Ethics of Responsibility', (2007) 3 *Law, Culture and the Humanities* 35, 38.
176 J. Waldron, 'Torture and Positive Law: Jurisprudence for the White House', (2005) 105 *Colum. L. Rev.* 1681, 1715.
177 S. Holmes, 'Is Defiance of Law a Proof of Success? Magical Thinking in the War on Terror', in Greenberg, *supra* n. 109, 128.
178 See, for example, Bufacchi and Arrigo, *supra* n. 9, 358.
179 Human Rights Watch, *'No Questions Asked': Intelligence Cooperation with Countries that Torture* (2010) 15.
180 Yuval Ginbar cites with approval the suggestion that the ticking bomb hypothetical is 'a load of rubbish', but includes in his work an annex listing ticking bomb scenarios, some of which he claims are 'real (or described as such)' without further analysis.: *supra* n. 169, 357–64.
181 Wisnewski, *supra* n. 5, 209.
182 Matthews, *supra* n. 7, 71, 73, 96, 98, 206, 207.
183 A.W. McCoy, *A Question of Torture: CIA Interrogation, From the Cold War to the War on Terror* (2006) 192.
184 *Id.* 193.
185 *Id.* McCoy does not discuss other examples from Israel which are also discussed in publically available sources.
186 For example, Brecher claims to identify factors which suggest that the 'the ticking bomb scenario remains a fantasy, and not a description of a rare but realistic possibility', *supra* n. 115, 22.
187 Sunstein, *supra* n. 106, 49.
188 This can also result in an exaggeration of risk.
189 Brecher, *supra* n. 115, 17.
190 K.L. Scheppele, 'Hypothetical Torture in the "War on Terrorism"', (2005) 1 *J. Nat'l Security L. & Pol'y* 285, 305.
191 *Id.* 323.
192 *Id.*
193 Holmes, *supra* n. 177, 127–8.
194 See, for example, A. Perliger *et al*, 'Policing Terrorism in Israel', (2009) 36 *Criminal Justice and Behavior* 1279, 1292 ('In 2005, the Israeli Police was able to prevent at least 15 suicide attacks in various stages of execution, and during 2006, no fewer than 50 Palestinians living in Israel illegally and intending either to carry out attacks or to assist others in doing so were detained by the police ... '). For older data, see for example, Israel Ministry of Foreign Affairs, 'Terrorist attacks prevented by the Israeli security forces – October/November 2001' (listing 16 serious terrorist attacks that were foiled). For an example from the United States, see: N. Jabali-Nash, 'California Highway Gunman Byron Williams Aimed for "Revolution", Say Cops', www.cbs.news.com 21 July 2010 (armed suspect arrested while travelling to attack two 'nonprofit groups').
195 For several examples of the Northern Ireland police thwarting terrorist attacks, see D. Doran, 'Remembrance Sunday bomb intercepted', independent.co.uk 13 November 2000; 'Huge van bomb intercepted', www.bbc.co.uk/news 15 June 2003; H. Mac-Donald, 'Dissident republican bomb plot foiled in Northern Ireland', *The Guardian* 31 December 2009; I. Graham, 'Northern Ireland police defuse huge bomb on Dublin road', *Reuters* 9 April 2011; A. Bloxham, 'The Queen in Ireland: bomb found on bus hours before historic state visit', www.telegraph.co.uk 17 May 2011.
196 K. Lasson, 'Torture, Truth Serum, and Ticking Bombs: Toward a Pragmatic Perspective of Coercive Interrogation', (2008) 39 *Loy. U. Chi. L.J.* 329, citing: A. Rabinovich, 'Suicide Bomber Thwarted', *Australian* 22 February 2007, 8 (discussing the arrest of a terrorist who was captured by Israeli security forces after he had planted a bomb and subsequently divulged its location, for reasons that are unknown. As a result, the bomb was located and the attack foiled). The Israel Ministry of Foreign Affairs publishes

details of terrorist attacks, as well as those that have been prevented by the Israeli security forces: www.mfa.gov.il/mfa/terrorism-%20obstacle%20to%20peace/ter rorism %20and%20islamic%20fundamentalism (accessed 1 February 2014).

197 A. Horne, *A Savage War of Peace: Algeria 1954–1962* (2006) 204–5.
198 *Id.* 205. It is not clear whether a bomb was ever found or even existed.
199 Cited by Brecher, *supra* n. 115, 21.
200 *PCATI, supra* n. 63.
201 *Id.* paras. 5.
202 Another document includes reference to a case with marked similarities to the first *PCATI* case suspect, but with a different name. *Letter dated 20 February 1997 from the Permanent Representative of Israel to the United Nations Office at Geneva addressed to the secretariat of the fifty-third session of the Commission on Human Rights* E/CN.4/1997/116, 5 March 1997.
203 *PCATI, supra* n. 63, para. 4.
204 A. Pedahzur, *The Israeli Secret Services and the Struggle Against Terrorism* (2009) 97–101. For discussion of the Wachsman case and the Israeli police and security force responses to the problem of kidnapping, see Perliger, *supra* n. 194, 1287–91.
205 *Id.* 99.
206 *Id.*
207 G. Frankel, 'Prison Tactics a Longtime Dilemma for Israel', *The Washington Post* 16 June 2004 A01. Of course, we do not know the details of the interrogation methods used in the Wachsman case, but Rabin's comment suggests that they may have been more severe than the techniques endorsed by the Landau Commission which noted that in some instances during interrogation, the 'exertion of a moderate measure of physical pressure cannot be avoided', *supra* n. 4, para. 4.7.
208 Brecher, *supra* n. 115, 86.
209 *Id. Infra* n. 221.
210 Brecher argues that if such an event were to take place '[n]othing is to be done. It is too late', and that if legalised torture were to be permitted 'we would have to accept all the [negative] consequences', *Id.* 87.
211 'Leicester City Council "not ready" for zombie attack', www.bbc.co.uk/news 10 June 2011 (discussing an enquiry made to Leicester City Council regarding its contingency plans in the event of a zombie attack. Unsurprisingly, the council had no such plans).
212 This point is forcefully made by Anthony Lake, *6 Nightmares: Real Threats in a Dangerous World and how America can Meet Them* (2000).
213 Bufacchi and Arrigo, *supra* n. 9. 360–2.
214 *Id.* 360.
215 *Id.*
216 *Id.*
217 *Id.* 358–9.
218 H. Shue, 'Torture in Dreamland: Disposing of the Ticking Bomb', (2005) 37 *Case W. Res. J. Int'l L.* 231, 233. On this point Shue assumes the hypothetical depicts the prevention of a terrorist attack by the use of interrogational torture. This is not how the hypothetical is always constructed. Shue precludes its use as a means of setting out a series of conditions that must be met for interrogational torture to be justified.
219 *Id.* 236–7.
220 *Id.* 231.
221 *Leon* v. *Wainwright* 734 F.2d 770 (11th Cir. 1984). In this case, the police detained a kidnapper who was attempting to collect a ransom. The police feared for the life of the kidnap victim so they threatened and choked the suspect until he disclosed the location of the victim who was subsequently rescued by the police. See also *Gäfgen* v. *Germany* Application no. 22978/05 (2010). For detailed discussion, see Chapter 1.
222 [1991] 93 Cr. App. R. 350.
223 *Id.* 352.

224 Allhoff, *supra* n. 110, 247.
225 Shue argues that the hypothetical is idealised because it contains a number of assumptions that are unlikely to exist in real life situations: Shue, *supra* n. 218, 233.
226 In Chapter 4 examples of counter-terrorism campaigns will be given where rules imposed on the use of interrogational torture have, in most instances, been liberally interpreted or entirely ignored.
227 Matthews repeatedly claims that empirical reality undermines the case for legalised torture: *supra* n. 7, 34. Wisnewski and Emerick argue that the hypothetical 'should have a basis in empirical reality' and go onto to argue that empirically, the hypothetical has no basis in reality: *supra* n. 6, 33.
228 P. Bobbitt, *Terror and Consent: Wars for the Twenty-First Century* (2008) 381. Here, Bobbitt is referring to the claim that torture never works as a tool of interrogation, but his observation could equally apply to the approach of those who wish to disparage the ticking bomb hypothetical.
229 C.R. Sunstein, 'Misfearing: A Reply', (2006) 119 *Harv. L. Rev.* 1110, 1119. See also C.R. Sunstein, *Laws of Fear: Beyond the Precautionary Principle* (2005) 104 (includes extensive discussion of confirmation and other biases in the context of counter-terrorism).
230 Willis and colleagues note that '[g]iven the tremendous uncertainties surrounding terrorism risk assessment, it is prudent to plan for the range of plausible futures that may play out', H.H. Willis *et al, Estimating Terrorism Risk* (2005) 55.

3

INTERROGATIONAL TORTURE AND THE QUESTION OF EFFECTIVENESS[1]

'Pain is truth; all else is subject to doubt.'[2]

'Did you tell them what they wanted to know? the judge asked. "I did not, Your Honour," the man said, and the judge banged his gavel. "Case dismissed. This man has not been tortured. Tortured men always talk".'[3]

The effectiveness of interrogational torture in producing the disclosure of timely and reliable intelligence often underpins discussion of its legalisation. The question of effectiveness has attracted attention from scholars,[4] journalists[5] and state officials.[6] As the quotes above suggest, the use of torture is often accompanied by certain assumptions regarding its effectiveness. The effectiveness claim is a pivotal part of the case for legalisation. As such, it must be critically examined. If there is little evidence that interrogational torture can produce intelligence to prevent an imminent terrorist attack, then its use is costly with no discernable benefit. This chapter identifies a range of factors that help to explain why the use of interrogational torture is ineffectual in ticking bomb cases. It will critically examine claims that interrogational torture has produced ticking bomb and infrastructure intelligence. Further, it will argue that there is a mismatch between the legalisation argument, which stipulates the need to use torture in a time-limited situation, and the available evidence, which suggests that virtually all the intelligence that is said to be produced by torture is in fact infrastructure intelligence. There is scant evidence that torture can work to produce timely and reliable ticking bomb intelligence. This does not provide a strong evidential base for arguing that torture is likely to produce the intelligence necessary to prevent a terrorist attack in time-limited circumstances.

The chapter will consider how effectiveness can be measured and the limitations of any such analysis. In keeping with the focus on empiricism, the chapter will engage in a detailed analysis of the intelligence gains that are said to have resulted from the use of interrogational torture and coercion in the CIA's 'High Value Detainee' programme, Northern Ireland, Algeria and Israel. This analysis will include an examination of some of the common themes and the limitations of the existing data. The chapter will also include a brief exploration of the alternatives to interrogational torture and implications for the torture debate. The chapter will conclude that there is little credible empirical evidence that interrogational torture works to produce the type of intelligence needed in the typical ticking bomb-type scenario.

The analysis in this chapter will allow for the development of an argument that fits within the consequentialist argument in this book. The notion of torture's effectiveness underpins its use by state officials based on a narrative that emphasises that it is necessary, effective, but with no evidence that it is more effective than non-coercive interrogation. One consequence of the institutional belief that torture has utility is that it is used to produce infrastructure intelligence and goes far beyond the prevention of imminent terrorist attacks. This is typical of the kind of consequentialist approach to the use of torture evidenced in previous chapters. This chapter continues the analysis by detailing the way in which the issue of torture's effectiveness is used to support a case for an expansive torture power.

1. Measuring effectiveness: ticking bomb and infrastructure intelligence

Intelligence can serve political, strategic or prosecutorial goals[7] and is pivotal in counter-terrorism or insurgency operations.[8] The intelligence gathering focus of states has altered in recent decades to reflect the existence of a 'new threat environment of asymmetric warfare' between states and terrorist groups.[9] This chapter reflects the shift in that it is concerned with the use of intelligence to disrupt the activities of terrorist groups. It distinguishes between *ticking bomb intelligence* and *infrastructure intelligence*. The former refers to intelligence concerning an imminent terrorist attack; the latter to intelligence involving such things as arms dumps, safe houses, internal organisation and the identity of terror cell members, recruiters and financiers. While the former may save lives by preventing imminent attacks, the latter can also save lives by disrupting the ability of terrorist groups to operate in an organised and efficient manner.[10] Such a distinction is rarely acknowledged in the existing literature[11] but is crucial in answering a key empirical question in the torture debate: does torture work in preventing imminent terrorist attacks? This question is of importance because the case for legalisation normally rests on its use in a time-limited situation where accurate, timely intelligence disclosures are essential.

The chapter will also seek to test a hypothesis that interrogational torture, if it works at all, is likely to produce significantly more infrastructure intelligence than ticking bomb intelligence. This hypothesis rests on two assumptions. First, information sufficient enough to prevent an imminent terrorist attack is likely to be known by only a small number of individuals whereas information regarding infrastructure is, by necessity, known more widely within terrorist groups. Thus a terrorist suspect will almost certainly possess knowledge of infrastructure and perhaps future plans. In contrast, knowledge of the location of a ticking bomb is likely to be known by very few people. Second, given the time-limited nature of imminent terrorist attacks, interrogators have but a short time to elicit the information they seek. This is less of a problem when they seek infrastructure intelligence when there is likely to be more time to gain information.

Some scholars have pointed to the difficulties of knowing whether or not torture is a reliable means of producing intelligence.[12] This poses a particular problem for proponents of legalised torture. If they cannot show that interrogational torture works to produce time-sensitive intelligence in more than an isolated number of cases then this creates serious problems for their argument. If this is true then creating an exception to the absolute prohibition permitting the use of torture with little proof that it works in emergency cases appears to be irresponsible. Evidence-based policy-making demands a better understanding of issues. Since some proponents argue that the use of interrogational torture would require evaluation only *after* its use[13] then it would appear that policy makers would be asked to legislate without inadequate knowledge. It has been argued that there is a danger that the debate over effectiveness becomes a 'numbers game' with one side citing an example of where torture worked and the other an example of where it did not.[14] However, this misses the point. A detailed examination of evidence is the only way of understanding its strengths, limitations, what it is we know at the moment and what we do not.

This chapter will examine evidence from a range of sources in an attempt to gain a better understanding of effectiveness. This enables us to discover whether there are any recurrent patterns running through the literature and assess whether a reliable body of evidence exists to support the claim that interrogational torture works in producing timely, accurate intelligence. In such an analysis it is necessary to take account of sources, the ability to verify factual claims[15] and the possibility that some effectiveness claims will be self-serving, inaccurate or untrue.[16] It has been argued that the value of intelligence gained from coercive methods in some prominent cases has been exaggerated[17] and there have been failures to realise the value of intelligence already possessed by state agencies and disclosures gained by non-coercive means.[18] This is an area that is complicated by government secrecy and the unwillingness of state agencies to produce detailed corroborative evidence to support factual claims.[19] While some of the examples of successful coercion to be found in the literature are impossible to verify, it would be contrary to more convincing evidence to suggest that we cannot make any determination. Analysis of this evidence also enables identification of the problems that characterise the use of interrogational torture. Indeed, throughout the historic and contemporary record there are a number of themes that are worthy of examination.

It is also crucial that we judge effectiveness by some measure. Given the importance of the ticking bomb argument to proponents of legalisation, this chapter will assume that to be successful intelligence gained from the use of interrogational torture needs to be reliable *and* timely in the sense of preventing an imminent act of terrorism. If intelligence gathered by torture fails to meet this measure then it has failed. If one considers this issue in the context of a legal regulatory framework then imminence would likely require some specific definition, otherwise there is significant danger that the law would not be tightly controlled and the state would possess an expansive power. In keeping with Chapter 2, imminence will be defined, for the purpose of this chapter, as an act of terrorism that will occur within 48 hours of the suspect's arrest. In terms of judging the effectiveness of torture, a shorter time frame is likely to narrow the instances where it can be argued that interrogational torture is effective, and likewise, a longer time frame will widen the evidential base. The greater the time element, the further the scenario moves away from the notion of imminence that forms a central pillar of the ticking bomb argument and the notion of an emergency power. This would also allow for the use of alternative means of intelligence gathering.

As noted in Chapter 1, repressive terrorism measures may be seen to work in certain instances, but they can also have wider societal impacts, including provoking a violent counter-reaction which may worsen terrorist violence.[20] This links to Ignatieff's 'effectiveness test' which considers whether counter-terrorism measures have political implications and 'make citizens more or less secure in the long run'.[21] Making such assessments might be very difficult. While governments are often eager to emphasise the alleged success of counter-terrorism measures such as the use of interrogational torture,[22] there are often many questions that are left unanswered. These include the frequency of false or inaccurate disclosures, the existence of disclosures that are impossible to verify, whether timely disclosures provide specific intelligence and the role of other intelligence gathering techniques in gaining intelligence. Many disclosures cannot be independently verified and it is largely unknown whether interrogators in individual cases have inadvertently or purposefully fed snippets of information to detainees which are then pieced together and fed back as a disclosure to other interrogators.

Scholars have expressed widely divergent views on the question of effectiveness. Some claim it is 'maximally ineffective ... in the acquisition of truth',[23] that there is 'abundant evidence that torture is not effective either as an interrogation tactic or an information-extracting device'[24] and that 'torture does not actually work: prisoners treated like those in Abu Ghraib will confess to anything'.[25] In contrast, proponents of legalisation claim torture is 'an excellent means of gathering information',[26] or is 'often an effective method of eliciting true information'.[27] Dershowitz claims that it 'sometimes' works[28] and engages in a form of reverse reasoning to suggest that interrogational torture sometimes works: 'It is precisely because torture sometimes does work and can sometimes prevent major disasters that it still exists in many parts of the world and has been totally eliminated from none.'[29] Here, Dershowitz makes a leap by simply assuming that torture exists around the globe for a rational reason, that is, as a means of preventing terrorism or other criminality. He cites no evidence to support this claim. Indeed, elsewhere he acknowledges that in countries such as Egypt, Saudi Arabia and the Philippines 'torture – including the lethal torture of purely political prisoners – is common and approved at the highest levels of government'.[30] When one examines evidence of torture it becomes apparent that it is used for a variety of reasons, including the victimisation of political opponents, human rights campaigners and journalists, the general suppression of dissent, as well as the persecution of cultural, racial and sexual minorities.[31] Judged by this evidence, the notion that torture exists because it works to 'prevent major disasters' is speculative. Likewise, Bagaric and Clarke suggest: 'If the considered view of the CIA was that torture was not effective in most cases, it seems incredulous that President Bush and Vice President Cheney would have so vigorously lobbied Congress to exempt the CIA from legislation ... that bans "cruel, inhuman and degrading treatment of prisoners ... "'[32] Bagaric and Clarke's suggestion that lobbying is evidence that torture works 'in most cases' is a claim for which they provide no supporting evidence.

At best, this is an inference drawn from behaviour. It assumes that governmental decision-making is always based on a rational, evidence-led consideration of options, with the decision-maker choosing 'the alternative that best advances his interests'.[33] Studies of governmental decision-making suggest that such rationality-based assumptions can be 'powerfully misleading'.[34] Indeed, there is some evidence to suggest that the use of torture to extract intelligence from terrorist suspects was discussed in the immediate aftermath of 9/11 and hardly suggests an evidence-led approach to the issue. In his book, *State of Denial*, Woodward, quotes President George W. Bush two days after 9/11, in conversation with Prince Bandar bin Sultan of Saudi Arabia: 'If we get somebody and we can't get them to cooperate, we'll hand them over to you.'[35] Government decisions to use torture are sometimes driven by fear and the need to be seen to act in order to allay public fear. In the context of interrogational torture, decisions may be made in the hope that they will produce some positive result[36] or because of the perceived need to gain confessions.[37] Such decisions cannot be simply equated with evidence that torture works. McCoy explains the decision to use torture: 'the powerful often turn to torture in times of crisis, not because it works but because it salves their fears and insecurities with the psychic balm of empowerment.'[38] Likewise, Ackerman argues: '[s]ecurity services can panic in the face of horrific tragedy. With officials in disarray, with rumours of impending attacks flying about, and with an outraged public demanding instant results, there will be overwhelming temptations to use indecent forms of interrogation. This is the last place to expect carefully nuanced responses.'[39]

There are three further issues that require consideration when judging the question of effectiveness. First, it has been suggested that the citation of evidence of interrogational torture being ineffective is of little irrelevance when considering models of legal regulation that would use torture in a targeted and controlled manner, inflicted for the purpose of averting catastrophe.[40] Bagaric and Clarke make this argument, yet they use evidence from the very same conflicts and counter-terrorism campaigns cited by their critics, to prove that torture works.[41] Unfortunately, many of their specific claims are either unverifiable, involve infrastructure, not ticking bomb intelligence or have been proven to be false.[42] Further, it is not the legal framework or specific context in which torture occurs that determines effectiveness, but human psychology and many other factors. Further, they rely on an assumption about human behaviour to support their argument that torture has utility. They state: 'we know as a fact that humans dislike pain and will try to avoid it.'[43] It has long been recognised, however, that the 'agony of torture created an incentive to speak, but not necessarily to speak the truth'.[44]

Second, attention should be given to the range of harms that interrogational torture is said to prevent. Terrorists engage in a wide range of criminal activity and it would be an error for any counter-terrorism strategy to focus only on ticking bomb scenarios. In Israel, it has been claimed that through the use of coercive interrogation methods, over a two-year period:

> some 90 planned terrorist attacks have been foiled. Among these planned attacks were some 10 potential suicide bombings; 7 car bombings; 15 kidnappings of soldiers and civilians; and some 60 attacks of different types, including the shooting of soldiers and civilians, hijacking of buses, stabbing and murder of ordinary Israelis and the placing of explosives.[45]

On its face, these statistics provide evidence that torture and other coercive interrogation methods have prevented a wide range of terrorist-related activity. However, the reference to 'planned' attacks means that it is not clear whether these activities were imminent, aspirational or if the disclosures were corroborated. Neither do we know what role other sources of intelligence played in preventing these terrorist plots. Further, it might be that a very small number of detainees disclosed multiple plots, or that this data was gathered by interrogating large numbers of detainees.[46] We simply do not know. This leads on to a third issue and that is whether such claims are, in fact, true.[47] Dershowitz acknowledges the limitations of some of the evidence in this area when he makes reference to a claim that as a result of the *PCATI* decision[48] 'at least one preventable act of terrorism has been allowed to take place'. But he notes that '[w]hether this claim is true, false, or somewhere in between is difficult to assess'.[49] This is a problem with state claims that torture has worked to produce intelligence in terrorist-related contexts and will be revisited later. The next section will examine some of the factors that impact on the potential utility of interrogational torture.

2. Three factors impacting on the question of effectiveness

The effectiveness of interrogational torture can potentially be influenced by a range of factors. Some relate to specific circumstances, the type of intelligence being sought, the urgency with which it is needed, as well as the training, competence and subjective judgements of interrogators and intelligence analysts. A detainee may be a skilled liar, be able to withstand coercion for long periods or he may simply not possess the intelligence that his interrogators are seeking.[50] In reality, there are likely to be a multitude of factors that influence the effectiveness, or otherwise, of interrogational torture in individual cases. The purpose of this section is to examine three of these factors. All three tend to inhibit the ability of interrogators to gain intelligence in time-limited situations.

a. The nature of intelligence

A key factor impacting on the question of effectiveness is the fragmentary nature of intelligence. Intelligence that is required in the context of the 'ticking bomb' is time limited. In such cases, interrogators require detailed, precise disclosures which may not be strongly corroborated or corroborated at all by intelligence from other sources. The problem was explained by Satre as '[t]he purpose of [torture] is to force from *one* tongue, amid its screams and its vomiting up of blood, the secret of *everything*'[51] (emphasis in original). In reality, 'intelligence is usually bitty and needs piecing together, assessing, judging … even the best of it never tells the whole story'.[52] In his book, *Securing the State*, Omand makes a similar point.[53] He notes that often 'raw intelligence represents a piece of a jigsaw that may fit one of several mixed-up puzzles … [and] … will need validating to ensure that its shape can be relied upon … then its likely place in one of the puzzles can be estimated'.[54] It is not only that intelligence may be fragmented, but also that authorities may already possess the intelligence being sought. In a report, the United States Intelligence Science Board notes that if the 'United States has information about an imminent, catastrophic attack, *and* has captured a person known to be knowledgeable might the authorities already have substantial intelligence [that might be useful for] prevention?'[55] (emphasis in original). Indeed, there are examples of state authorities seeking disclosures through the use of interrogational torture when they already possess the information sought, through the use of informers.[56] This is an important element in the analysis of torture as an effective means of intelligence gathering. Acknowledging the fragmentary nature of intelligence does not mean that a victim of interrogational torture can never provide intelligence that will prevent an imminent attack, but it does suggest it is unlikely. Further, the intelligence jigsaw may help to explain the observation of some scholars who have argued that interrogational torture has only produced 'useful intelligence' when it has been used on a mass scale.[57] In these instances it has also been used alongside other intelligence gathering techniques.

In contrast to ticking bomb intelligence, fragmented disclosures of infrastructure intelligence may help to build a picture of a terrorist group, its members, supporters and activities. The CIA's HVD programme provides evidence of the way in which intelligence from various detainees was used to provide a more detailed understanding of al Qaeda:

> [The CIA] frequently uses the information from one detainee, as well as other sources, to vet the information of another detainee. Although lower-level detainees provide less information than the high value detainees, information

from these detainees has, on many occasions, supplied the information needed to probe the high value detainees further [redacted] the triangulation of intelligence provides a fuller knowledge of Al-Qa'ida activities than would be possible from a single detainee. For example, Mustafa Ahmad Adam al-Hawsawi, the Al-Qa'ida financier who was captured with Khalid Shaykh Muhammad, provided the Agency's first intelligence pertaining to [redacted] another participant in the 9/11 terrorist plot … [58]

More limited, fractured intelligence may provide an important means by which interrogators can more effectively question detainees and provide a means by which they can judge the accuracy of new disclosures or existing information. In a CIA Directorate of Intelligence report concerning the HVD programme, it has been noted that intelligence 'from one detainee can be used in debriefing another detainee in a "building block" process'.[59] For example, it has also been claimed that interrogations were most productive with Mohammed al-Qahtani, the so-called '20th hijacker' when he was presented with evidence provided by other detainees, in particular Khalid Sheikh Mohammed.[60] This evidence raises further questions regarding the effectiveness of interrogational torture and other forms of coercion to produce timely and reliable intelligence disclosures. If the successful use of interrogational torture requires the detention of other detainees to encourage disclosure this will be of little use in cases of imminent threat where authorities have detained a single individual.

The threat posed by terrorist groups has required a shift of focus within the intelligence community. Powers has noted that for US intelligence agencies '[d]efining and describing "the threat" was easier during the forty years of cold war with the USSR', than when dealing with the 'amorphous threat of terrorism which requires significant co-operation with foreign intelligence agencies'.[61] The threat of terrorism has also required intelligence analysis to shift away from considering the possibility of single events 'with a more fluid approach giving a sense of the range of possible outcomes with fuzzy numbers for the probability of the major ones'.[62] Indeed, the challenges of intelligence analysis continue to create problems in counter-terrorism work. The 9/11 terrorist attacks could have been prevented had US authorities made better use of intelligence it already possessed prior to 9/11. For example, the 9/11 Commission noted that new and existing intelligence concerning the role of Khalid Sheik Mohammed with other plotters provided a 'late opportunity' to prevent the attack, but was 'not put together' by the CIA or pursued further.[63] Similarly, a fuller investigation of the 9/11 plotter Zacarias Moussaoui and his activities 'might have derailed the plot'.[64] Moussaoui is an interesting case in point given that Alan Dershowitz has argued that Moussaoui could have been a candidate for the use of interrogational torture. He concludes that in this case, the 'cost-benefit analysis for employing … non-lethal torture seems overwhelming'.[65] This is a statement made with the benefit of hindsight. In fact, prior to 9/11 there was disagreement within the FBI as to whether Moussaoui posed a terrorist threat.[66]

Intelligence services employ analysts to evaluate the value of detainees as sources of information.[67] Intelligence analysts can also assist in identifying particular lines of questioning. The quality of analysis is a crucial element in judging effectiveness and in decisions to use torture. There is, however, evidence of analysts failing to consider the reliability of intelligence or of particular interpretations placed on that intelligence.[68] Research involving police officers suggests that some exhibit an over-confidence in being able to identify when a suspect is lying and that 'accusatorial' interview styles result in a greater number of baseless accusations of lying.[69] In the context of interrogational torture, faulty decision-making can result in the production of false, or 'extraneous information' which 'distracts, rather than supports, valid interrogations'[70] and can result in individuals being subject to interrogational torture when those methods are either unnecessary or targeted against individuals who do not possess the intelligence being sought.

b. Terrorist cells and networks, 'lone wolfs' and the question of effectiveness

The effectiveness of interrogational torture is influenced by the organisational structure of terrorist groups that may impact on the knowledge of those involved in terrorist activity. An important factor, which is likely to have impact on intelligence gathering is the fact that some terrorist groups deliberately structure themselves to reduce the impact of infiltration, eavesdropping and interrogation. An example of this type of structural change can be found in the history of the IRA. In an internal document entitled *Staff Report* dated 1976, the IRA leadership acknowledged the impact of interrogations on its members and operations: 'The three-day and seven-day detention orders are breaking volunteers and it is the Republican Army's fault for not indoctrinating volunteers with the psychological strength to resist interrogation.'[71] As a result of this problem the IRA decided to change its organisational structure from one that mimicked the British hierarchal army structure, to a 'cell' structure consisting of a small number of volunteers (the document refers to four) who would carry out operations independently of other cells.[72] In his analysis of coercive interrogation in Northern Ireland, Peter Taylor explained that the idea behind this change was that if individuals were questioned, they might be able to disclose information about their own cell members and operations, but they would know little about the operations and membership of other cells.[73] He notes: 'At best [interrogation] could destroy a cell, but not a whole battalion. It made infiltration more difficult too. If information was leaked, it was easier for the leadership to identify the source.'[74] The organisational change did not mean that cells operated in an entirely independent manner, but were controlled through senior members of the IRA, with cells having no control over weapons or explosives.[75] Al Qaeda has adopted a similar strategy. Farrall notes that the group:

> is not a traditional hierarchical terrorist organization ... and it does not exercise full command and control over its branch and franchises: [I]t operates as a

devolved network hierarchy ... al Qaeda's core members focus on exercising strategic command and control to ensure the centralization of the organization's actions and message, rather than directly managing its branch and franchises.[76]

It has also been observed that al Qaeda has adapted to the well-publicised use of highly coercive interrogation techniques by the CIA. In giving evidence before the US Senate Judiciary Committee, John E. Cloonan, a retired special agent of the FBI, who had experience of interrogating senior al Qaeda operatives, explained how the terror network has responded to the use of torture and coercion:

> Bin Laden and his advisors often refer to US intelligence and law enforcement agents as 'blood' people. This means simply this: We, according to bin Laden, use torture to extract information. Bin Laden has theorized that the most loyal al Qaeda sympathizer will break within 72 hours and give up operational information. Therefore, he has kept operational details about impending attacks strictly compartmentalized. In other words, those in the know or with a need to know were limited to a few trusted followers. My experiences and those of my former FBI colleagues would certainly support this conclusion.[77]

While cell structures and the 'compartmentalisation' of knowledge may hinder the ability of a terrorist from identifying other group members and detailing future actions, there will also be other organisational forms that undermine effective intelligence gathering. For example, terror groups may divide into cells with no central orga- nisation or leadership. This kind of structure has been referred to as Leaderless Resistance. One of the leading proponents of Leaderless Resistance, Louis Beam, has described it as:

> A system of organization that is based upon the cell organization, but does not have any central control or direction ... Utilizing the Leaderless Resistance concept, all individuals and groups operate independently of each other, and never report to a central headquarters or single leader for direction or instruction ... [78]

It can be argued that al Qaeda inspires and motivates the actions of some jihadists who accept al Qaeda's message but over whom the group's leaders have no direct contact or control.[79] In recent years there have been several domestic cases of individuals, inspired by the ideology of jihad who, acting alone have been involved in a range of terrorist-related activity.[80]

A further means by which terrorists can minimise the chances of others divulging their plans is by operating individually. The term 'lone wolf' has been coined by some right-wing extremists in the United States to refer to individuals who are engaged in violent or terrorist acts, but not as part of a centrally organised group.[81] By their very nature, terrorist acts committed by 'lone wolfs' are unlikely to be prevented by interrogational torture. Other people are not directly involved in the planning of attacks and are unlikely to be aware of specific acts or plans. This makes it difficult for state authorities to uncover these types of activities irrespective of the intelligence gathering methods employed. A classic example of a 'lone wolf' was David Copeland, a self-confessed Nazi who, in 1999, targeted black people, Asians and gays in three bombings in London, killing three people and injuring over one hundred others. After the first two bombings, an image of Copeland taken from CCTV footage was released to the media. Someone who knew Copeland contacted the police and he was subsequently arrested. Further explosive devices were found after his arrest.[82] While Copeland was partly inspired by neo-Nazi literature which *inter alia* encouraged acts of violence against racial minorities, he acted alone and no-one appears to have had prior knowledge of his specific plans. Again, historic examples of 'lone wolfs' abound[83] as well as those acting as 'lone wolfs' in pursuit of goals shared by others who are a part of a larger terrorist organisation.[84]

Structural arguments clearly impact on the potential effectiveness of interrogational torture. Cell members can provide important infrastructure intelligence. Genuine 'lone wolfs' cannot provide wider information about terrorist plots because they are not part of a larger terrorist grouping. If authorities are fortunate enough to have detained a lone wolf prior to the detonation of a bomb, then he will have exact knowledge of the location of the bomb in a way that cell members may not. A lone wolf will have information about future plans and the location of weaponry, but of course, if he is acting alone, he will be unable to pursue his plans. The point of this analysis is to note that the knowledge held by individual terrorists is context-specific and will vary from case-to-case. Some terrorist groups, however, are organised in such a way so as to frustrate infiltration and other forms of intelligence gathering by state authorities. This is a matter that must be considered relevant when examining the effectiveness of interrogational torture.

c. Individual detainee characteristics

The effectiveness of any form of interrogation is likely to be influenced by the background and characteristics of the detainee, as well as the knowledge he possesses. In the development of the CIA's High Value Detainee interrogation programme (HVD), memoranda produced by the Office of Legal Counsel (OLC) stated that interrogation techniques required consideration of individual characteristics, including the medical and psychological state of detainees, as well as their responsiveness to questioning and level of co-operation.[85] There was also recognition of the general characteristics of high-value detainees. The CIA's *Background Paper* notes: 'HVDs are well-trained, often battle-hardened terrorist operatives, and highly committed to jihad. They are intelligent and resourceful leaders and able to resist standard interrogation approaches.'[86] As well as these factors, another reason why some terrorists may be resistant to interrogation is that groups prepare their recruits for the possibility of capture and interrogation. In its so called *Green Book*, the IRA, for example, instructed volunteers to 'SAY NOTHING, SIGN NOTHING, SEE NOTHING, HEAR NOTHING'[87] (emphasis in original). To reinforce these instructions, the IRA killed volunteers who co-operated with the authorities.[88] An al Qaeda manual recovered during a police raid in Manchester contained instructions on giving interrogators false information regarding a 'brother' who organised terrorist activity. Included within the document is a suggestion that 'each brother should mention a story that suits his personal status and the province of his residence' and 'coordination should be maintained with all brothers'.[89] Further evidence of this is provided by Omar Nasiri who infiltrated jihadist cells, mosques and training camps while working for European intelligence services. While at one camp, he recounted training to resist interrogation. He gave the example of a 17 year old who was interrogated by Chechen trainees. During the mock interrogation they slapped and threatened him and fired their guns within centimetres of his feet. When the trainee finally broke: 'he had given his interrogators more than they wanted, and made his army sound much stronger than it really was'.[90] Of course, the combination of a strong commitment to a cause and training to resist interrogation may lead some to assume that hardened terrorists will not disclose intelligence in response to rapport building techniques. In reality, however, there is evidence of this approach resulting in valuable intelligence disclosures.[91]

A further matter that impacts on the effectiveness of interrogational torture is the level of knowledge possessed by the detainee. There are several important aspects to this issue that must be considered. First, interrogational torture is sometimes used on the basis of an assumption that the detainee knows or should know ticking bomb or infrastructure intelligence. In its HVD programme, the CIA took the view that a determination that someone was of high value depended on their knowledge of imminent attacks, membership of particular terrorist groups and their potential future threat to the United States.[92] However, the HVD programme produced no intelligence concerning imminent attacks.[93] One reason for why interrogational torture may be of limited value in producing ticking bomb intelligence is the possibility that the detainee did not possess intelligence regarding an imminent attack because there were no plots of an imminent nature in existence. A second issue is that some caution must be shown when interpreting the significance of individual intelligence disclosures. As already noted, intelligence can be fragmented and may require piecing together with information gleaned from other sources and with the co-operation of the security services of other nations.[94] Finally, knowledge of ticking bomb intelligence will be dependent on how closely a detainee has been involved in a plot. Where terrorist groups are geographically dispersed and operating as a network of loosely affiliated cells it is unlikely that any single detainee is going to be aware of every detail of any plot, unless they have been intimately involved in the planning and execution of a specific plot.

This analysis has made clear that there are a number of impediments to state agencies gaining ticking bomb intelligence. Indeed, these difficulties tend to be masked by the fact that agencies also pursue infrastructure intelligence. This does not mean that interrogational torture can never work to gain accurate, time-limited intelligence. However, as the next section shows, there is scant evidence that interrogational torture works to produce ticking bomb intelligence which is central to the case for legalisation.

3. The effectiveness of interrogational torture: an examination of evidence

a. The CIA and its interrogation manuals

Since the 1950s the CIA has conducted research involving the study of human behaviour and psychology. One of the reasons for this work has been to develop methods of gathering intelligence from detainees during interrogation.[95] In 1996, following a Freedom of Information Act request by *The Baltimore Sun* newspaper, the CIA released two manuals which explain the use of physical and psychological interrogation methods and potential drawbacks in the use of such techniques. The first manual is entitled: KUBARK, *Counterintelligence Interrogation – July 1963*.[96] The second is dated from 1983 and is entitled: *Human Resource Exploitation Training Manual*.[97] This later manual, which appears to be based on the KUBARK manual, explicitly refers to the ineffectiveness of torture: 'Experience indicates that the use of force is not necessary to gain cooperation of sources. Use of force is a poor technique, yields unreliable results, may damage subsequent collection efforts, and can induce the source to say what he thinks the interrogator wants to hear.'[98] The KUBARK manual states: 'In fact, most people underestimate their capacity to withstand pain ... In general, direct physical brutality creates only resentment, hostility, and further defiance.'[99] An illustration of this phenomenon is the experience of Henri Alleg, who, while detained by French interrogators in Algeria in 1957, was severely tortured. Alleg recounts shouting at his interrogators on one occasion: 'You can bring back your magneto! I'm ready for you! I'm not afraid of you!'[100] Indeed, Alleg illustrates the way in which torture can invoke further defiance of interrogators.

Notwithstanding such assertions, both CIA manuals detail the use of psychological techniques and physical coercion that can be used to obtain intelligence.[101] They provide a useful means of assessing the claim that torture has utility in producing timely and reliable intelligence. Bagaric and Clarke state: 'Humans have an intense desire to avoid pain, no matter how short term, and most will comply with the demands of a torturer to avoid the pain. Often even the threat of torture alone will evoke cooperation.'[102] They cite no evidence in support of this claim. The KUBARK manual states that threats could be 'worse than useless'[103] although there is evidence that detainee threats[104] or threats against family members[105] can illicit information. While some of these disclosures are accurate, there is no evidence on which to judge their overall effectiveness.

The KUBARK manual also notes that there are detainees who are able to withstand pain to a much greater degree than others,[106] and of particular relevance to the terrorist who has deeply embedded religious or political beliefs, it states: '[p]ersons of considerable moral or intellectual stature often find in pain inflicted by others a confirmation of the belief that they are in the hands of inferiors, and their resolve not to submit is strengthened.'[107] This was a point acknowledged by Bentham, 'anger mixing itself with the sensation of pain will have a peculiar tendency to give force to obstinacy'.[108] Indeed, there is evidence from Northern Ireland that some suspected terrorists were motivated to resist when brutalised by interrogators.[109] Both manuals emphasise the importance of creating rapport during interrogations and the need for control, skill, professionalism and patience on the part of interrogators.[110] Events in Iraq illustrate well the fact that the use of extreme physical brutality does not necessarily gain cooperation. For example, after a series of severe beatings, Iraqi Major General Abed Hamed Mowhoush died in US military custody. Having shown 'moderate cooperation' initially without the use of coercion, it was decided that in order to gain further intelligence, interrogational torture would be used. Prior to his death 'a secret CIA-sponsored group of Iraqi paramilitaries, working with Army interrogators, had beaten Mowhoush nearly senseless, using fists, a club and a rubber hose'. This did not result in further disclosures.[111]

A problem with interrogational torture is that detainees may disclose false information in order to stop further torture. This is a particular problem where authorities are seeking information in a true 'ticking bomb' situation where there is pressure to obtain accurate and timely information and where independent verification of disclosures is unlikely. In an interview conducted with Khalid Sheikh Mohammed by the International Committee of the Red Cross, he explained why he had given false information: 'During the harshest period of the interrogation I gave a lot of false information in order to satisfy what I believed the interrogators wished to hear in order to make the ill-treatment stop … I'm sure the false information … wasted a lot of their time.'[112] Irrespective of the truth of this specific claim, this problem has been acknowledged by the CIA.[113] The KUBARK manual makes specific reference to this problem:

> Intense pain is quite likely to produce false confessions, concocted as a means of escaping from distress. A time-consuming delay results, while investigation is conducted and the admissions are proven untrue. During this respite the interrogatee can pull himself together. He may even use the time to think up new, more complex 'admissions' that will take still longer to disprove.[114]

Prior to their release from Guantánamo Bay in 2004, three British detainees falsely admitted to appearing in a video with Osama bin Laden. One of the detainees, Shafiq Rasul, gave the following explanation for his false confession: 'The reason I did this was because of the previous five or six weeks of being held in isolation and being taken to interrogation for hours on end, short shackled and being treated in that way … I was desperate for it to end and therefore eventually I just gave in and admitted to being in the video.'[115] Rasul and another British inmate at

Guantánamo Bay, Asif Iqbal, claimed that coercion also resulted in false accusations being made by some detainees against fellow detainees.[116] This suggests that measures short of the severe infliction of pain or life-threatening methods such as water-boarding have the potential to produce inaccurate information in order to stop the coercion.[117] The Public Committee Against Torture in Israel cites a case from the Tel Aviv-Jaffa District Court in 2003. In acquitting the defendant, the court observed: 'GSS interrogators have confirmed in their testimonies, and it has been evidenced in protocols that were recorded, that the accused reached a state in which he announced to them that he is prepared to sign anything they wrote … '[118]

While a body of evidence certainly exists which supports various assertions set out in the CIA manuals, it should also be acknowledged that US authorities claimed the detainees at Guantánamo Bay produced 'enormously valuable intelligence'.[119] These claims, however, have been doubted. For example, Lieutenant Colonel Anthony Christino, who for six months prior to his retirement had regular access to the intelligence coming from Guantánamo Bay, has argued that its value has been 'wildly exaggerated'[120] and that the system of interrogation adopted at Guantánamo Bay makes intelligence 'inherently unreliable'.[121] Joshua Dratel has claimed that there is a consensus amongst 'intelligence, military and criminal investigators' that the intelligence coming from Guantánamo Bay 'has been minimal and of little value' and that the US government has 'not pointed to a single piece of information gleaned from Guantánamo Bay detainees'.[122] However, in 2005, the US Department of Defense disclosed information derived from 'more than 4,000 reports [that] capture information provided by … [Guantánamo] detainees'.[123] Disclosures were said to involve infrastructure intelligence, including information about the financing of terrorist groups, the identity of al Qaeda operatives who have not been apprehended and explosives trainers, details of bomb making and training of operatives.[124] The report claims that 'much' of the information disclosed is 'corroborated by other intelligence reporting'.[125] Assuming this assessment is accurate, it is worth noting that one cannot necessarily assume that these disclosures indicate that torture or other form of coercion work. This is because the use of coercion varied between agencies working at Guantánamo Bay and was not necessarily used in every interrogation,[126] although it should be acknowledged that the conditions of confinement were inherently coercive.

More recent disclosures result from the publication of documents by Wikileaks which provides important additional data.[127] In 765 detainee files there is discussion of the intelligence disclosures of Guantánamo Bay detainees, their reliability and potential threat level. While the files suggest that a significant amount of intelligence was gained from interrogations it is also evident that a significant proportion of detainees were viewed as 'withholding information' or 'refusing to discuss', being 'uncooperative', 'unreliable', 'partially truthful' or 'deceptive'.[128] The identity of one detainee, who was at Guantánamo Bay for nearly five years, remained unknown and his file described him as 'highly evasive and deceptive … and his activities and timeline are not well understood'.[129] A number of files also suggest that certain detainees have received counter-interrogation training which over an extended period appear to have inhibited the ability of interrogators to gain information.[130] Some files also question the accuracy and reliability of disclosures. Mohammed Basardah, for example, is described as having provided 'invaluable tactical and strategic information about al-Qaida and extremist operations and activities … '[131] and describes him as being of 'high intelligence value'.[132] However, the memo also notes: '[i]t seems many … detainees are willing to reveal self-incriminating information to him. Detainee's first-hand knowledge in reporting remains in question. Any information should be adequately verified thorough other sources before being utilized.'[133] As a result of these kinds of concerns, the evidence of some Guantánamo Bay detainees, including Basardah, has been deemed as unreliable in legal proceedings.[134]

This section begins to provide an indication as to the themes that are evident in the existing literature. The CIA manuals cannot provide a definitive description of the effectiveness of torture or the view of the CIA for all time.[135] However, if the claims in the manuals are read in light of the wider contemporary and historic literature it becomes clear that they have value in warning of the problems and potential counter-productive effects of using torture and other coercive interrogation methods.

b. The CIA's 'High-Value Detainee' programme[136]

The CIA's HVD programme has received a significant amount of attention in the media, amongst politicians and the general public. A series of memos and reports have been made publicly available that provide evidence concerning the workings and effectiveness of this programme. Inquiries examining the circumstances surrounding the approval and use of coercive techniques in the programme have been conducted by the US Department of Justice,[137] FBI,[138] CIA[139] and United States senate.[140] The purpose of this section is not to recount these investigations in detail, but instead, to examine the claim that the techniques 'produced vital intelligence that saved lives'.[141]

The programme was initially developed following the March 2002 capture of the most senior al Qaeda detainee at the time, Abu Zubaydah, and in response to the pressure the CIA 'was under … to do everything possible to prevent additional terrorist attacks' and a belief that 'a more robust approach was necessary to elicit threat information from Abu Zubaydah and possibly from other senior Al-Qa'ida high value detainees'.[142] The HVD programme comprised ten 'Enhanced Interrogation Techniques' (EITs): the attention grasp, walling, the facial hold, the facial or insult slap, cramped confinement, sleep deprivation,[143] placing an insect in a confinement box, wall standing, stress positions and waterboarding.[144] The purpose underlying the use of the techniques was to encourage compliance amongst HVDs. Further, in a US Department of Justice Office of Legal Counsel (OLC) memo concerning the use and legality of EITs on Zubaydah, it was stated that the purpose of the techniques was to 'dislocate his expectations regarding the treatment he believes he will receive'.[145] In an OLC memo dated 30 May 2005, former US Assistant Attorney General Stephen Bradbury, noted an assessment by the CIA that Khalid Sheikh Mohammed and Zubaydah were withholding important information about future attacks: '[they] expressed their belief that the general US population was "weak", lacked resilience, and would be unable to "do what was necessary" to prevent the terrorists from succeeding in their goals.'[146] In the same memo it was claimed that following the use of waterboarding, Zubaydah told interrogators: 'brothers who are captured and interrogated are permitted by Allah to provide information when they believe they have "reached the limit of their ability to withhold it" in the face of psychological and physical hardships.'[147]

The use of EITs, along with the legal opinions that underpinned them has attracted immense controversy, as well as consideration of whether former Bush Administration officials should face criminal prosecution.[148] Many of the techniques that were authorised for use by the CIA were 'reverse engineered'[149] from Survival, Evasion, Resistance, Escape (SERE) techniques used by the United States military in order to train military personnel to resist coercive interrogation if captured by enemy forces. As noted in a US Senate Armed Service report, these techniques were partly based:

> ... on Chinese Communist techniques used during the Korean war to elicit false confessions, [and] included stripping students of their clothing, placing them in stress positions, putting hoods over their heads, disrupting their sleep, treating them like animals, subjecting them to loud music and flashing lights, and exposing them to extreme temperatures.[150]

The CIA consulted with two psychologists with experience of the SERE training techniques in order to write 'a paper on Al-Qa'ida's resistance to interrogation techniques'. Subsequent to this, they 'developed a list of new and more aggressive EITs that they recommended for use in interrogations'.[151] According to a source quoted by Mayer, the CIA 'struggled to design an interrogation and detention program on the fly [and] turned to psychologists in its own scientific division for advice about what might work to "break" terror suspects'.[152] Welch has observed that giving EITs scientific credibility through the use of psychologists gave them the allure of reliability and respectability.[153] The CIA sought to use a range of coercive techniques in its interrogation of HVDs. Lawyers working in the OLC were consulted as to the legality of these proposed methods,[154] key members of Congress were informed[155] and Bush Administration approval given. It is evident that the CIA consulted with a number of individuals who had experience of working on SERE training programmes in order to ascertain their effect on those who were subject to the techniques. As a result of this consultation a number of specific factual claims were included in the OLC memos. For example, in one memo it was claimed that waterboarding was an extremely effective means of interrogation when used on Naval trainees: '[i]t was also reported to be almost 100 percent effective in producing cooperation among the trainees.'[156] This assertion gives some indication of the speculative nature of the decision to use techniques such as waterboarding on HVDs. It is self-evident that the use of waterboarding on trainees for the purpose of helping them understand techniques to which they might be subjected when captured is very different from being forcibly and repeatedly subjected to the technique while in CIA custody.[157] Further, Naval trainees are not terrorists and are unlikely to possess the degree of motivation to resist found amongst HVDs committed to the terrorist cause. The relevance of this experience in assessing the SERE techniques was summed up in an OLC memo: 'the SERE waterboard experience is so different from the subsequent Agency usage as to make it almost irrelevant.'[158]

Documentation from the CIA suggests that EITs may have only provided limited assistance in producing *timely* intelligence disclosures. In a document entitled the *Background Paper* the CIA provided information to the Department of Justice, which was then used by the OLC to assess the legal standing of interrogations where EITs were used in combination. The paper provides important information concerning the extent to which it can be said EITs are likely to produce ticking bomb intelligence. The memo refers to a '30-day approval period' for techniques and the potential for further approvals to be given.[159] The approval period was recognition that the interrogation methods were not necessarily expected to have an immediate effect. In addition, the document states that '[o]n average, the actual use of interrogation technique[s] [redacted] can vary upwards to fifteen days based on the resilience of the HVD'.[160] On this basis it is doubtful whether EITs would provide ticking bomb intelligence particularly where authorities only have hours or a few days to find a device. A further complication arises through the repetitive use of EITs. In an OLC memo, based on information provided by the CIA, it stated 'repetition will not be substantial because the techniques generally lose their effectiveness after several repetitions'.[161] This is an important admission given that Khalid Sheikh Mohammed and Zubaydah were waterboarded 183 times and 'at least' 83 times, respectively.[162] Either the statement regarding effectiveness is inaccurate, or perhaps interrogators continued to use methods in the hope of gaining further results. Indeed, the CIA-OIG report noted that the EITs were being used on the basis of assumptions regarding what high-level detainees 'should know'.[163] This is complicated by the difficulties in identifying which techniques led to disclosures.[164]

The second reason why the HVD programme would likely not produce intelligence to prevent imminent attacks relates to the system of OLC memos that were required for the use of EITs. In the case of an actual ticking bomb this might well cause significant difficulty. In such an instance, the granting of legal authorisation would have to be done within an extremely narrow time frame. Yet, some of the OLC memos that have been disclosed are in excess of 40 pages.[165] Even with a large staff it is likely that such a memo might take several days, weeks or even months to finalise and approve. When discussing the aftermath of the capture of Zubaydah, George Tenet recounts that it took five months to establish the legality of EITs 'in situations like this you don't call in the tough guys; you call in the lawyers'. He noted that it took until August of 2002 'to get clear guidance on what Agency officers could legally do'.[166] Of course, one response to this problem would be to abandon the use of such memos or to prepare them in advance. However, this would not take account of individual detainees and their specific vulnerabilities and raises the question about the extent to which interrogators could be said to be engaging in lawful activity and may expose them to subsequent prosecution. If a torture warrant system was adopted as suggested by Dershowitz, the HVD programme suggests that the legal and factual issues that would require judicial consideration would not result in quick decision-making. It is doubtful that such a system could respond quickly to an imminent attack of the sort often portrayed in the ticking bomb hypothetical.[167]

c. Results of the HVD programme: an evaluation

The response to the release of government documents which discuss the claimed effectiveness of the HVD programme has been varied. For some, the documents prove the value of the HVD programme,[168] while scholars have expressed 'scepticism' that the EITs produced useful intelligence disclosures.[169] Indeed, it has been claimed that the value of the intelligence produced was largely illusory with detainees lying to stop the infliction of coercion.[170] A CIA document makes reference to this problem: '[d]etainees by virtue of their circumstances, have an adversarial relationship with their debriefers; they often try [to] pass incomplete or intentionally misleading information … '[171] Despite these potential problems, the available documentation contains a number of claims regarding the general effectiveness of the HVD programme. A memo written by Assistant Attorney General Stephen Bradbury, states 'the CIA advises us that the program has been virtually indispensible to the task of deriving actionable intelligence from other forms of collection'.[172] He also makes reference to an 'effectiveness memo' which details the intelligence gains achieved by the use of EITs: '[the CIA believes that] the intelligence acquired from these interrogations has been a key reason why al-Qa'ida has failed to launch a spectacular attack in the West since 11 September 2001.'[173] The 'effectiveness memo' has yet to be publically released and this has led Vice President Dick Cheney to call for the release of documents that he argues show that EITs worked.[174] However, it should be noted that a number of documents already exist which purport to show that EITs produced a wide range of intelligence gains.[175]

In 2009, a report of the Central Intelligence Agency's Office of Inspector General was released following a Freedom of Information Act request by the American Civil Liberties Union. The report was published in 2004 and reviewed the agency's interrogation activities from September 2001 until October 2003.[176] The report discusses the effectiveness of the EITs used to interrogate detainees. The document's analysis of effectiveness begins with a note of caution: '[m]easuring the effectiveness of EITs … is a … subjective process and not without some concern.'[177] However, the report was unambiguous in noting the role of EITs in gaining intelligence: 'The detention of terrorists has prevented them from engaging in further terrorist activity, and their interrogation has provided intelligence that has enabled the identification and apprehension of other terrorists, warned of terrorists[sic] plots planned for the United States and around the world … '[178] The report states that the EITs produced intelligence regarding a number of plots involving attacks in the United States, England and Pakistan.[179] Three of the detainees, Abu Zubaydah, Al-Nashiri and Khalid Sheikh Mohammed, were waterboarded in the 'belief that each of the three detainees possessed perishable information about imminent threats against the United States'.[180] However, the report also noted that '[t]his review did not uncover any evidence that these plots were imminent'.[181] The belief that these three detainees knew of imminent threats presumably derived from the identity of the detainees rather than on intelligence suggesting that they knew of plans for an imminent attack. Indeed, Abu Zubaydah was captured in March 2002 and it has been claimed that he was not waterboarded until August.[182] If this were true he would certainly not possess any active ticking bomb intelligence. Instead, his only use would be as a source of infrastructure intelligence.

When Khalid Sheikh Mohammed resisted giving information about future attacks, it is claimed he said '[s]oon you will know'.[183] This could have provided a reasonable basis on which to assume he knew of imminent attacks; but equally could have been the bluster of a defiant terrorist. Similarly, in a US Department of Justice Office of Professional Responsibility report, it was found that none of the enhanced interrogations involved the disclosure of ticking bomb intelligence:

> To our knowledge, none of the information presented to [the Office of Legal Counsel] about Abu Zubaydah, KSM, Al-Nashiri, or the other detainees subjected to EITs approached the level of imminence and certainty associated with the 'ticking time bomb' scenario. Although the OLC attorneys had good reasons to believe that the detainees possessed valuable intelligence about terrorist operations in general, there is no indication that they had any basis to believe the CIA had specific information about terrorist operations that were underway, or that posed immediate threats.[184]

In March 2002, the first HVD to be captured by the US was Abu Zubaydah who was the 'most senior Al-Qa'ida member in U.S. custody at that time'.[185] He was the subject of a specific OLC memo dated 1 August 2002 in which the legality of various EITs was considered.[186] The memo states that the question of the use of further techniques was raised because the CIA 'interrogation team is certain that he has additional information that he refuses to divulge', including information regarding terrorist networks and future attacks.[187] The necessity of these techniques and the intelligence produced by them has been the subject of ongoing disagreement and is worthy of close analysis. The OIG report acknowledged that Zubaydah provided intelligence before the use of EITs. The number of intelligence reports produced by non-coercive methods and EITs were redacted, thus making a determination of relative utility impossible:

> Prior to the use of EITs, Abu Zubaydah provided information for [redacted] intelligence reports ... During the period between the end of the use of the

waterboard and 30 April 2003, he provided information for approximately [redacted] additional reports. It is not possible to say definitively that the waterboard is the reason for Abu Zubaydah's increased production, or if another factor, such as the length of detention, was the catalyst. Since the use of the waterboard however, Abu Zubaydah has appeared to be cooperative.[188]

As the report acknowledged, Zubaydah co-operated *before* the use of the waterboard. Further, the testimony of a former supervisory special agent of the FBI who initially interrogated Zubaydah following his capture challenges the narrative produced by the CIA. Ali Soufan and a colleague questioned Zubaydah using non-coercive techniques. They built rapport with him and, as a result, Zubaydah disclosed actionable intelligence,[189] including information that Soufan claims led to the thwarting of an 'attack in the works'.[190] Zubaydah also disclosed that Khalid Sheikh Mohammed was the mastermind behind the 9/11 attacks[191] and other classified information.[192] Prior to this disclosure, it was known that a person named 'Muktar' played a pivotal role in the planning of the 9/11 attacks, but it was not known that 'Muktar' was Khalid Sheikh Mohammed.[193] Zubaydah's disclosure of intelligence, including the identity of 'Muktar' using 'traditional interrogation' was acknowledged by Jose Rodriguez, who at the time of the HVD programme, was director of the CIA's Counterterrorism Center.[194]

Despite the apparent success of non-coercive methods, a CIA interrogation team arrived at the location where Zubaydah was detained and began to use coercive methods. Soufan claims:

> The new techniques did not produce results as Abu Zubaydah shut down and stopped talking. At that time nudity and low-level sleep deprivation (between 24 and 48 hours) was being used. After a few days of getting no information, and after repeated inquiries from DC asking why all of sudden no information was being transmitted (when before there had been a steady stream), we again were given control of the interrogation. We then returned to using [non coercive methods]. Within a few hours, Abu Zubaydah again started talking and gave us important actionable intelligence.[195]

Soufan claims that the non-coercive techniques resulted in the naming of Jose Padilla who was later captured and convicted of terrorist offences in the United States.[196] Some former Bush administration officials have declared that Soufan's claims regarding the identification of Khalid Sheikh Mohammed as 'Muktar' and Padilla are 'simply false'.[197] However, Soufan's FBI colleague confirmed that Zubaydah admitted his own identify or the identification of Mohammed as 'Muktar' through the use of rapport building techniques.[198]

The HVD programme has resulted in a number of other widely publicised claims regarding the programme's successes. Three examples provide an indication of how confident assertions can turn out to be false when subjected to closer analysis. First, in a 2007 interview, John Kiriakou, a retired member of the CIA, claimed that when Abu Zubaydah was waterboarded he broke after 35 seconds and subsequently cooperated.[199] Specifically, a 'short time afterwards, in the next day or so, he told his interrogator that Allah had visited him in his cell during the night and told him to cooperate because his cooperation would make it easier on the other brothers who had been captured. And from that day on he answered every question.'[200] This claim is clearly false when one considers the fact that Zubaydah was subjected to a range of techniques and was waterboarded on dozens of occasions. The second example attracted a great deal of international media attention. In his memoir, former US President George W. Bush claimed that enhanced interrogation prevented terrorist attacks on Heathrow airport and Canary Wharf.[201] This was not a new claim, however, and has been made in earlier CIA documents.[202] While these plots appear to have been real, Peter Clarke, the head of Scotland Yard's counter-terrorism unit at the time of the Heathrow plot stated: 'The deduction that what was being planned was an attack against airliners was entirely based upon intelligence gathered in the UK.'[203] This refutation of the value of EITs is particularly telling as it is made by someone with an intimate knowledge of the case. Furthermore, the British police uncovered evidence of a plot involving Canary Wharf and other targets resulting from the arrest of the Heathrow plotters and an examination of their documents and computers.[204]

The third example involved the killing of Osama bin Laden by US Navy Seals in Pakistan. A series of conflicting claims were made regarding the role of EITs in the discovery of his location.[205] A number of former Bush administrative and intelligence officials claimed the use of EITs were important in identifying the name of a courier used by bin Laden that eventually led to his hideout. The former director of the CIA's Counter Terrorism Center, Jose Rodriguez, claimed that: 'Information provided by KSM and Abu Faraj al-Libbi about bin Laden's courier [during the HVD programme] was the lead information that eventually led to the location of [bin Laden's] compound and the operation that led to his death.'[206] Other commentators disagreed.[207] The truth reflects the fragmentary nature of intelligence discussed earlier. Indeed, former Vice President Dick Cheney claimed that EITs 'played a role ... [as well as] *a number of other factors*'[208] (emphasis added). It seems sensible to view EITs in light of other intelligence sources, including the tracking of the phone calls of the courier close to bin Laden.[209] The most authoritative view on the subject emerges from Leon Panetta, who as Director of the CIA, told Senator John McCain in 2011, that:

> Nearly 10 years of intensive intelligence work led the CIA to conclude that Bin Ladin was likely hiding at the compound in Abbottabad, Pakistan there was no one 'essential and indispensible' key piece of information that led us to this conclusion. Rather, the intelligence picture was developed via painstaking collection and analysis. Multiple streams of intelligence – including from detainees, but also from multiple other sources – led CIA analysts to conclude that Bin Ladin was at this compound. Some of the detainees who provided useful information about the facilitator/courier's role had been

subjected to enhanced interrogation techniques. Whether those techniques were the 'only timely and effective way' to obtain such information is a matter of debate and cannot be established definitively. What is definitive is that that information was only a part of multiple streams of intelligence that led us to Bin Ladin.

Let me further point out that we first learned about the facilitator/courier's *nom de guerre* from a detainee not in CIA custody in 2002. It is also important to note that some detainees who were subjected to enhanced interrogation techniques attempted to provide false or misleading information about the facilitator/courier. These attempts to falsify the facilitator/courier's role were alerting.

In the end, no detainee in CIA custody revealed the facilitator/courier's full true name or specific whereabouts. This information was discovered through other intelligence means[210].

Even if one is to take the claims that the use of EITs had some role in uncovering bin Laden's location, its utility appears to be distant in light of other factors and the lengthy passage of time between the end of the HVD programme and the actual death of bin Laden. This hardly provides compelling evidence of the utility of torture, particularly as a means of gaining all the intelligence necessary to locate bin Laden. Thus an essential element of any case for the legalisation of interrogational torture is absent. Instead, the fragmentary nature of intelligence and the painstaking way in which it is gathered is further confirmed.

This is further confirmed by a report of the CIA's Directorate of Intelligence concerning the HVD programme which stated: 'Detainee information must be corroborated using multiple sources of intelligence; uncorroborated information from detainees must be regarded with some degree of suspicion.'[211] This raises the question of which HVD programme disclosures were corroborated as part of a jigsaw of other intelligence. Further, if disclosures were corroborated using 'multiple sources of intelligence', then in at least some instances it is reasonable to assume that fragments of intelligence were already known to the CIA. In such cases, it is unclear as to the extent to which the HVD programme may have led to concrete results. Indeed, the Directorate of Intelligence report notes the fractured nature of intelligence: 'As with information from other collection streams, detainee reporting is often incomplete or too general to lead directly to arrests; instead, detainees provide critical pieces of the puzzle, which, when combined with other reporting, have helped direct an investigation's focus and led to the capture of terrorists.'[212] Finally, while the document refers to the 'unquestionable utility of detainee reporting' it goes on: '[d]etainees have been known to pass incomplete or intentional misleading information; moreover, we assess that each detainee very likely has information that he will not reveal [redacted].'[213] On the basis of the current literature it is not possible to determine the extent of these problems.

Given the lack of specifics in CIA disclosures it is important to use other means to test claims of success on the part of EITs. At his Combat Status Review Tribunal hearing at Guantanamo Bay in 2007, Khalid Sheikh Mohammed admitted to his involvement in more than two dozen plots and acts of terrorism.[214] The admissions have been questioned on the basis that Mohammed was known to be 'prone to exaggeration' and wished to 'promote his own importance'.[215] The veracity of at least one of his specific admissions has also been questioned. For example, in his hearing Mohammed stated: 'I was responsible for planning, training, surveying, and financing the New (or Second) Wave attacks against the following skyscrapers after 9/11: a. Library Tower, California; b. Sears Tower, Chicago; c. Plaza Bank, Washington state; d. The Empire State Building, New York City.'[216] It has been argued that Mohammed's disclosures resulted from the use of waterboarding and other EITs and were the primary reason for preventing these attacks.[217] An earlier OLC memo refers to the yet-to-be-released *Effectiveness Memo*, thus: 'You have informed us that the interrogation of KSM … led to the discovery of a KSM plot, the "Second Wave", "to use East Asian operatives to crash a hijacked airliner into" a building [the Library Tower] in Los Angeles … You have informed us that information obtained from KSM also led to the … discovery of the Guraba Cell, a 17-member Jemaah Islamiyah cell tasked with executing the "Second Wave"'.[218]

By contrast, it has been argued that the Library Tower plot was prevented prior to Mohammed's capture and use of EITs.[219] This claim is based on an assertion by President George W. Bush, thus: 'In 2002, we broke up a plot by KSM to hijack an airplane and fly it into the tallest building on the West Coast [the Library Tower].'[220] In a 2006 White House press briefing concerning homeland security and counter-terrorism, Frances Fragos Townsend stated that the Library Tower plot was 'disrupted' in 2002 and 2003. According to Townsend, Mohammed led efforts to carry out attacks on the West Coast of the United States after the 9/11 attacks. Members of a cell were recruited in Asia by the cell leader who was arrested in early 2002. At this point, according to Townsend 'the other members of the cell believed that the West coast plot was cancelled'.[221] Mohammed, of course, was detained in March 2003. These assertions suggest that the Library Tower plot was not disrupted as a result of the HVD programme. However, fourteen months after Townsend's briefing, the Director of the CIA, General Michael V. Hayden, gave a classified statement before the US Senate Select Committee on Intelligence. In this statement he noted that one of the West coast al Qaeda plotters, named Hambali, who was detained as a result of the HVD programme in 2003, 'was considering pursuing this plot and his efforts were disrupted by his detention'.[222] It is impossible to know the extent to which the West Coast plot was still active and realistically achievable once the original cell leader and others, including Mohammed, were detained. In the post-9/11 security environment, to successfully carry out such an attack would have been virtually impossible. Further 'considering' the pursuit of a plot is certainly not the same as there being a credible threat. Of course, it is possible that the HVD programme played a disruptive role, but this is, to some degree, speculative given uncertainties over the credibility of the plot. The Library Tower plot is illustrative of a wider problem in that there is much about the programme we do not know, including the relative importance of intelligence sources outside of the HVD programme. However, recent disclosures suggest that the HVD programme successes have been significantly exaggerated.[223] Such an acknowledgement is essential given that former Bush administration officials[224] and prominent politicians in the United States advocate the re-introduction of EITs.[225]

The Senate Select Committee on Intelligence Study on the CIA Detention and Interrogation Program

At the time of writing, a US Senate Select Committee on Intelligence report that examines the use of EITs by the CIA has yet to be released into the public domain. It is claimed to be nearly 6,300 pages in length[226] and is alleged to show that the use of EITs by the CIA did not produce significant intelligence disclosures and that the CIA misled Congress and the White House on a number of matters, including the effectiveness of these techniques.[227] The report took three years to complete and involved the examination of six million pages of internal CIA memos and other records.[228] Several US government agencies, including the CIA, have been given the opportunity to review the report and respond to its contents.[229] While accepting some of the report's findings,[230] the CIA has highlighted what it claims are 'significant errors'.[231] Despite repeated calls for the release of the report,[232] there are ongoing talks within government concerning its contents and there is no planned publication date at the time of writing.[233] The controversy over the committee's findings has continued with the chairwoman of the Senate Intelligence Committee, Dianne Feinstein, accusing the CIA of spying on the committee's work and intimidating investigators.[234] Allegations concerning the alleged actions of some CIA employees are currently the subject of an internal investigation by the Agency's Inspector General.[235]

The Senate report has also been the subject of various leaks to the press. Some of the more recent disclosures are of particular importance to this chapter. For example, leaks suggest that the use of EITs as part of the HVD programme did not provide critical intelligence of use in tracking down Osama bin Laden, but disclosures were made either before the use of EITs or months afterwards.[236] On the basis of disclosures by unnamed sources familiar with the contents of the report, the *Washington Post* has reported that the CIA made false or misleading claims regarding the success of the HVD programme, including the attribution of intelligence gains to the use of EITs when the intelligence was gained by other means. It is also claimed that the CIA exaggerated the importance and seniority of particular HVD detainees and that the most valuable intelligence disclosures regarding al Qaeda did not result from the HVD programme and that the use of EITs continued even after detainees were co-operating.[237]

These findings raise serious questions regarding the effectiveness of EITs. There is increasing reason to believe that the intelligence gains attributed to the use of EITs are a mixture of exaggeration, wishful thinking and outright falsehood. Even if one accepts the claims that have been made by the CIA at face value, there is no evidence that EITs prevented a single imminent attack. Instead, the alleged intelligence gains concerned infrastructure, not ticking bombs. So where these claims are cited in support of the use or legalisation of interrogational torture,[238] they can only be cited in support of an expansive torture power that would include attempts to gain infrastructure, as well as ticking bomb situations. A similar trend exists in other counter-terrorism campaigns, as the next two examples will illustrate.

d. Algeria

In the 1950s, French military and police used interrogational torture extensively in order to gain intelligence in its bid to crush a rebellion against its rule in Algeria and tackle a small terrorist group, the Front de Libèration Nationale (FLN).[239] In examining the effectiveness of interrogational torture, Levinson quotes a review of several books published in the *New York Review of Books*, thus: 'Was torture effective? ... torture enabled the French to gather information about future terrorist strikes and to destroy the infrastructure of terror in Algiers.'[240] The problem here is how one defines effectiveness. The review notes: '[t]orture failed not only to repress the yearning for independence among Algerians, it increased popular support for the FLN,[241] contributing to the transformation of a small vanguard into a revolutionary party with mass support ... Indeed, France's tactics helped the FLN to win over Algerian moderates ... '[242] By contrast, other scholars rely on the second-hand assertions of media commentators to support their claim that interrogational torture worked in defeating the FLN.[243]

One historical source, largely ignored in the contemporary torture debate literature, provides insight into the actions of the French state and some of the reasoning underpinning the use of torture. A report authored in 1955 by the Civil Inspector-General Wuillaume, gives an indication of how the use of torture and other forms of coercion were viewed from within the French government and police.[244] The report notes that there was 'disquiet shown by all sections of the police' resulting *inter alia* from 'the strict instructions issued to them that violence was not to be used on pain of severe punishment'.[245] He found that of the 61 detainees he interviewed, 21 out of the 61 said that they had suffered no violence during interrogation and suggested that the total number of torture victims must be 'fairly high'.[246] These prisoners did not know each other and Wuillaume was concerned to ensure that they did not have the opportunity to concoct stories between them. The report details the use of a range of interrogation techniques, including beatings, drowning and electrocution.[247] He states that he was privately assured by officers 'that the effectiveness of these methods was proved',[248] and reported that the police argued 'they would be severely handicapped without them'.[249] However, Wuillaume also noted that he could not corroborate these claims: 'I myself am in no position to assert that these practices were effective and am compelled to rely on the statements of those who assured me of this and who, it should be noted, were highly thought of by their superiors.'[250]

In his treatise *Torture and Democracy* and other work, Rejali paints a very different picture than that suggested by proponents of legalisation.[251] Rather than achieving a military victory against terrorists through the use of torture, Rejali argues that 'the French won by applying overwhelming force in an extremely constrained space, not by superior intelligence gathered through torture … What made the difference for the French in Algiers was not torture, but the accurate intelligence obtained through public cooperation and informants.'[252] He also argues: 'In fact, no rank-and-file soldier has related a tale of how he personally, through timely interrogation, produced decisive information that stopped a ticking bomb.'[253] Rejali examines a wide range of sources in order to identify cases where the use of torture did result in the discovery of life-saving intelligence. He notes that there exist a very small number of documented cases in which torture did result in disclosures, none of which appear to involve ticking bomb intelligence. Disclosures under torture tended to involve such things as the location of safe houses and identity of accomplices and other infrastructure intelligence, as well as false leads or outdated intelligence.[254] Rejali argues that while '[a] few less important FLN members were more pliable under torture … it is a dismal record even if one counts all the ambiguous accounts'.[255] He goes on to detail an example of successful interrogational torture where a messenger disclosed the hideout of an FLN leader. However, Rejali notes: '[b]ut that was not new. Informants had identified this FLN safe house months ago; the French had been too busy to raid it.'[256] Thus, the alleged success of interrogational torture in Algeria is contested, and indeed, one of the few scholars to carefully analyse the evidence emanating from this conflict concludes that there is no evidence that torture produced valuable intelligence that prevented imminent terrorist attacks. Indeed, the documentary record suggests a record of failure, delay and error.

e. Northern Ireland

In August 1971, fourteen men who were thought to be linked with the Irish Republican Army (IRA) were subjected to 'interrogation in depth' (also known as the 'five techniques'): wall standing, hooding, subjection to noise, sleep deprivation and deprivation of food and water.[257] The fourteen were 'thought to possess considerable knowledge of the IRA but … were considered unlikely to respond to normal police questioning'.[258] The use of the techniques was underpinned by 'historic narratives' suggesting the techniques worked and by a belief that normal policing techniques would be ineffective.[259] This latter view was expressed by a member of the Royal Ulster Constabulary, thus: '[Terrorists] are not going to admit [to their activities] and face the rest of their lifetime in prison by being given tea and buns.'[260]

The use of the 'five techniques', having been held to be a violation of Article 3 by the ECtHR,[261] was earlier examined by an inquiry chaired by Lord Chief Justice Parker.[262] The resulting majority report concluded that the techniques had yielded very significant infrastructure intelligence gains, including the identification of

'700 members of both IRA factions' and the 'discovery of individual responsibility for about 85 incidents recorded on police files'.[263] The majority observed that the seizure of arms, ammunitions and explosives 'increased markedly' after 9 August when internment and the five techniques were introduced.[264] This increase in intelligence disclosures, the majority argued, resulted 'either directly or indirectly from information obtained by interrogation in depth'.[265] It is evident that there is an omission in the Parker Report's assessment of evidence. There is no discussion of the contribution of other sources of intelligence, such as informants, voluntary disclosures and electronic surveillance. The majority report, however, was unequivocal that coercion did result in crucial disclosures: 'There is no doubt that the information obtained by [interrogation in depth] directly and indirectly was responsible for the saving of lives of innocent citizens.'[266] The majority also noted that interrogation 'sometimes had the effect of establishing the innocence of both other wanted people and of the detainee himself' and that incorrect information was given 'in a few cases'.[267]

In judging the effectiveness of these methods the minority report, while acknowledging that a 'considerable quantity of intelligence information was obtained'[268] observed that after 9 August 'there was a sudden and considerable increase in the number of people arrested and questioned so that a dramatic increase in intelligence information was in any case to be expected'.[269] Likewise, Taylor notes:

> There was a limit to how many rounds of ammunition, pounds of explosives and piles of weapons fourteen men could reveal, especially when some had only the slightest IRA connections. But the 'guinea pigs' were only fourteen of the 3,000 suspects interrogated by the RUC in the year that followed internment.[270]

It has been argued that the value of intelligence said to have been gathered through interrogation in-depth in Northern Ireland was exaggerated.[271] In his book *The Guineapigs*, McGuffin describes both the Parker Report's claim that the 'five techniques' saved lives as 'grotesque and ludicrous'.[272] He provides no evidence to substantiate this sweeping rejection of the claims made in the Parker Report. Further, as a point of contradiction, he concedes that the use of coercive methods or their threatened use resulted in some detainees disclosing information 'hence the rise in the arrest figures and arms hauls'.[273]

Recent attention has been given to a document found in the National Archives which amounts to a summary of the intelligence gains that are said have been achieved through the use of the 'five techniques'. The document refers to a range of intelligence gains, including 'details of possible IRA operations, arms caches, safe houses, communications ... '.[274] These gains are similar to those discussed in the Parker Report, but there is no corroboration offered.[275] The discovery of this document has been met with some scepticism. Brecher argues that while the information is 'possibly correct', it 'cannot be assumed to be so'.[276] Sands denies that the document provides 'real support' for the claim that coercion produced intelligence disclosures and refers to it as 'self-serving'.[277] He goes on: '[i]t should be treated as what it appears to be: an advocacy document that was written to provide political justification for the five techniques and the embrace of cruelty.'[278] It is also worth noting that the Parker report itself provides reason to doubt blanket claims about the utility of these techniques. The minority report noted that '[s]ome of the 14 [detainees] were only too anxious to give information ... from the start' without the need for coercion.[279] If this is true, it may simply have resulted from fear of what would happen if the detainees in question did not cooperate. Either way, it muddies the waters still further. Thus, even if one accepts that some intelligence was gained through the use of the five techniques, there is no way of comparing intelligence gained from coercive and standard interrogation techniques.

There can be little doubt that it would be helpful if further information were provided to substantiate the claims that are made in the Parker Report and National Archives document, but unless one is to argue that the five techniques never worked, it appears unwise to summarily dismiss all the claims made in these documents. Instead, what is required is a more sophisticated analysis. The five techniques were not used in isolation – in at least some instances they were accompanied by threats and physical violence.[280] This in itself raises doubts regarding the extent to which it can be said that the five techniques produced intelligence disclosures. Further, similar to many of the other examples of successful interrogational torture and coercion cited in this chapter, consideration would also have to be given to other intelligence gathering techniques which, in the context of the torture debate, are often ignored. It is to that issue that this chapter will now turn.

f. The effectiveness of alternatives to interrogational torture

In the literature concerning the effectiveness of interrogational torture, reference is often made to alternative interrogation methods which are less coercive or even non-coercive, including: rapport building techniques,[281] the use of truth serum,[282] polygraph machines[283] and brain imaging.[284] It is common to find it claimed that such techniques are potentially as, or more effective than interrogational torture in securing timely and reliable disclosures.[285] Indeed, there is anecdotal evidence from terrorists themselves indicating that rapport building may be more effective than brutality.[286] However, there are fundamental problems with such comparative claims. There are no scientific studies in which such techniques have been compared. Claims of success can 'rarely be tested in a controlled environment'.[287] Even if such data were available, it does not answer the moral and legal question of what should be done where non-coercive techniques have been tried, have failed and interrogational torture is the last remaining option for interrogators. Proponents of legalisation would no doubt argue it is irrelevant that there exist alternatives which might be more effective overall if they failed in *that* instance. Another means of addressing the use of alternatives to interrogational torture is provided by the Israeli-based human rights group B'Tselem, which, instead of denying that coercion sometimes produces intelligence, argues that alternative methods could also be successful:

> ... those who make this argument have not provided a shred of evidence that physical force is the only or the most effective means to prevent attacks. It is not enough to represent cases in which the [General Security Service], after using force during interrogations, succeeded in preventing terrorist attacks, because we do not know what the result would have been had the GSS used other methods instead.[288]

It has also been argued that interrogational torture can become a distraction from using other methods of intelligence gathering. For example, in a recent interview former US Vice President Dick Cheney was asked whether EITs should be reinstated if the US were to capture a new high-value target, Cheney replied: 'I certainly would advocate it. I'd be a strong supporter of it.'[289] In the context of Algeria, Rejali has argued that torture became so entrenched that 'engaging in torture prevented the use of ordinary – and more effective – policing skills'.[290] Others have argued that detainee interrogation is only a limited source of intelligence. A former member of the British security service MI5, Tom Parker, has suggested that often 'detainees aren't valuable' and what is required is '"being creative" about human intelligence gathering, such as infiltration and eavesdropping'.[291]

In the HVD programme it was claimed that waterboarding was used against Khalid Sheikh Mohammed and Abu Zubaydah because 'standard interrogation techniques were not working'.[292] What is readily apparent, however, is that standard techniques appear to have been given little opportunity to produce intelligence. A CIA *Background Paper* which explained the combined use of techniques as part of the HVD programme explains that: 'once detainees have arrived at a "Black Site" and have been given medical and psychological interviews they are interrogated using an "initial interview". This interview is designed to "assess the initial resistance posture of the HVD."'[293] The document notes that the 'standard of participation is set very high ... The HVD would have to willingly provide information on actionable threats and location information on High-Value targets at large – not lower level information – for the interrogators to continue with the neutral approach.'[294] The *Background Paper* makes clear that detainees were informed that co-operation would result in an immediate improvement in conditions.[295] But here lies a problem – standard interrogation techniques may or may not get immediate results, but these techniques are predicated on the need to win and maintain the detainee's trust and build rapport between the interrogator and detainee. In the context of high-value detainees this may take time, but it is evident that the HVD interrogation programme was not intended to give interrogators using these standard techniques the time to work. The HVD programme only recognised co-operation over a 'very high' threshold and categorised any co-operation below the threshold as an indication of failure. The evidence suggests that the EITs also took time to work,[296] but they were not judged by the same high threshold as 'standard' interrogation techniques. The unwillingness to properly use rapport building techniques and the rapid use of EITs suggests that the HVD programme failed what Ignatieff refers to as the 'last-resort test' for coercive counter-terrorism measures: 'have less coercive measures been tried and failed?'[297]

Some have argued that the intelligence disclosures resulting from the use of EITs could have been gained by non-coercive methods. In response to questions during a press conference in 2009, President Barack Obama stated: 'I am absolutely convinced it was the right thing to do [to prohibit the use of EITs] – not because there might not have been information that was yielded by these various detainees who were subjected to this treatment, but because we could have gotten this information in other ways, in ways that were consistent with our values ... '[298] In another press conference, a month later, President Obama stated: 'I know some have argued that brutal methods like waterboarding were necessary to keep us safe. I could not disagree more. As Commander-in-Chief, I see the intelligence ... I categorically reject the assertion that these are the most effective means of inter-rogation ... '[299] A similar argument is made by the FBI counter-terrorism agent Ali Soufan when he states in the context of Abu Zubaydah: [t]here was no ... intelligence ... that wasn't or couldn't have been gained from regular tactics.'[300] It is worth noting of course, that neither President Obama, nor Ali Soufan has denied that EITs produced valuable intelligence, only that the intelligence could have been gained by other methods. Such claims might, in fact, be true but ultimately they constitute speculation.

Perhaps a more concrete way of approaching this issue is to consider the role of alternatives to interrogational torture in the CIA's war with al Qaeda. Former Director of the CIA, George Tenet, makes clear his view that the use of EITs were an essential and effective means of acquiring intelligence.[301] However, he also refers to the importance of other information sources: 'from our interrogation of KSM and other senior al-Qa'ida members, *and our examination of documents found on them,* we learned many things ... '[302] (emphasis added). Tenet also makes specific reference to Abu Zubaydah who he claimed: 'provided a motherlode of informa-tion, and not just from his interrogation. We were able to exploit data found on his cell phone, computer, and documents in his possession that greatly added to our understanding of his contacts and involvement in terrorism plotting.'[303] In a report authored by the CIA's Directorate of Intelligence reference is made to the value of 'detainee disclosures',[304] as well as the 'large volumes of documents and computer data seized in raids'.[305] While this short section in the report is heavily redacted, it notes that important information was found on a computer, including contact details of terrorist recruits and the identity of 'a key al-Qa'ida financial operative and facilitator of the 11 September attacks'. The report also notes that the documentation could be used 'in confronting detainees to persuade them to talk about topics they would otherwise not reveal'.[306] Given the amount of attention that has been given to the use of EITs by the CIA in reports and news media, it is unfortunate that so little attention has been given to the role of other intelligence sources. It leaves open the possibility that sources of intelligence outside of EITs played a crucial role in some of the intelligence gains discussed in the CIA documentation. This provides further reason to show some degree of caution when attributing success to the HVD programme's use of EITs.

Evidence suggests that the HVD programme and Guantánamo interrogations could take days, weeks and months to secure intelligence disclosures. In some instances detainees had not fully disclosed what they knew after years of detention and interrogation. Further, there are several other reasons to question the value of coercive methods based on the CIA's own documentation. First, as noted by the CIA's OIG report, it is no easy task to establish what works when differing interrogation methods are used and the effectiveness of most individual techniques cannot be determined. Second, there is the fact that because there is so much focus on the use of EITs, we know relatively little about the role of non-coercive methods in gaining intelligence in any of the case studies examined here. We know that intelligence was gathered from documents, computers and other sources, but we have no indication as to its real significance compared to the use of EITs.

4. Conclusion: the problem of mismatch

To some, this chapter may send out the 'pernicious message' that torture may work as a means of intelligence gathering in terrorism cases.[307] Such a simplistic response, however, would be inappropriate. There can be little doubt that interrogational torture and other forms of coercion do sometimes work to produce disclosures. To suggest such a claim is 'sheer fantasy' indicates an unwillingness to seriously engage with the historic and contemporary literature.[308] Indeed, the IRA and al Qaeda have, at different times, organised themselves into cell structures or compartmentalised knowledge on the assumption that intelligence will be disclosed during interrogation.[309] The fact that interrogational torture can be said to have worked in at least some cases does not make torture a good thing. It remains an evil. As Matthews argues, an architect or engineer could design a death camp, 'but the design's effectiveness is no virtue'.[310] One of the crucial issues to arise out of the analysis in this chapter is the evidential mismatch that exists in the case for legalised interrogational torture.

The use of torture and other coercive interrogation methods in Algeria, Northern Ireland and as part of the CIA's HVD programme have not resulted in the disclosure of ticking bomb intelligence.[311] There is no evidence that torture has prevented imminent terrorist attacks that would take place within 30 minutes,[312] 48 hours or any other specific time frame. In the wider literature there are a handful of examples of threats, brutality or torture resulting in timely and accurate intelligence disclosures which either did prevent or could have prevented imminent harm.[313] However, this is an extremely thin record. The cautious tone found in the CIA's KUBARK manual discussed in this chapter must also be viewed in the light of wider contemporary findings. While there is undoubtedly supporting evidence for some of the problems the manual identifies, evidence discussed in this chapter suggests that coercive methods may produce infrastructure intelligence and confirms the hypothesis set out at the beginning of this chapter that if interrogational torture produces intelligence; it is more likely to be infrastructure, rather than ticking bomb intelligence.

Even if one assumes for the moment that the claims of infrastructure gains are entirely accurate (and there is good reason to question the reliability of many claims of success), this does not help the case for legalised torture. This is because there is an evidential mismatch at the heart of the case for legalised interrogational torture. While the case normally rests on ticking bomb-type scenarios, where intelligence is required to prevent an imminent attack, the evidence on effectiveness overwhelmingly relates to infrastructure intelligence. Of course, one response to this evidential mismatch could be to argue that torture should be used to illicit infrastructure intelligence which, as already noted, may also result in the prevention of terrorist attacks in the longer term by disrupting the ability of terrorist groups to operate effectively. This would certainly fit within the logic of consequentialism. However, the problem with such a proposal is that a torture law based on such a widely defined definition of intelligence would result in an expansive use of interrogational torture. This is because virtually *every* terrorist possesses infrastructure intelligence and a law allowing for the use of interrogational torture in such cases would dramatically depart from any notion of an emergency power. Such a power would be used frequently, along with cases of error, abuse and ineffectiveness.

The claim that interrogational torture or coercion has produced intelligence of any sort cannot be taken at face value as it is telling only part of the story. As noted earlier, intelligence is often fragmented and data from multiple sources may be required in order to build an accurate picture of events and future threats. Further, interrogations often involve the use of multiple techniques, which makes it difficult to know what works.[314] This creates a level of complexity that is often unacknowledged. Further, data that have been released are often vague and leaves many questions unanswered. Jurisdictions that use torture or other forms of coercion often attract criticism and it might be the case that intelligence gained by alternative means is downplayed so torture can be seen to have worked. It is also clear the state officials lie or exaggerate. In the absence of solid data that indicate the extent to which intelligence may have been gathered from other sources, such as informants or electronic surveillance, there is no way of knowing that interrogational torture is a better technique than the alternatives.

Finally, we have to consider the implication of this analysis for the case made by the proponents of legalisation. They have not begun to deal with the fact that there is a *virtually no* reliable evidence suggesting that timely and reliable intelligence can be gathered by coercive means in emergency situations. Further, in accordance with the 48 hour test set out at the beginning of this chapter, there is *no* credible, verifiable evidence at all of torture preventing a terrorist attack within 48 hours of a suspect being arrested. In fact, it is not all clear that evidence exists of such an example if one is to extend the time frame further, in part because examples cited by the Israeli government are so vague and open to differing interpretations.[315] As a result, there exists an extremely thin evidential record upon which to argue for the legalisation of interrogational torture in ticking bomb cases on grounds of effectiveness. The use of infrastructure intelligence gains in the case for legalisation is even more problematic. The evidential base might be a little stronger, but such intelligence gains have nothing to do with obtaining sufficient intelligence to prevent an imminent terrorist attack. If the case for torture is simply expanded to allow for its use to gather infrastructure intelligence then it can no longer be seen as an emergency power. The next chapter will look at the implications of this notion of an expansive power in more detail.

Notes

1 Some small and occasional sections of text in this chapter were originally published elsewhere: P. Rumney, 'The Torture Debate: A Perspective from the United Kingdom', in J. Moran and M. Phythian (eds.), *Intelligence Security and Policing: the UK Response to the War on Terror* (2008). The author expresses his thanks to Palgrave Macmillan for permission to re-use this material.

2 J.M. Coetzee, *Waiting for the Barbarians* (2000) 5.

3 T.E. Kennedy, *In the Company of Angels* (2010).

4 See, most recently, L. Hajjar, 'Does Torture Work? A Sociolegal Assessment of the Practice in Historical and Global Perspective', (2009) 5 *Ann. Rev. Law Soc. Sci.* 311 (arguing that interrogational torture is harmful and ineffective).

5 See, for example, M. Robbins, 'Does Torture Work?' www.guardian.co.uk 4 November 2010 (arguing for the need of scientific evidence before it is argued that it works).

6 See, for example, J. Yoo, *War by Other Means: An Insider's Account of the War on Terror* (2006) ch. 7 (former lawyer in the US Department of Justice, Office of Legal Counsel discussing evidence that coercive interrogation produces actionable intelligence).

7 Bamford distinguishes between background, operational and criminal intelligence, 'all of which are used for very different purposes: to aid policy decisions, to locate and engage the "enemy" and for criminal prosecutions'. B.W.C. Bamford, 'The Role and Effectiveness of Intelligence in Northern Ireland', (2005) 20 *Intelligence and National Security* 581, 586.

8 M. Kress and R. Szechtman, 'Why Defeating Insurgencies Is Hard: The Effect of Intelligence in Counterinsurgency Operations—A Best-Case Scenario', (2009) 57 *Operations Research* 583 (noting *inter alia* the importance of intelligence in defeating insurgency and that states 'cannot eradicate ... insurgency by force alone').

9 Hon. James R. Schlesinger, *The Report of the Independent Panel to Review Department of Defense Detention Operations* (2004) 64 (hereafter Schlesinger Report).

10 Klerks has also suggested that targeting terrorist network members with specific skills can seriously inhibit the ability of terror networks to function effectively: P. Klerks, 'The Network Paradigm Applied to Criminal Organisations: Theoretical nitpicking or a relevant doctrine for investigators? Recent developments in the Netherlands', (2001) 24 *Connections* 53.

11 Tamar Meisels argues: 'methods that require prolonged endurance, can rarely, if ever, be justified by any argument about immediate necessity. They are more likely to be used in order to gather general intelligence information. This is an important point, which is often missed and rarely stressed.' *The Trouble with Terror: Liberty, Security, and the Response to Terrorism* (2008) 188. It would appear that the distinction between ticking bomb and infrastructure intelligence is similar to Meisel's reference to intelligence that is of 'immediate necessity' and 'general information'.

12 S. Levinson, 'Contemplating Torture', in S. Levinson (ed.), *Torture: A Collection* (2004) 33. Marcy Strauss notes: 'evaluating the efficacy of torture requires information not

currently available and perhaps, unknowable'. 'Torture', (2004) 48 *N.Y.L. Sch. L. Rev.* 201, 263.

13 Posner and Vermeule suggest evaluation of the use of interrogational torture by experts and various other forms of oversight: *Terror in the Balance: Security, Liberty, and the Courts* (2007) 211, 213.

14 M. Bagaric and J. Clarke, *Torture: When the Unthinkable is Morally Permissible* (2007) 58.

15 In an early account of the CIA's 'High Value Detainee' programme by Ronald Kessler, several claims are clearly wide of the mark when compared to later disclosures by the CIA. For example, he claims: 'The CIA fuelled [press reports of coercion] hoping to instil fear ... [it] found that torture was not needed and, in any case, it produced bad information. Simply offering them tea and sympathy was often enough to get al Qaeda members to talk ... Most al Qaeda members cooperated after a day or two.' R. Kessler, *The CIA at War: Inside the Secret Campaign Against Terror* (2003) 277.

16 P. Rumney, 'The Effectiveness of Coercive Interrogation: Scholarly and Judicial Responses,' (2005) 44 *Crime, Law and Social Change* 465, 484, n 38; P. Rumney, 'Is Coercive Interrogation of Terrorist Suspects Effective? A Response to Bagaric and Clarke', (2006) 40 *U.S.F.L. Rev.* 479, 499.

17 D. Froomkin, 'Bush and the Torture tapes', www.washingtonpost.com 7 December 2007.

18 *The 9/11 Commission Report: Final Report of the National Commission on Terrorist Attacks Upon the United States* (2004) ch. 8 (discussing intelligence already in possession of US authorities which could have potentially prevented the 9/11 attacks).

19 S. Lum *et al*, 'Are Counter-terrorism Strategies Effective? The Results of the Campbell Systematic Review on Counter-terrorism Evaluation Research', (2006) 2 *Journal of Experimental Criminology* 489, 491.

20 For discussion, see Chapter 1 nn. 116–47 and accompanying text: P. Rumney, 'Making Things Worse? Interrogational Torture as a Counter-terrorism Strategy' (2013) 12 *Contemporary Issues in Law* 339.

21 M. Ignatieff, *The Lesser Evil: Political Ethics in an Age of Terror* (2004) 24.

22 'George W. Bush Claims UK Lives "Saved by Waterboarding"', www.bbc.co.uk/news 9 November 2010.

23 R. Matthews, *The Absolute Violation: Why Torture Must be Prohibited* (2008) 219.

24 H.H. Koh, 'A World Without Torture,' (2005) 43 *Col. J. Trans. L.* 641, 653.

25 G. Kassimeris, 'The Warrior's Dishonour', in G. Kassimeris (ed.), *Warrior's Dishonour: Barbarity, Morality and Torture in Modern Warfare* (2006) 14.

26 M. Bagaric and J. Clarke, 'Not Enough Official Torture in the World? The Circumstances in Which Torture Is Morally Justifiable', (2005) 39 *University of San Francisco Law Review* 581. In subsequent writings Bagaric and Clarke argue that it is an 'effective' interrogation tool: *supra* n. 14, ch. 6.

27 R.A. Posner, *Not a Suicide Pact: The Constitution in a Time of National Emergency* (2006) 81.

28 A.M. Dershowitz, *Why Terrorism Works: Understanding the Threat, Responding to the Challenge* (2002) 137.

29 *Id*. 138.

30 A. Dershowitz, *The Case For Israel* (2003) 135.

31 See, for example, Amnesty International's Prisoners and People at Risk campaign: www.amnestyusa.org/our-work/issues/prisoners-and-people-at-risk (accessed 1 February 2014); Human Rights Watch, *In a Time of Torture: The Assault on Justice in Egypt's Crackdown on Homosexual Conduct* (2004).

32 M. Bagaric and J. Clarke, 'Tortured responses (a reply to our critics): Physically Persuading Suspects is Morally Preferable to Allowing the Innocent to be Murdered', (2006) 40 U.S.F.L. Rev. 703, 718.

33 G. Allison and P. Zelikow, *Essence of Decision: Explaining the Cuban Missile Crisis* 2nd ed. (1999) 49.

34 *Id*. 19.

35 B. Woodward, *State of Denial: Bush at War, Part III* (2006) 80.
36 It is evident that in the context of the Central Intelligence Agency's use of 'Enhanced Interrogation Techniques' there was a significant amount of speculation as to the potential effectiveness of the techniques prior to their use and continuing uncertainty subsequent to their use. See *infra* nn. 156–64, 177 and accompanying text.
37 It has been argued that, historically, in certain Continental European legal systems and in modern-day Israel there is evidence of a heavy reliance on coercion to gain convictions: J.H. Langbein, *Torture and the Law of Proof: Europe and England in the Ancien Régime* (2006); L. Hajjar, *Courting Conflict: The Israeli Military Court System in the West Bank and Gaza* (2005).
38 A.W. McCoy, *A Question of Torture: CIA Interrogation, from the Cold War to the War on Terror* (2006) 207.
39 B. Ackerman, *Before the Next Attack: Preserving Civil Liberties in an Age of Terrorism* (2006) 108–9.
40 Bagaric and Clarke, *supra* n. 14, 61.
41 *Id.* 54–7.
42 They cite examples from Algeria, Israel and the War on Terror, as well as the infamous case of Abdul Hakim Murad who was tortured for more than two months by Philippines authorities. The torture in this case has been widely mischaracterised as preventing imminent terrorist attacks on the Pope and American airliners. These claims appear to be untrue and involve a misreading of source material by Alan Dershowitz and others. See McCoy, *supra* n. 38, 110–2; Rumney, *supra* n. 16, 487–8.
43 Bagaric and Clarke, *supra* n. 32, 720.
44 J.H. Langbein, 'The Legal History of Torture', in Levinson, *supra* n. 12, 97. This is a point that has been repeatedly reiterated in the historic literature: 'Whatever one thinks of torture, one cannot seriously dispute its utility. Coerced confessions do not possess a high degree of reliability – commentators have at least, since ancient Greece, remarked upon the manifest unreliability of admissions gleaned through torture': M. Plaxton, 'Justifying Absolute Prohibitions on Torture as if Consequences Mattered', in Kassimeris, *supra* n. 25, 206. A book, written in the fifteenth century, described and advocated the use of torture in order to obtain confessions from suspected witches. It provided repeated warnings regarding false confessions, thus: 'For some are so soft-hearted and feeble-minded that at the least torture they will confess anything, whether it be true or not': *The Malleus Maleficarum* (1971) 225, 229, 243. Indeed, there is good evidence that suspects with mental health problems are susceptible to making false admissions within the criminal justice system: A.D. Redlich *et al*, 'Self-Reported False Confessions and False Guilty Pleas among Offenders with Mental Illness', (2010) 34 *Law Hum. Behav.* 79. Further, largely benign interrogation tactics can also lead to false confessions: J.T. Perillo and S.N. Kassin, 'Inside Interrogation: The Lie, the Bluff, and False Confessions', (2011) 35 *Law Hum. Behav.* 327. The proponents of legalisation do not consider the problem of terrorist suspects with vulnerabilities, and specifically, those with mental health problems or those who attention-seek, who may make false admissions leading to the use of torture in order to gain more intelligence, which would, of course, be false.
45 *Letter dated 20 February 1997 from the Permanent Representative of Israel to the United Nations Office at Geneva addressed to the secretariat of the fifty-third session of the Commission on Human Rights* E/CN.4/1997/116, 5 March 1997.
46 For discussion of this phenomenon in the context of Northern Ireland see *infra* nn. 265–70 and accompanying text.
47 There is also evidence that members of the Israeli security services have committed acts of perjury: B'Tselem, *Legislation Allowing the Use of Physical Force and Mental Coercion in Interrogations by the General Security Service* (2000) 52–3.
48 *Public Committee Against Torture in Israel* v. *The State of Israel* (1999) 38 ILM 1471.
49 A.M. Dershowitz, *Why Terrorism Works: Understanding the threat, responding to the challenge* (2002) 150.

50 The problem of correctly identifying those who possess intelligence is another difficulty that impacts on the issue of effectiveness. Further, Card has noted that the victims of interrogational torture 'have no convincing way to demonstrate their ignorance to a torturer': C. Card, 'Ticking Bombs and Interrogations', (2008) 2 *Crim. Law and Philos.* 1, 12.

51 J. Paul Satre 'A Victory', in H. Alleg, *The Question* (1958) xxxix. A similar point is made by Chris Mackey who was a member of the US intelligence corps based in Afghanistan. He notes 'In the movies, one key evil genius knows all and conveniently spills the pertinent information in a quick two-minute stretch. Real espionage doesn't work that way. Interrogators find tiny bits of truth, fragments of information, slivers of data': C. Mackey and G. Miller, *The Interrogator's War: Inside the Secret War Against al Qaeda* (2004) xxv.

52 E. Manningham-Buller, 'The International Terrorist Threat to the United Kingdom', in P. Hennessy, (ed.), *The New Protective State: Government, Intelligence and Terrorism* (2007) 70.

53 D. Omand, *Securing the State* (2010).

54 *Id.* 139. See also Schlesinger Report, *supra* n. 9, 65.

55 Intelligence Science Board, *Intelligence Interviewing Teaching Materials and Case Studies: A Report from the Study of Educing Information* (2009) 41.

56 See D. Rejali, *Torture and Democracy* (2007) 491.

57 McCoy, *supra* n. 38, 198.

58 Central Intelligence Agency-Office of Inspector General, *Counterterrorism Detention and Interrogation Activities (September 2001–October 2003)* 7 May 2004, para. 214 (hereafter CIA-OIG).

59 Central Intelligence Agency-Directorate of Intelligence, *Detainee Reporting Pivotal for the War Against Al Qa'ida* 3 June 2005, 2 (hereafter CIA-DOI).

60 'Inside the Interrogation of Detainee 063', *Time* 12 June 2005. See also *id.* 6 (referring to the use of detainee disclosures to 'leverage' intelligence from other detainees).

61 T. Powers, *Intelligence Wars: American Secret History from Hitler to al-Qaeda* (2004) 396, ch. 25.

62 *Id.* 401.

63 9/11 Commission Report, *supra* n. 18, 276–7.

64 *Id.* 276.

65 Dershowitz, *supra* n. 28, 144.

66 9/11 Commission Report, *supra* n. 18, 276.

67 For an excellent discussion, see: P. Gill and M. Phythian, *Intelligence in an Insecure World* (2006) ch. 5.

68 This problem is discussed by Gill and Phythian in relation to the flawed intelligence assessments which wrongly suggested that prior to the Gulf War, Iraq possessed WMD: *id.* 131 and ch. 7 generally.

69 S.M. Kassin *et al*, 'Comparative Study of College Students and Police Investigators', (2005) 29 *Law and Human Behavior* 211 (finding police officers more confident than students in their judgements, but students were found to be better able to identify falsehoods); A. Vrij *et al*, 'Cues to Deception and Ability to Detect Lies as a Function of Police Interview Styles', (2007) 31 *Law and Human Behavior* 499 ('accusatorial interview style resulted in more false allegations [of lying]'). For discussion of these issues in the context of the legal regulation of interrogation, see the excellent: G.C. Thomas III and R.A. Leo, *Confessions of Guilt: From Torture to Miranda and Beyond* (2012).

70 *Testimony of Douglas A. Johnson before Judiciary Hearing on the Nomination of the Honorable Alberto R. Gonzales, Counsel to President George W. Bush, to be the Attorney General of the United States* 6 January 2005, 9–10.

71 T.P. Coogan, *The IRA* (1987) 578.

72 P. Taylor, *Beating the Terrorists? Interrogation in Omagh, Gough and Castlereagh* (1980) 205.

73 *Id.* 205–6.

74 *Id.*
75 Coogan, *supra* n. 71, 577–80.
76 L. Farrall, 'How al Qaeda Works: What the Organization's Subsidiaries Say About its Strength', *Foreign Affairs* March/April 2011, 128, 133–4.
77 'Statement of John E. Cloonan, Retired Special Agent, West Caldwell, New Jersey', in US Senate Committee on the Judiciary, *Coercive Interrogation Techniques: Do They Work, are They Reliable, and What did the FBI Know About Them?* 10 June 2008, 34.
78 L. Beam, 'Leadership Resistance', *The Seditionist* February 1992 www.louisbeam.com/leaderless.htm (accessed 1 February 2014).
79 For an excellent discussion of this phenomenon in the context of jihadist terrorism, see M. Sageman, *Leaderless Jihad: Terror Networks in the Twenty-First Century* (2008).
80 K. Pilling, 'Jihadi Terror Obsession led to Pair's Conviction', *The Independent* 23 June 2010 (noting the case of Ishaq Kanmi who was jailed for seven years for encouraging others to commit acts of terror); D. Gardham, 'Terrorist Isa Ibrahim was a "Lone Wolf" who Radicalised Himself', *The Telegraph* 17 July 2009 (discussing the case of Isa Ibrahim who was inspired by the teachings of radical preachers and online bomb making manuals).
81 See, for example, J. Coates, *Armed and Dangerous: The Rise of the Survivalist Right* (1995) ch. 6 (discussing *inter alia* the case of David Lewis Rice, who in 1985 beat and stabbed to death a family of four, including two children, because he believed the father was a communist and Jew).
82 BBC, 'The Nailbomber', *Panorama* 30 June 2000.
83 In the context of Europe and the United States of America, see, for example, J. Merriman, *The Dynamite Club: How a Bombing in Fin-de-Siecle Paris Ignited the Age of Modern Terror* (2009) 138, 213; J.T. McCann, *Terrorism on American Soil: A Concise History of Plots and Perpetrators from the Famous to the Forgotten* (2006).
84 This could be seen in the actions of European anarchists in the nineteenth century: Merriman, *id.* ch. X.
85 For discussion, see, for example, Central Intelligence Agency, *Background Paper on CIA's Combined Use of Interrogation Techniques* (2004) 3 (hereafter *Background Paper*).
86 *Id.* 17.
87 Coogan, *supra* n. 71, 711. This of course was recognised in the IRA's Staff Report as being inadequate.
88 E. Moloney, *A Secret History of the IRA* (2002) 134.
89 Al Qaeda, *The al Qaeda Manual* (undated) 66–7.
90 O. Nasiri, *Inside the Jihad: My Life with Al Qaeda* (2006) 183.
91 See, for example, M. Alexander and J.R Bruning, *How to Break a Terrorist: The US Interrogators who Used Brains, not Brutality, to Take Down the Deadliest Man in Iraq* (2008) (examining the impact of a variety of non-coercive techniques, including rapport building, trickery and rapid questioning which led to the discovery of the hideout of Abu Mousab al Zarqawi, leader of al Qaeda in Iraq. This resulted in an air raid that killed Zarqawi). See also: A.H. Soufan and D. Freedman, *The Black Banners: Inside the Hunt for Al-Qaeda* (2011) (discussing the successful use of rapport building in gaining intelligence disclosures from terrorist suspects).
92 Fax for Daniel Levin, Assistant Attorney General, Office of Legal Counsel, from [name redacted] Assistant General Counsel, CIA; 4 January 2005, quoted in: OLC, *Re: Application of United States Obligations Under Article 16 of the Convention Against Torture to Certain Techniques that May Be Used in the Interrogation of High Value al Qaeda Detainees* 30 May 2005, 5.
93 *Infra* n. 184 and accompanying text.
94 Omand, *supra* n. 53, 302.
95 For a detailed discussion, see McCoy, *supra* n. 38, ch. 2.
96 KUBARK, *Counterintelligence Interrogation – July 1963* (1963).
97 *Human Resource Exploitation Training Manual* (1983). A substantial part of the 1983 manual appears to be based upon the content of the 1963 manual.

98 This warning appears before the manual's introduction, in a section entitled: 'Prohibition Against Use of Force': *Id.*
99 KUBARK, *supra* n. 96, 90. Internal quotation marks omitted.
100 Alleg, *supra* n. 51, 77. 'Magneto' refers to a device used by interrogators to electrocute prisoners.
101 KUBARK, *supra* n. 96, 52–104.
102 Bagaric and Clarke, *supra* n. 26, 588–9.
103 KUBARK, *supra* n. 96, 92.
104 *Gäfgen* v. *Germany* (application no. 22978/05) (a threat of torture led a suspect to disclose the location of the body of a child he had kidnapped).
105 Lt. Gen. Randall M. Schmidt, *Investigation into FBI Allegations of Detainee Abuse at Guantanamo Bay, Cuba Detention Facility – Executive Summary* (2005) 24–5 (discussing the case of a detainee who was threatened with death and things 'worse' than physical pain. He was also told that his 'family had been captured by the United States and that they were in danger'. The detainee later responded by stating that he ' ... was not willing to continue to protect others to the detriment of himself and his family').
106 KUBARK, *supra* n. 96, 93.
107 *Id.* 94. For a possible example of this phenomenon, see B'Tselem, *supra* n. 47, 52 (referring to the interrogation of a Hamas member by the Israeli security forces).
108 W.L. Twining and P.E. Twining, 'Bentham *on* Torture', (1973) 24 *N.I.L.Q.* 305, 315.
109 A. Feldman, *Formations of Violence: The Narrative of the Body and Political Terror in Northern Ireland* (1991) 133, 139, 141.
110 See, for example, KUBARK, *supra* n. 96, 10–4.
111 J. White, 'Documents Tell of Brutal Improvisation by GIs', *Washington Post* 3 August 2005, A01.
112 International Committee of the Red Cross, *ICRC Report on the Treatment of Fourteen 'High Value Detainees' in CIA Custody* (2007) 37.
113 *Infra* n. 171 and accompanying text.
114 KUBARK, *supra* n. 96, 94. For an example of a false confession induced by the Israeli security forces, see B'Tselem, *supra* n. 47, 52.
115 S. Rasul *et al, Composite Statement: Detention in Afghanistan and Guantánamo Bay* (2004) para. 199.
116 D. Rose, *Guantánamo: America's War on Human Rights* (2004) 104–5.
117 The three British detainees have provided detailed accounts of their psychological and physical suffering as a result of coercion that included being exposed to extremes of temperature, being chained for long periods of time, the use of stress positions and dogs to frighten them: Rasul, *supra* n. 115.
118 Public Committee Against Torture in Israel, *Back to a Routine of Torture* (2003) 86.
119 M. Bright, 'Guantánamo has "failed to prevent terror attacks"', *The Observer* (London) 3 October 2004. See also K.T. Rhem, 'Guantánamo Detainees Still Yielding Valuable Intelligence', *American Forces Press Service* 16 March 2005 (quoting Army Brig. Gen. Jay Hood, commander of the Joint Task Force at Guantánamo Bay: 'Initially we had a lot to do to learn about the nature of our detainees. Many of them used aliases; many of them were not forthcoming with us in describing who they were and what their activities on the battlefield were ... But over the last couple years, we've gained a great deal of information on them and intelligence from them.')
120 Bright, *id.*
121 Rose, *supra* n. 116, 117. See also: A. Applebaum, 'The Torture Myth', *Washington Post* 12 January 2005, 21.
122 J. Dratel, 'The Curious Debate', in K.J. Greenberg (ed.), *The Torture Debate in America* (2006) 114.
123 US Department of Defense, *JTF-GTMO Information in Detainees* (2005) 1.
124 *Id.* 1–4.

125 *Id.* 1. The release of hundreds of *Guantánamo* detainee files by Wikileaks suggests that much of this corroboration comes from other detainees.

126 E. Saar and V. Novak, *Inside the Wire: A Military Intelligence Soldier's Eyewitness Account of Life at Guantánamo* (2005); US Department of Justice–Office of the Inspector General, *A Review of the FBI's Involvement in and Observations of Detainee Interrogations in Guantánamo Bay, Afghanistan, and Iraq* (2008) 53 (hereafter DOJ-FBI) (noting 'tension' and 'stark differences' between FBI, military and US intelligence agency policies and interrogation techniques'). Though it must be acknowledged that the conditions of confinement at Guantánamo were inherently coercive.

127 Wikileaks, *GITMO Files* http://wikileaks.ch/gitmo (accessed: 1 February 2014).

128 See, for example, ISN 000011; ISN 000489; ISN 001016; ISN 001103; ISN 0001457.

129 ISN 001030, 4.

130 See, for example, ISN 001056; ISN 000493; ISN 001104.

131 ISN 000252, 5.

132 *Id.* 12.

133 *Id.*

134 *El Gharani v. Bush* 593 F.Supp.2d 144 (2009); *Ahmed v. Obama* 613 F.Supp.2d 51 (2009).

135 Bagaric and Clarke, *supra* n. 14, 55.

136 Hereinafter 'HVD programme'.

137 US Department of Justice-Office of Professional Responsibility, *Investigation into the Office of Legal Counsel's Memoranda Concerning Issues Relating to the Central Intelligence Agency's Use of 'Enhanced Interrogation Techniques' on Suspected Terrorists* (2009) (hereafter DOJ-OPR).

138 DOJ-FBI, *supra* n. 126.

139 CIA-OIG, *supra* n. 58.

140 *Senate Armed Services Committee Inquiry into the Treatment of Detainees in US Custody* (2008).

141 M.A. Thiessen, *Courting Disaster: How the CIA Kept America Safe and How Barack Obama is Inviting the Next Attack* (2010) 125.

142 CIA-OIG, *supra* n. 58, para. 4. There is some dispute over the value of Zubaydah as a detainee. It has been argued that the Bush Administration exaggerated his value: Froomkin, *supra* n. 17. By contrast, the CIA has claimed that his interrogation resulted in the disclosure of valuable intelligence: CIA-OIG, *supra* n. 58, paras. 216–23.

143 The literature existing prior to the HVD programme suggested that sleep deprivation impacted on accurate disclosures: M. Blagrove, 'Effects of Length of Sleep Deprivation on Interrogative Suggestibility', (1996) 2 *Journal of Experimental Psychology: Applied* 48 (suggested sleep deprivation may increase suggestibility).

144 Office of Legal Counsel, *Memorandum for John Rizzo Acting General Counsel of the Central Intelligence Agency: Interrogation of al Qaeda Operative* 1 August 2002, 2.

145 *Id.* 1–2.

146 Office of Legal Counsel, *Re: Application of United States Obligations Under Article 16 of the Convention Against Torture to Certain Techniques that May Be Used in the Interrogation of High Value al Qaeda Detainees* 30 May 2005, 9.

147 *Id.*

148 For example, it has been argued that lawyers who wrote opinions authorising the use of EITs may be guilty of criminal offences: J.D. Ohlin, 'The Torture Lawyers', (2010) 51 *Harv. Int'l L.J.* 193.

149 S. Shane, 'Soviet-Style "Torture" Becomes Interrogation', *The New York Times* 3 June 2007.

150 Committee on Armed Service, *supra* n. 140, xiii.

151 CIA–OIG, *supra* n. 58, para. 32.

152 J. Mayer, *The Dark Side: The Inside Story of How the War on Terror Turned into a War on American Ideals* (2008) 162.

153 For discussion, see: M. Welch, 'American "Pain-ology" in the War on Terror: a Critique of "Scientific" Torture', (2009) 13 *Theoretical Criminology* 451; M. Welch, 'Illusion in Truth Seeking: The Perils of Interrogation and Torture in the War on Terror', (2010–11) 37 *Social Justice* 123. The scientific basis for coercive interrogation methods has been doubted. Steven M. Kleinman notes: 'Claims from some members of the operational community as to the alleged effectiveness of coercive methods in educing meaningful information from resistant sources are, at best, anecdotal in nature and would be, in the author's view, unlikely to withstand the rigors of sound scientific inquiry.' 'KUBARK Counterintelligence Interrogation Review: Observations of an Interrogator – Lessons Learned and Avenues for Further Research', in Intelligence Science Board, *Educing Information, Interrogation: Science and Art* (2006) 130, n. 91. See also early evidence that some coercive methods can hinder accurate memory recall: P. Solomon MD *et al*, *Sensory Deprivation: A Symposium Held at Harvard Medical School* (1961).

154 CIA-OIG, *supra* n. 58, paras. 36–44.

155 *Id*. para. 45.

156 OLC, Memorandum for John Rizzo, Acting Attorney General of the Central Intelligence Agency, *Interrogation of an al Qaeda Operative* 1 August 2002, 6.

157 SERE training has been described, thus: 'Few courses in the military are as physically or emotionally challenging as the captive phase of SERE training … ' D. Couch, *Chosen Soldier: The Making of a Special Forces Warrior* (2007) 369. This does raise the question of whether it was waterboarding that was so effective on Naval trainees or it was the general harshness of the training that resulted in disclosures.

158 *Techniques Memo*, *infra* n. 165, 41 n. 51.

159 *Background Paper*, *supra* n. 85, 17.

160 *Id*.

161 OLC, *supra* 156, 2.

162 CIA-OIG, *supra* n. 58, paras. 223, 225. For discussion, see S. Shane, 'Waterboarding Used 266 Times on 2 Suspects', *The New York Times* 19 April 2009.

163 CIA-OIG, *supra* n. 58, para. 205.

164 R. Suskind, *The One Percent Doctrine: Deep Inside America's Pursuit of its Enemies Since 9/11* (2006) 118 (quoting a US official in regards to the Zubaydah interrogation, thus: 'Once you go down this road-and try everything—it's hard to know what worked').

165 See, for example, OLC, *Re: Application of United States Obligations Under Article 16 of the Convention Against Torture to Certain Techniques that May Be Used in the Interrogation of High Value al Qaeda Detainees* 30 May 2005 (40 pages); OLC, *Re: Application of 18 USC §§ 2340–2340A to Certain Techniques That May be Used in the Interrogation of a High Value al Qaeda Detainee* 10 May 2005 (*Techniques Memo* – 46 pages); OLC, *Re: Application of 18 USC §§ 2340–2340A to the Combined Use of Certain Techniques in the Interrogation of High Value al Qaeda Detainees* 10 May 2005 (*Combined Use* – 19 pages).

166 G. Tenet, *At the Center of the Storm: My Years at the CIA* (2007) 241. This claim is disputed by an FBI agent who was present at the start of the CIA interrogation of Zubaydah claiming that he was being subject.

167 Posner and Vermeule acknowledge this problem, noting that: '[t]he torture warrant serves its purpose only when there are no time constraints'. Posner and Vermeule, *supra* n. 13, 209.

168 For a lengthy discussion, see Thiessen, *supra* n. 141, ch. 3.

169 P. Sands, 'Publish and be Damned, Mr Cheney', www.guardian.co.uk (accessed 21 April 2009).

170 M. Thompson and B. Ghosh, 'Did Waterboarding Prevent Terrorism Attacks?' *Time* 21 April 2009.

171 OLC, 30 May memo, *supra* n. 165, 8.

172 *Id*. 11.

173 *Id*. 8 citing: Memorandum for Steven G. Bradbury, Principal Deputy Assistant Attorney General, Office of Legal Counsel, from [redacted] DCI Counterterrorist Center, *Re:*

Effectiveness of the CIA Counterintelligence Interrogation Techniques 2 (2 March 2005) (hereafter *Effectiveness Memo*).

174 'Cheney Enters "Torture" Memos Row', www.bbc.co.uk/news 21 April 2009 ('There are reports that show specifically what we gained as a result of this activity. They have not been declassified. I formally ask that they be declassified now.').

175 See, for example, CIA-OIG, *supra* n. 58, paras. 211–25.

176 *Id.*

177 *Id.* para. 211.

178 *Id.*

179 *Id.* para. 217.

180 *Id.* para. 222.

181 *Id.*

182 *Id.* para. 223. Soufan's account of the CIA's treatment of Zubaydah suggests that highly coercive techniques were employed before August 2002.

183 *Id.*

184 DOJ-OPR, *supra* n. 137, para. 212.

185 CIA-OIG, *supra* n. 58, para. 30.

186 OLC, *supra* n. 152.

187 *Id.* 1.

188 CIA-OIG, *supra* n. 58, para. 223. See also: P. Finn and J. Warrick, 'Detainee's Harsh Treatment Foiled No Plots', *The New York Times* 29 March 2009 (suggesting *inter alia* that Zubaydah's importance was exaggerated by the Bush Administration). A confidential CIA briefing in April 2003 to US Senators described the disclosures from Zubaydah and another HVD as 'founts' of useful information 'though it seems clear that they have not, even under enhanced techniques, revealed everything they know of importance'. CIA, Memorandum for the Record, 'Member Briefing', 2 April 2003.

189 DOJ-OIG, *supra* n. 137, 68.

190 A.H. Soufan and D. Freedman, *The Black Banners: Inside the Hunt for Al-Qaeda* (2011) 378. The reference to an imminent attack was to Jose Padilla. There is no doubt that Padilla wished to engage in acts of terrorism on US soil, such as the use of a radiological bomb, but it is open to question whether such an attack was imminent or if Padilla would ever have the means to carry out such an attack.

191 *Id.* 385–9. It has been reported that when George Tenet was told of Zubaydah's initial disclosures he was delighted until he learned that the disclosure had been made to the FBI. Mayer, *supra* n. 152, 156.

192 Soufan and Freedman's book contains a significant number of redactions that were stipulated by the Central Intelligence Agency: *supra* n. 190, xi.

193 *Id.* 386. See also: United States Senate Committee on the Judiciary, 'Testimony of Ali Soufan', 13 May 2009. By contrast, Soufan's colleague reported to the FBI that CIA interrogators had claimed Zubaydah was only providing 'throw-away information': DOJ-FBI, *supra* n. 126. 68. This is a surprising characterisation given the importance of discovering the identity of 'Muktar' and does raise some questions as to why the CIA would be so dismissive of this disclosure. Indeed, in a report of the Office of the Director of National Intelligence this particular disclosure was described as 'important': *Summary of the High Value Terrorist Detainee Program* (undated).

194 A. Davidson, 'I really resent you using the word "torture": Q and A with Jose Rodriguez', *The New Yorker* 19 July 2012. Rodriguez muddies the water somewhat by claiming that sleep deprivation was used as part of the 'traditional' methods employed. See also the CIA-OIG report concerning disclosures by Zubaydah: *supra* n. 58, para. 216.

195 Soufan, United States Senate testimony, *supra* n. 193.

196 'Padilla Given Long Jail Sentence', www.bbc.co.uk/news 23 January 2008.

197 Thiessen, *supra* n. 141, 86, 87.

198 DOJ-FBI, *supra* n. 126, 68, 322 and 325.

199 R. Esposito and B. Ross, 'Coming in From the Cold: CIA Spy Calls Waterboarding Necessary But Torture', http://abcnews.go.com 10 December 2007.
200 Transcript of ABC News Interview with John Kiriakou, 17. This document can be accessed via the following link: http://abcnews.go.com/images/Blotter/brianross_kiriakou_transcript1_blotter071210.pdf (accessed 1 February 2014).
201 C. McCreal, 'Bush on Torture: Waterboarding Helped Prevent Attacks on London', *The Guardian* 9 November 2010.
202 For example, the Heathrow plot was referred to by the CIA, *supra* n. 59, 5.
203 J. Mayer, 'Counterfactual: A Curious History of the C.I.A.'s Secret Interrogation Program', *The New Yorker* 29 March 2010. This attack was also foiled by infiltration of a terrorist cell: 'Agent Infiltrated Terror Cell, US says', www.CNN.com 11 August 2011.
204 S. O'Neill and D. Byers, 'Airline Terror Trial: Heathrow, Canary Wharf and nuclear plants in bomb plot', *The Times* 5 April 2008.
205 S. Shane and C. Savage, 'Bin Laden Raid Revives Debate on Value of Torture', *The New York Times* 3 May 2011.
206 M. Calabresi, 'Ex-CIA Counterterror Chief: "Enhanced Interrogation" Led U.S. to bin Laden', *Time* 4 May 2011.
207 M. Alexander, 'Tortured logic: Waterboarding Didn't Help U.S. get Bin Laden' *UCLA Today* 6 May 2011.
208 'Waterboarding Helped Find Osama bin Laden, Dick Cheney Says', www.montreal gazette.com 8 May 2011.
209 'Osama bin Laden Killed: Phone Call by Courier led US to their Target', www.Tele graph.co.uk 3 May 2011.
210 G. Sargent, 'Private Letter from CIA Chief Undercuts Claim Torture was Key to Killing Bin Laden', *Washington Post* 16 May 2011.
211 CIA-DOI, *supra* n. 59, 9.
212 *Id.* 1.
213 *Id.* ii.
214 *Verbatim Transcript of Combatant Status Review Tribunal Hearing for ISN 10024* (2007) 19.
215 A. Zagorin, 'Can KSM's Confession be Believed?' *Time* 15 March 2007.
216 *Supra* n. 214, 18.
217 Thiessen, *supra* n. 141, 48.
218 OLC, *supra* n. 165, 10 (May 30 memo).
219 T. Noah, 'Water-Bored', www.Slate.com 21 April 2009.
220 White House, *Fact Sheet: Keeping America Safe from Attack – President Bush Discusses Intelligence Showing the Importance of Defeating Al Qaeda in Iraq* 23 May 2007.
221 White House, *Press Briefing on the West Coast Terrorist Plot by Frances Fragos Townsend, Assistant to the President for Homeland Security and Counterterrorism* 9 February 2006.
222 General M.V. Hayden, *Classified Statement of the Record* Senate Select Committee on Intelligence, 12 April 2007, 6. Hayden's reference to 'considering' is hardly suggestive of an active plot. Terrorists have many ideas but this is hardly evidence of a credible plot.
223 For discussion, see *infra* nn. 226–37 and accompanying text.
224 *Infra* n. 289 and accompanying text.
225 For example, during her attempt to secure the Presidential nomination of the Republican Party for the 2012 Presidential election, Congresswoman Michele Bachmann said: 'If I were president, I would be willing to use waterboarding. I think it was very effective. It gained information for our country … '. D. Farber, 'John McCain Hits GOP Hopefuls over Waterboarding', http://cbsnews.com (accessed 14 November 2012).
226 J. Mayer, 'Top CIA Lawyers Sides with Senate Torture Report', *The New Yorker* 17 October 2013.
227 M. Mazzetti and S. Shane, 'Senate and CIA Spar over Secret Report on Interrogation Program', *The New York Times* 19 July 2013.

228 J. Yager, 'Senate Intel Panel Approves Torture Report' *The Hill* 13 December 2012.
229 M. Mazzetti and S. Shane, 'Senate and C.I.A. Spar Over Secret Report on Interrogation Program', *The New York Times* 19 July 2013.
230 Despite this, in recent hearings the General Counsel of the CIA Stephen W. Preston contradicted assertions of the CIA when he stated that during the HVD programme's existence: 'briefings to the Committees included inaccurate information related to aspects of the program' (at 9). He also stated that the CIA's disclosure of information regarding to the Office of Legal Counsel regarding the HVD programme 'fell well short of our current practices' (p 8). Mayer, *supra* n. 226 (page references are to a document containing questions and answers available within Mayer's story).
231 *Id.*
232 *Statement by Senator John McCain on Intelligence Committee Report on Torture* 13 December 2012.
233 In April 2014, a majority of the Senate Intelligence Committee voted to partially declassify sections of the report: S. Ackerman, 'Senate Committee Votes to Declassify Parts of CIA Torture Report', www.theguardian.com 3 April 2014.
234 G. Miller *et al*, 'Feinstein: CIA Searched Intelligence Committee Computers', www.washingtonpost.com 11 March 2014 (accessed 3 April 2014).
235 M. Mazzetti, 'C.I.A. Employees Face New Inquiry Amid Clashes on Detention Program', www.nytimes.com 4 March 2014 (accessed 3 April 2014).
236 G. Miller *et al*, 'CIA Misled on Interrogation Program, Senate Report Says', www.washingtonpost.com 1 April 2014 (accessed 3 April 2014).
237 *Id.*
238 P. Wehner, 'Morality and Enhanced Interrogation Techniques', *Commentary* www.commentarymagazine.com/pods-author/peter-wehner (accessed: 1 February 2014) (pointing to some of the complex moral and legal issues in the torture debate, including the possibility that the use of EITs might be used as a recruiting tool).
239 For discussion, see A. Horne, *A Savage War of Peace: Algeria 1954–1962* (2006) ch. 4.
240 A. Shatz, 'The Torture of Algiers', *New York Review of Books* 21 November 2002, 53, 57, cited in: S. Levinson, 'Contemplating Torture: An Introduction', in S. Levinson, *Torture: A Collection* (2004) 34.
241 The Front de Libèration Nationale (FLN) began as a small underground organisation violently opposed to French rule in Algeria: J.M. Todd, *Algeria 1830–2000: A Short History* (2004) 27; Horne, *supra* n 239, ch. 4.
242 Shatz, *supra* n. 240, 57.
243 For example, Bagaric and Clarke rely on A. Palmer, 'Is Torture Always Wrong?' *The Spectator* 24 September 2005, 40, cited in *supra* n. 14, 54, n. 6.
244 Office of the Governor-General, Civil Inspectorate-General in Algeria, Algiers, 2 March 1955, cited in P. Vidal-Naquet, *Torture: Cancer of Democracy, France and Algeria 1954–62* (1963).
245 *Id.* 169. This would be appear to be a disingenuous criticism by officers given that amount of abuse found by Wuillaume and others.
246 *Id.* 171.
247 *Id.* 171–3.
248 *Id.* 170, 177.
249 *Id.* 177.
250 *Id.* 176–7.
251 For example, Bagaric and Clarke, *supra* n. 14, 54.
252 Shatz notes that the French legal system had great difficulty controlling the French armed forces and their activities in Algiers, *supra* n. 240, 57.
253 D. Rejali, 'Does Torture Work?' www.slate.com (accessed 21 June 2004).
254 D. Rejali, *Torture and Democracy* (2007) 487–92.
255 *Id.* 491.
256 *Id.*

257 *Ireland* v. *United Kingdom* [1978] 2 EHRR 25, para. 96.
258 S. Newbery, 'Intelligence and Controversial British Interrogation Techniques: The Northern Ireland Case, 1971–72,' (2009) 20 *Irish Studies in International Affairs* 103, 115. Quoting a Ministry of Defence document.
259 *Id.* 106.
260 C. Ryder, *The RUC 1922–1997: A Force Under Fire* (1997) 197.
261 *Supra* n. 257, para. 167.
262 *Report of the Committee of Privy Counsellors Appointed to Consider Authorised Procedures for the Interrogation of Persons Suspected of Terrorism* (1972) (hereinafter the Parker Report).
263 *Id.* para. 20.
264 *Id.* para. 21
265 *Id.* paras. 20–1. The reference to 'indirect' appears to refer to a 'snowball' effect whereby coerced information led to further disclosures using conventional policing techniques (para. 23).
266 *Id.* para. 24.
267 *Id.* paras. 18, 22.
268 *Id.* para. 14(a).
269 *Id.* para. 14(b)(ii).
270 P. Taylor, *Beating the Terrorists? Interrogation in Omagh, Gough and Castlereagh* (1980) 20–1.
271 T. Parker, 'Counterterrorism Policies in the United Kingdom', in P.B. Heymann and J.N. Kayyem, *Preserving Liberty in an Age of Terror* (2005) 123.
272 J. McGuffin, *The Guineapigs* (1974) 106. Similarly, David Omand describes the intelligence gains resulting from the use of interrogation in-depth as 'very limited' and 'at the cost of a propaganda disaster'. D. Omand, 'The Dilemmas of Using Secret Intelligence for Public Security', in Hennessy (ed.), *supra* n. 53, 149.
273 McGuffin, *id.* 108.
274 *Intelligence Gained from Interrogations in Northern Ireland*, undated, DEFE 13/958, The National Archives, in S. Newbery, 'Interrogation, Intelligence and the Issue of Human Rights', (2009) 24 *Intelligence and National Security* 631, 635.
275 While the Parker Report did contain some analysis to this effect, it was very limited.
276 B. Brecher, 'Why Torture Remains Unjustified', (2009) 24 *Intelligence and National Security* 636, 636.
277 P. Sands, 'Evidence of Utility? A Legal Perspective', (2009) 24 *Intelligence and National Security* 638, 639–40.
278 *Id.* 639. Sands noted that there is no 'hard information' to corroborate the claims such as an 'interrogation log'. It is worth noting that such information could be forged and may be of little corroborative value.
279 Parker Report, *supra* n. 262, para. 4(b)(i). The majority report also appeared to recognise this, but claimed that most of the disclosures resulted from the use of the five techniques (para. 21).
280 I. Cobain, *Cruel Britannia: A Secret History of Torture* (2012) ch. 6; Taylor, *supra* n. 270.
281 For examples of the successful use of non-coercive techniques, see *supra* n. 91.
282 K. Lasson, 'Torture, Truth Serum, and Ticking Bombs: Toward a Pragmatic Perspective of Coercive Interrogation', (2008) 39 *Loyola University Chicago Law Journal* 329; L. M. Keller, 'Is Truth Serum Torture?' (2005) 20 *Am. U. Int'l L. Rev.* 521.
283 B. Dedman, 'New Anti-terror Weapon: Hand-held Lie Detector', www.msnbc.com 9 April 2008; A. Ananthaswamy, 'AI lie detection could help crack terror cells' *New Scientist* 14 March, 2011. Some Guantánamo detainees have also been the subject of polygraph tests. See, for example, ISN 000117.
284 J. Wild, 'Brain Imaging Ready to Detect Terrorists, Say Neuroscientists', (2005) 437 *Nature* 22 September, 457.
285 P. Rumney and M. O'Boyle, 'The Torture Debate', *New Law Journal* 9 November 2007, 1567 (discussing comments by Amnesty International pertaining to the use of the 'five techniques' in Northern Ireland).

286 Feldman, *supra* n. 109, 131 (referring to a Republican terrorist recounting that brutality increased his anger and determination to resist whereas 'the [interrogators] who are being nice lower your defences').
287 D. Cole, *Enemy Aliens: Double Standards and Constitutional Freedoms in the War on Terrorism* (2005) 184.
288 B'Tselem, *supra* n. 47, 49.
289 'Dick Cheney Calls for the Return of Enhanced Interrogation', www.telegraph.co.uk 9 May 2011. Such claims tend to ignore evidence that non-coercive techniques have also resulted in crucial intelligence disclosures.
290 Rejali, *supra* n. 56.
291 J. Mayer, 'Outsourcing Torture', *The New Yorker* 14 February 2005.
292 OLC, *supra* n. 146, 8. The Director of Central Intelligence Interrogation Guidelines define '"standard interrogation techniques" as techniques that do not incorporate significant physical or psychological pressure': CIA-OIG, *supra* n. 58, para. 63.
293 *Background Paper, supra* n. 85, 3.
294 *Id.*
295 *Id.* 10
296 *Supra* n. 16 and accompanying text.
297 Ignatieff, *supra* n. 21, 24.
298 White House Office of the Press Secretary, *News Conference by the President* 29 April 2009.
299 White House Office of the Press Secretary, *Remarks by the President on National Security* 21 May 2009.
300 A. Soufan, 'My Tortured Decision', *The New York Times* 23 April 2009.
301 Tenet, *supra* n. 166, 255.
302 *Id.*
303 *Id.* 242.
304 CIA, *supra* n. 59, 1, 3, 4 (noting that 'reporting from high value al-Qa'ida detainees has become a crucial pillar of US counterterrorism efforts', and has created many 'actionable leads' for law enforcement and has 'helped thwart a number of al-Qa'ida plots').
305 *Id.* 8.
306 *Id.*
307 P. Sands, 'Torture is Illegal – and it Never Works', www.guardian.co.uk 24 November 2008.
308 D. Manderson, 'Another Modest Proposal: In Defence of the Prohibition Against Torture', in M. Gani and P. Mathew (eds.), *Fresh Perspectives on the War on Terror* (2008) 41.
309 *Supra* nn. 72–4 and accompanying text and Cloonan, *supra* n. 77 and accompanying text.
310 Matthews, *supra* n. 23, 218.
311 Despite claims that the use of coercive methods in Israel has foiled attacks, the nature of this claim must be carefully analysed with an acknowledgement that there is no supporting evidence for these claims: *supra* nn. 45–9 and accompanying text. Further, where details are given they often do not meet the ticking bomb-type standard often portrayed in the ticking bomb scenarios put forward by proponents: Chapter 2, nn. 203–6 and accompanying text.
312 Bagaric and Clarke, *supra* n. 14, 44 (setting out a scenario involving a bomb on an aircraft that will explode in 30 minutes).
313 See *Leon* v. *Wainwright* 734 F 2d 770 (11th Cir., 1984); *Gäfgen* v. *Germany* (application no. 22978/05). See also the Wachsman case in Chapter 2, nn. 207–10 and accompanying text. All of which are discussed in Chapter 2. The absence of further supporting evidence might result from the fact that detainees as part of the HVD programme, for example, never possessed such intelligence. However, even if this is true, it means that the proponents lack a compelling body of evidence to prove their claims.
314 Suskind, *supra* n. 164.
315 *Supra* n. 45–9 and accompanying text.

4

TORTURE STATUTES, SLIPPERY SLOPES AND THE CHALLENGES OF REGULATION[1]

'[The] prisoner should be manacled at the wrists with his feet upon the ground and his hands [stretched up] as high as he was [able to] reach against the wall.' (1592)[2]

'The individual stands about four to five feet from a wall, with his feet spread approximately to shoulder width His arms are stretched out in front of him, with his fingers resting on the wall. His fingers support all of his body weight ... ' (2002)[3]

As these quotes demonstrate, the regulation of torture and other coercion techniques has a long history. In the last decade a variety of regulatory models have been proposed that would serve to allow state officials to torture terrorist suspects in order to gain intelligence. These have included the use of the defences of necessity[4] and self-defence,[5] the notion of civil disobedience[6] and defining torture in such a way as to restrict its application to certain interrogation techniques.[7] However, most scholars who have argued in favour of legalisation propose the creation of an exception to the absolute prohibition that would allow for the use interrogational torture, but only in emergency situations.[8] Few of these scholars have considered in detail the principles, procedures or safeguards that would underpin such a regulatory arrangement.[9] This chapter will argue that while the use of a law-based regulatory arrangement might give the impression of precision and control, the reality of interrogational torture and of emergency powers generally suggests that legalisation would lead to significant regulatory difficulties. The chapter will consider the challenges of drafting a torture statute and will pay particular attention to a comparison between a legal standards approach to regulation and a more narrowly drafted rule-based law. This will assist in illustrating the potential difficulties of interpreting a legal provision in circumstances of urgency while maintaining tight control of the torture power.[10]

This chapter will examine the question of regulation within the analytical framework of so-called slippery slope arguments (hereafter SSAs) which suggest that a policy or legal reform will likely lead to a series of undesirable or unintended consequences that legal regulation is unlikely to prevent. SSAs are a classic consequentialist argument against legal reform and provide the final element of the cumulative argument that the case for legalised interrogational torture is inherently expansive and difficult to control. This chapter will continue to build this argument in order to construct an empirically-based SSA. It has been suggested that the use of SSAs in the context of legalisation are an 'argument of caution, not a debate stopper'.[11] Here, it is argued that the strength of SSAs against legalisation depend on the nature and probability of slippage. One of the problems that this chapter seeks to address is the fact that SSAs are often poorly used in the torture debate. Many opponents of legalisation make exaggerated claims while proponents offer unsupported denials that slippage would be a problem at all. This chapter will analyse various types of slippery slopes that might occur if torture were legalised and will do so with the support of empirical evidence. In so doing, it will utilise the theory of slippery slopes offered by Lode,[12] Schauer[13] and Volokh[14] who have contributed important works on SSAs, their nature and limitations. In conclusion, it will be argued that there are many differing types of empirically supported SSA that are likely to occur, irrespective of the type of regulation used to constrain a torture power.

1. Drafting a torture statute

Perhaps one of the surprising aspects of the torture debate is that no scholar, as yet, has ventured to propose the actual wording of an exception to the absolute prohibition. While the proponents of legalised torture have examined a range of policy and philosophical arguments to support their case none have gone beyond setting down general principles or variables to be used for determining when interrogational torture should be legally or morally permissible.[15] The absence of such explicit wording has, of course, been taken as a sign of weakness in the case for legalised torture. In his analysis of Dershowitz's case for the use of torture warrants,[16] Brecher argues:

> Nowhere in *Why Terrorism Works* or anywhere else is there a draft wording, however embryonic, of the legislation proposed. That might seem surprising. But it is not. For any attempt legislatively to specify the circumstances in which such a warrant might be granted, the conditions governing who would grant it and to whom, and what it would permit and what not, would require a basis of just that realism which the ticking bomb scenario precludes.[17]

It is not unusual for scholars favouring legal reform to omit the wording of proposed legalisation. After all, scholars do not usually draft legislation. However, there are compelling reasons for examining how such a statute might be worded. First, it is difficult to adequately discuss legalised torture without, at some point, confronting the explicit regulatory framework and statutory language that would empower the state to torture a terrorist suspect. Second, by examining the possible wording of such a statute, even one that is narrowly drafted, we can identify many of the long-observed difficulties that characterise statutory interpretation.[18] In particular, we identify the demands that statutory language would place on state officials and the interpretative dilemmas faced by officials working in a time-limited, stressful environment. Finally, a draft statute will assist in identifying particular areas of possible slippage.

Proposals for the legalisation of interrogational torture are goal-orientated. The aim of a torture law is to create a framework in which torture can be regulated in a controlled manner for the benefit of the wider community by preventing imminent acts of terrorism or criminality.[19] Seen in this way, the legal regulation of torture falls within a utilitarian 'public interest theor[y] of regulation' that 'attribute[s] to legislators and others responsible for the design and implementation of regulation a desire to pursue collective goals with the aim of promoting the general welfare of the community'.[20] A consequentialist theory of regulation however, requires a detailed analysis of the potential consequences of the legalisation of interrogational torture and this is where an examination of SSAs is crucial.

The ability of law to effectively control legalised torture has been the subject of important historical work. In his analysis of the historic use of torture in Continental Europe, Langbein has shown that legalised torture existed in many European nations for several hundred years.[21] In Continental Europe, the widespread use of torture resulted from the adoption of the Roman-canon law of proof in criminal trials. A conviction required either the evidence of two eye witnesses or a confession by the accused. Circumstantial evidence against the accused was not sufficient to form the basis of a conviction.[22] Unsurprisingly, this standard made the gaining of proof necessary to convict a person of a crime very difficult. Consequently, the use of torture to extract confessions was seen as a crucial tool in order to secure convictions.[23] On the face of it, many of these laws appeared to provide procedural protections and restraints on the use of torture. In order for torture to be authorised 'half proof against the suspect' was required. Half proof was constituted by one eye witness to the crime or circumstantial evidence sufficient to suggest the guilt of the accused.[24] Further, investigation under torture could only be used in cases involving capital crimes and certain people were exempted from the use of torture, including pregnant women and children.[25] Some laws also required the presence of a doctor when certain forms of torture were being used[26] and to avoid false confessions 'torture was supposed to be employed in such a way that the accused would also confess to details of the crime'.[27]

These supposed safeguards should be viewed with caution. Langbein notes that judges enjoyed 'considerable discretion'[28] and the safeguards intended to protect the innocent were 'quite imperfect'.[29] There was also a fundamental problem in the enforcement of laws regulating torture: 'If the judge did engage in suggestive questioning, even accidently, that could seldom be detected or prevented … In many jurisdictions the requirement [that a confession be verified] was not enforced, or was indifferently enforced.'[30] Further, before torture could be used the judge was expected to verify that a crime had occurred in the first place, but Langbein notes that if 'it had been rigorously enforced, the European witch craze could not have claimed its countless victims'.[31] Indeed, torture was not always limited to securing a confession prior to conviction. In several countries it was also permitted after conviction.[32] Langbein suggests that this system of regulation may have led to its use in other contexts: '[the] system of torture incident to the Roman-canon statutory proofs did not prevent, and indeed probably helped inspire, some other uses of torture.'[33]

In contrast to the position in Continental Europe, Langbein and others[34] have examined the use of torture warrants under English law. Langbein examined 81 torture warrants issued either by the monarch or Privy Council between 1540 and 1640.[35] It was easier to gain a conviction under English law than in Continental Europe and this rendered torture largely unnecessary.[36] While there existed 'no established procedural safeguards' torture in England was used in a limited manner.[37] Although he could not be sure that torture was not used in a small number of additional cases, Langbein concluded: '[t]orture in England remained a very exceptional practice of the highest central authorities … Relative to the thousands of felony investigations each year, the number of torture cases was miniscule.'[38] The Privy Council had a discretionary power to order torture, but did not do so often: '[it] could impose torture without fear of formal legal or constitutional restraints, but it had practical incentives to use torture sparingly [as it] did not want to frighten or alienate any sector of the political community needlessly.'[39] This finding appears counter-intuitive. The Privy Council operated without formal restraint at a time of national crises. Langbein's notes that during this period there was the English Reformation along with the 'growth of Spanish power [which] induced a sense of extreme national peril about domestic plots and foreign intrigue'.[40] Yet, even at a time of crisis it would appear that torture was used on a limited basis and is a rejection of the slippage thesis.[41] The limited use of torture appears to have resulted from the centralisation of the torture power and the fact that authority to authorise torture had not been delegated.[42] However, there is another aspect to Langbein's analysis that may support an SSA. First, while most torture warrants were issued for crimes such as sedition and treason; warrants were also issued for murder, robbery, counterfeiting and theft.[43] While Dershowitz notes that torture was used under English law to save lives, this is misleading because it was clearly used for other reasons, too.[44] Further, mistakes were made. Torture was used on some individuals who were innocent of wrongdoing.[45]

This analysis illustrates some of the ways in which a regulatory regime can be subject to slippage. This early evidence mirrors more recent examples of slippage in the use of interrogational torture. It should be noted that the English use of torture is also a rare instance of torture being used in a limited and largely controlled manner. In the next section the issue of regulation will be further examined through analysis of two regulatory regimes.

a. Bagaric and Clarke's torture variables

Bagaric and Clarke argue that torture can be morally and legally justified in order to avert a 'grave risk'[46] with the aim of 'inflict[ing] the minimum degree of harm necessary to obtain the relevant information' to prevent terrorist attacks.[47] To assist in the decision-making process they identify five variables which they argue are 'relevant in determining whether torture is permissible and the degree of torture that is appropriate'.[48] These variables would be given a numerical value and then an equation used to determine whether the situation passes a certain 'threshold level' that would allow for the use of interrogational torture.[49] The five variables are:

> (1) the number of lives at risk; (2) the immediacy of the harm; (3) the availability of other means to acquire the information; (4) the level of wrongdoing of the agent; and (5) the likelihood that the agent actually does possess the relevant information. Where (1), (2), (4) and (5) rate highly and (3) is low, all forms of harm may be inflicted on the agent – even if this results in death.[50]

These variables suggest a set of standards as opposed to rules. Standards differ from rules in the 'extent to which efforts to give content to the law are undertaken before or after individuals act'.[51] Rules set out permissible conduct in advance and allow decision-makers to determine questions of fact, while standards are more vague and give greater discretion to decision-makers in terms of prohibited conduct and when to invoke the powers available to them.[52] Standards therefore have the characteristic of giving the decision-maker a wider degree of discretion to act in light of unpredictable situations, thus avoiding the 'rigidity' of rules.[53] In the context of Northern Ireland, a majority of the Parker Committee in 1972 made a similar recommendation when they favoured 'guidelines as opposed to rules because we recognise that it may sometimes be impracticable to comply fully with them'.[54] Bagaric and Clarke's variables are so vague that they provide only limited guidance to decision-makers and may result in inconsistent decisions. This is because the 'linguistic impression' of vaguely-worded variables 'increases the slippery slope risk'.[55] Vague wording ('availability of other means', 'likelihood', and 'level of wrongdoing') may increase the possibility that extraneous factors (such as fear or animosity), will influence decision-making. Although it should be acknowledged that these factors could influence decision-making under any regulatory regime. Legal standards may involve state officials spending precious time and effort endeavouring to understand the meaning of words and phrases at a point when time is extremely limited.[56] Further, it is inevitable that a torture law would be the subject of litigation, as any statutory language is likely to give rise to competing interpretations.[57] This may lead to further delay or uncertainty.

It has been suggested that vaguely worded standards may encourage greater deliberation by decision-makers.[58] This can only occur where there is time for such deliberation. Further, in circumstances of stress and urgency it is likely that standards would be interpreted in an inconsistent manner by different decision-makers. Further, vaguely worded standards may lack clarity in terms of the consequences of wrongdoing. Such uncertainty may discourage action, lead to recklessness[59] or hinder accountability. By contrast, a rule-based approach may deter a decision-maker from making a decision that could have beneficial results. However, rules also possess important strengths. They may force greater and more careful consideration by decision-makers which may reduce the likelihood of error,[60] but may also be a cause of delay.

Other problems are also apparent. These are best illustrated by reference to one of the ticking bomb hypotheticals Bagaric and Clarke posit in their work. In summary, they make reference to a situation in which a terrorist group has 'activated' a bomb on an unknown plane carrying a least 300 people. The group announces that the bomb will detonate in 30 minutes but disclose no further details. The authorities immediately capture the terrorist group leader who has been under surveillance. He refuses to disclose the location of the bomb.[61] Bagaric and Clarke suggest that torture is an appropriate means of extracting the information required.[62] This hypothetical, however, illustrates that the variables suggested by Bagaric and Clarke are inadequate in that one must also consider an additional variable. Would the information disclosed actually prevent the terrorist attack? In their hypothetical, even if the terrorist leader immediately disclosed the information required, how would the authorities be able to act within 30 minutes to land the plane, remove the passengers or even confirm that the bomb was on *that* particular plane? The time frame is so short that it is unlikely that torture would lead to any beneficial result. Any misleading or false information supplied by the terrorist leader is likely to make any further torture pointless.

Many of the facts that require interpretation as part of Bagaric and Clarke's variables are going to be incomplete or uncertain. Indeed, Gill and Phythian have noted that decision-makers sometimes have 'unrealistic expectations of what [intelligence] can deliver'.[63] To assist in such a decision-making process, Bagaric and Clarke propose that torture should only be used where the 'application of the variables exceeds a threshold level'.[64] This threshold level appears to serve two purposes. The first is to provide a trigger which permits the use of torture. Second, it determines the type of torture to be used: 'the higher the [numerical value] the more severe the forms of torture that are permissible'.[65] This approach is problematic. It suggests a mechanistic relationship between torture and intelligence disclosures – the more severe the torture; the more likely truth will be produced. The problem, of course, is that there is simply no reliable evidence that the more severe the torture the more likely it will produce results.[66] Indeed, it might produce results, but not necessarily truthful or fully accurate disclosures.[67] Further, Bagaric and Clarke argue that: '[t]here is no bright line that can be drawn concerning the point at which the "torture threshold" should be set' and recognise that this creates a significant degree of imprecision.[68] In earlier work they note that '[m]ore precision can, however, be obtained by first ascribing unit ranges to each of the … variables (depending on their relative importance), then applying the formula to a range of hypothetical situations, and then making a judgment about the numerical point at which torture is acceptable'.[69] There is a danger however, that the use of numerical values does little more than mask a series of subjective and impressionistic judgements. To inflict torture on the basis of such judgements creates a serious risk of slippage.

Even if one accepts that it is possible to craft variables with a greater degree of precision these variables are heavily reliant on the evidence being considered by decision-makers which cannot be assumed to be complete or accurate in all cases.[70] Further, the problem of the politicisation of intelligence and the failure to ask tough questions about its reliability or completeness is recognised.[71] Given the international nature of the terrorist threat it might be that authorities are alerted to an alleged threat by foreign intelligence services, including those that use torture.[72] This intelligence might be unreliable but there would be little time for proper evaluation. Bagaric and Clarke do not explain how a numerical value can be given to something when the reliability of evidence cannot be properly assessed. There might be cases where the reliability issue is straightforward but the challenge to regulation involves hard cases where there is information, from whatever, source, where reliability cannot be assessed. These problems raise serious doubts about Bagaric and Clarke's assertion that the pointed nature of their variables would lead to the conclusion that 'there is no basis for believing that torture will be sanctioned in inappropriate circumstances'.[73]

b. A rule-based approach to regulation

In contrast to Bagaric and Clarke's torture variables, this section will consider whether a narrower, rule-based approach would result in a more tightly controlled torture power. This is *not* a legal reform proposal, it is a means by which to test the slippage argument made in this chapter. This rule-based approach will be critically examined in order to illustrate some of the interpretative difficulties associated with such a law.

Section 1

(1) A judicial warrant authorising the use of torture will be granted in the following circumstances:

(a) There is proof beyond a reasonable doubt that the detained person is participating in a terrorist plot and possesses knowledge of an imminent act of terrorism and this knowledge would be sufficient to prevent that imminent attack, and

(b) the act of terrorism will pose a substantial risk of harm to human life or property, and

(c) at the time of the warrant application the detained person is 18 years or older.

(2) Imminent refers to an act of terrorism which will take place within 48 hours of the arrest of the detainee.

(3) The use of torture will be permitted for a maximum of sixty minutes from when the torture is first applied. Once torture is first applied, the sixty minutes will run continuously and cannot be divided into shorter time periods.

(4) Warrants will only be granted on one occasion per detainee. No further warrants will be issued under any circumstances for a detained person who has been the subject of a previous warrant.

There are a number of observations that can be made about the wording. This language sets out the *core* of the torture power. In reality, however, any functioning torture law would require the drafting of a detailed set of provisions. These provisions may not all be contained in statute and might be found within internal agency guidelines[74] which may run the risk of inhibiting transparency.[75] Further, many matters have been omitted[76] including, legal representation of the suspect(s), costs of representation, medical supervision of the interrogation[77] and psychological evaluation of the suspect;[78] appointment of judges; number and seniority of judges who would authorise a warrant; a detailed definition of terrorism;[79] compensation arrangements for those tortured who were, in fact, innocent of wrongdoing; training and other measures designed to prevent the well-recognised harms suffered by interrogators[80] and provisions for the unauthorised use of interrogational torture.[81] This draft statute would also require a unilateral abrogation from Article 3 ECHR and the judiciary to forego any consideration of Article 3 under its interpretative obligations in the Human Rights Act 1998.[82]

There are a number of other issues that also require attention. The draft statute does not list any permissible torture technique(s). While some scholars have suggested the use of a certain specific technique such as a 'sterilized needle shoved under the fingernails',[83] there is no scientific basis upon which to judge the effectiveness of any specific technique or combination of techniques. Posner and Vermeule suggest that a 'good rule would limit agents to the minimum amount of coercion that is necessary'.[84] As with Bagaric and Clarke's proposal this suggests a mechanistic relationship between the intensity of torture and truth. The question of identifying the *type* of torture that would produce the best results is an issue that must be considered in determining the desirability of regulating torture. As noted in Chapter 3, this is a complex question and there are many uncertainties. There is also the question of when torture would cease. Suppose that a suspect disclosures the location of a bomb within the first few minutes of interrogation. Should torture cease? Clearly such a disclosure will have to be investigated, but what if the suspect is lying? Brecher makes the point that this dilemma could lead to continuing the torture 'just in case' and he asks 'if that is justified here, why not elsewhere?'.[85] This is a particular problem in light of the fact that suspects may lie to stop torture.[86] The problem for interrogators is that they simply will not know if the disclosure is reliable until it is checked out. The draft statute could impose a prohibition on any torture once a disclosure has been made, but this leaves a significant margin for discretion on the part of state officials. What would count as a disclosure? Further, in such time-limited circumstances state officials would be particularly vulnerable to the disclosure of inaccurate information.

The statute applies to those aged 18 years and over. Restricting the use of torture on the grounds of age is itself problematic as it undermines the consequentialist goals of legalisation. Consequentialist reasoning leads some proponents of torture to favour its use against children,[87] while others, such as Dershowitz, insist on some limits otherwise 'we risk hurtling down a slippery slope into the abyss of amorality and ultimately tyranny'.[88] It may be that under the logic of consequentialism Dershowitz concedes too much. The reason is that if the minimum age of a person subject to torture is too high then it fails to acknowledge the nature of the current terrorist threat. For example, in the context of jihadist inspired terrorism, teenagers are often targeted for indoctrination and research examining the age of European jihadists at the time of arrest found that some were as young as 16 and 17.[89] The proponents of legalisation often make reference to the way in which the law regulates the use of lethal force by police officers and suggest torture should be similarly regulated.[90] However, this has implications for the case for legalisation. In the United States of America, for example, police officers regularly use lethal force against children who are deemed to possess weapons.[91] If the regulation of police use of lethal force is a template for controlling the power to torture, then proponents such as Dershowitz need to fully explain why children should not be tortured. If, of course, torturing a child is so different from shooting a child that the law should treat each differently, then this raises the question as to why the use of lethal force is offered as an example of regulation in the first place.

One of the most obvious criticisms of this draft statute is that it contains so many procedural safeguards that it would be difficult to invoke. It reflects what Posner and Vermeule refer to when they accuse 'liberal legalists' of being 'addicted to process' and tend to 'ignore or to underestimate the costs of process'.[92] The requirement that the detained person possess information concerning an imminent attack specifically narrows the scope of the statute to cover ticking bomb intelligence. Likewise, the requirement that the information would be enough to prevent the terrorist attack has the potential of making the law unworkable. How could authorities prove that information they did not possess would be sufficient to prevent an attack? Indeed, how could they prove beyond a reasonable doubt that a detainee knew the exact information required? While the standard of proof could be reduced, in reality, any torture law that required state officials to satisfy a particular standard of proof would face difficulties, unless the standard was reduced to such an extent that it became largely meaningless.

A similar difficulty exists in establishing whether the specific information that is being sought from a detainee will actually prevent a terrorist attack. A terror cell member may admit that he knows a bomb has been planted in London, but may claim that he does not know precisely where the bomb is located. It is not difficult to imagine that his initial admission might be enough to satisfy a court beyond a reasonable doubt that he is withholding intelligence that would assist in preventing the attack. If he makes no admissions at all then state officials might be seen to be making a much more speculative application for judicial authorisation. However, would cell membership be enough to justify torture? This may depend on the standard of proof applied and may satisfy the variables set out by Bagaric and Clarke. Indeed, based on consequentialist reasoning it could be argued that information that might indirectly lead to the location of the bomb, for example, the identity of other cell members, would have utility. In this way we start to see a drift from ticking bomb intelligence to infrastructure intelligence.

There is an important distinction to be made between the *knowledge* that a suspect knows the location of a bomb and a *belief* that they know or could know. It cannot be assumed that terrorist group leaders or cell member possesses sought-after intelligence given that many terrorist groups compartmentalise knowledge precisely to frustrate counter-terrorism measures.[93] Under the draft statute the torture of senior al Qaeda figures such as Khalid Sheikh Mohammed would not be justified. While Mohammed was a leading member of a terrorist network and linked to various attacks, including 9/11, there appears to no credible evidence he possessed knowledge of imminent attacks.[94] If he were to be tortured it would have to be based on an *assumption* of knowledge of imminent attacks. Indeed, the CIA-OIG report noted that the CIA 'had very little hard knowledge' of what al Qaeda's leaders might know, so this led to CIA 'analysts to speculate about what a detainee "should know" … ' and if they failed to answer a questions then the 'assumption … was that the detainee was holding back' and EITs were used.[95] In section 1(2) imminence is defined as involving an attack due to take place within 48 hours of the detainee's arrest. The requirement that there be evidence of an imminent attack would preclude the use of torture merely as a means of gaining a confession.[96] If applied, this would avoid the type of slippage seen in other jurisdictions that interpret imminence widely and allow for the use of torture and coercion in infrastructure intelligence-type cases.[97] However, there might be attempts by police officers to circumvent this rule by delaying arrest and making clear that a torture warrant will be sought as a way of attempting to coerce compliance.[98]

Section 1(3) is an attempt to prevent state officials circumventing the one hour window by splitting it into shorter periods of time or finding additional wrong-doing upon which to justify further torture. There is evidence in the historical literature of interrogators doing exactly this to avoid limitations placed upon them. In her study of witch hunting in Germany in the sixteenth and seventeenth centuries, Roper cites Jesuit Friedrich Spee's *Cautio criminalis*, published in 1631. Here, Spee, who heard the pleas of innocence of condemned witches, 'describes the ways in which hangmen got around the system – since an hour's torture is permitted, they divide the hour into two or three parts and stretch it over several days; or they evade restrictions on repeated torture by arguing that since more than one offence has be committed, the accused can be tortured again on a different point'.[99] There is another potential problem with this section – it may increase the severity of torture as the end of sixty minutes nears. With no means of applying for another warrant (section 1(4)), interrogators may be left to use increasingly horrific acts to secure intelligence, whether true or false. This might be avoided if a specific technique were listed in the statute, but given that the statute ultimately allows for the use of torture, this is hardly limiting. If section 1(3) and the other provisions were interpreted narrowly then the torture power would be unlikely to be used except in astonishingly rare circumstances. However, this observation fails to take account of the various mechanisms by which slippage can occur in the interpretation and enforcement of rules. It is to this issue that the rest of the chapter will now turn.

2. When consequences matter: slippery slopes and unintended consequences

Objections to legal change are often expressed through the use of rachet,[100] floodgates, wedge[101] and slippery slope arguments which suggest that a policy or legal reform will likely lead to a series of undesirable or unintended consequences.[102] SSAs are normally described as involving a series of incremental or 'small analogous' steps from a starting point (A) which then lead to the bottom of the slope (B) and are so objectionable that the law or policy represented by (A) should be opposed.[103] Thus, in many instances, the proponents of an SSA will object to (A), (B) and every incremental step in between.[104] Slippery slope arguments are a 'staple of debates about topics from free speech and privacy to church-state relations, gun control and euthanasia'.[105] Indeed, such arguments are so common that Lode observes that they are used in an 'amazing array' of debates[106] and Schauer notes that the 'slippery slope metaphor pervades legal argument'.[107]

There is also another version of an SSA which is less a slippery slope and more akin to jumping off a cliff[108] and is sometimes referred to as a 'one step slippery slope'.[109] Similar to an SSA, there is a starting point (A) and end point (B), but there are no incremental steps between (A) and (B).[110] This form of slippage will be termed 'Acute Slippage' (hereafter AS). In the context of interrogational torture, AS would exist where, for example, the police arrest a terrorist suspect, gain authorisation to use torture and afterwards it becomes apparent that the suspect is in fact, innocent of all wrongdoing and possesses no intelligence of value. Such an instance of mistaken identity would be a classic instance of AS. This is to be contrasted with the incremental steps that take place in a classic slippery slope. While these two forms of slippage are distinct, the mechanisms by which they come about may be very similar; involving errors, misjudgements, distorted reasoning or psychological processes that contributes to the slide or fall from (A) to (B).

One of the main reasons for the commonality of SSAs in legal debate is that it is *always* possible to find potential negative consequences. As a result, the use of SSAs has not gone unchallenged. SSAs have been criticised for lacking empirical support and therefore being 'very weak',[111] being invoked 'in a less than rigorous manner'[112] and for masking emotional responses to particular reform proposals.[113] As a result, some scholars have suggested that SSAs are best avoided when more convincing arguments are available.[114] Indeed, SSAs can be difficult to prove because they are predictive of what *may* happen in the future if a particular policy or reform is adopted. As such, they are difficult to prove but may be likely enough to require the rejection of the contested policy or law reform. They also require evidential support and an explanation as to how policy or law (A) will lead to (B),[115] including the identification of the 'means through which slippery slopes may actually operate'.[116] The growing literature on this topic has sought to identify the mechanisms that lead to slippage.[117] In the context of interrogational torture, these mechanisms and the empirical evidence on which they rest help to identify potential areas of vulnerability for a regulatory regime. In this way, one can distinguish between credible SSAs and ones that are unduly speculative or extremely unlikely.[118]

It must also be acknowledged that slippage may not result in longer-term consequences that are necessarily negative, or at least no more negative than doing nothing. Spielthenner notes that when discussing slippage in conditions of uncertainty a slope *may* have consequences other than an inevitable slide downwards and may even lead to positive consequences.[119] In the context of interrogational torture the fall off the cliff or 'small analogous' steps that lead from (A) to (B) may have two contradictory outcomes. First, the use of interrogational torture beyond the constraints of a torture law may, in fact, save lives. Second, where slippage and its mechanisms are identified they may lead to the ultimate rejection of interrogational torture as a counter-terrorism strategy. For example, the torture of an innocent person which results in death may cause such a public outcry that a torture law could be seen as too costly and be repealed by legislators.[120]

While some scholars take the view that the dangers of slippage must lead to the rejection of the case for legalisation,[121] this must surely depend on the nature of the slippage claim being made. Opponents of interrogational torture make repeated claims that its use cannot be controlled and thus slippage is not so much a possible consequence of the use of torture but is an inherent characteristic.[122] Amnesty International has argued: 'States that use torture and ill-treatment use it broadly ... We have not found a single state which tortures "only once," or only in a few extreme cases.'[123] Similarly, Shue argues that 'history does not present us with a government that used torture selectively and judiciously' [footnote omitted][124] and 'if anyone knows a case, I would appreciate an e-mail giving its name'.[125] If the legalisation of interrogational torture would be impossible to control[126] or result in a slow, but inevitable slide towards eventual totalitarianism, then such an argument, if proven, would be extremely powerful. The use of 'liberal democratic torture' could never be deemed acceptable if it led to the destruction of institutions and the society it was intended to protect. Though democratic nations are certainly sufficiently resilient to withstand the isolated use of interrogational torture, notions of liberalism and democracy will be compromised.[127] Similarly, if institutionalisation through legal regulation led to the creation of 'evil habits and dispositions'[128] then it might be argued that such a consequence could do serious damage to society generally. Another possible way of invoking an SSA is to suggest that slippage raises the cost of legalising interrogational torture, to a point that is intolerable given the unlikely benefits to be derived from its use.[129] This view acknowledges that slippage is going to take place but is unlikely to destroy democratic institutions. It is this latter view that is preferred by this author as it accords more closely with the available empirical evidence, which will be discussed later in this chapter.

The use of SSAs has been described by Williams as the 'trump card of the traditionalist' who opposes legal reform[130] and are in essence used to bolster a pre-existing objection to a particular law or policy. SSAs, however, also perform an essential function in warning of the negative consequences of reform. This is particularly the case where the state seeks to acquire power to prevent future harm. John Stuart Mill acknowledged that it is 'one of the undisputed functions of government to take precautions against crime before it has been committed', but this power 'is far more likely to be abused, to the prejudice of liberty, than powers to detect and punish' crime.[131] Those who propose the legalisation of interrogational torture reject such warnings. Bagaric and Clarke claim that 'there is no evidence to suggest that the lawful violation of fundamental human interests will necessarily lead to a violation of fundamental rights where the pre-conditions for the activity are clearly delineated and controlled'.[132] Of course, Bagaric and Clarke do not appear concerned that a legal-based system of torture might actually encourage torture rather than reduce it. Further, they claim that SSAs in the context of torture are not evidenced[133] and 'cannot be plucked out of thin air'.[134] Likewise, Posner and Vermeule argue that there is no evidence that the use of torture leads to a 'culture of torture' and the 'purposes for which officials use coercion will expand' to *inter alia* 'extracting confessions from suspects in routine criminal cases'.[135] They appear to define slippage primarily in the context of coercion being used for purposes other than intelligence gathering. This is a very narrow form of slippage and as this chapter develops it will become clear that their assessment of evidence is wide of the mark because they have not fully engaged with the empirical literature concerning slippage as part of a consequentialist analysis.

While the proponents of legalisation overstate their argument regarding the question of slippage, the opponents make striking claims that require careful analysis. In terms of the predictive element of an SSA care must be taken in the evidence that is cited in support of particular propositions. Brecher refers to a host of countries where torture has led to negative consequences.[136] For example, he states: '[b]oth judiciary and politicians (let alone others) in Nazi Germany, in Argentina under military dictatorship, in the ex-Soviet Union – to name but a very few – increasingly sacrificed such of their scruples as remained for "the greater good", as what was once unthinkable came to be normalized.'[137] While the Nazis justified policy on the grounds that it was in the interests of the German people or state, there were many factors that underpinned Nazi policy, including anti-Semitism and a commitment to violent totalitarian rule.[138] Brecher's argument simplistically links utilitarianism with the horrors of Nazi rule. This is like trying to discredit the idea of democratic elections because the Nazis used the electoral process to gain political leverage in Germany prior to seizing power. Matthews also refers to the use of torture by the Argentinian junta in the 1970s, pointing out that the torturers also murdered, raped, robbed and intimidated witnesses and the media. The lesson from this experience, he argues, is that '[t]he nature of torture makes such additional violence inevitable, and history supports the view that it is neither controlled nor controllable'.[139] Perhaps so, but it might well be unwise to refer to the use of torture in a dictatorship and then formulate a general consequentialist theory on this basis.

Likewise, Bufacchi and Arrigo argue that torture leaves deep wounds within societies in which it is used: ' ... in country after country where alleged national security threats have resulted in the torture of domestic enemies – including Algeria, South Africa, Chile, Argentina, Uruguay, El Salvador, Guatemala, Ireland – human rights researchers have shown the failures of various programs of social repair. Part of the difficulty of social repair is the high proportion of innocents who are tortured'[140] (internal citations omitted). This is a problematic assessment because Bufacchi and Arrigo do not acknowledge the array of human rights abuses and other factors that can impact social repair,[141] as well as perceptions of group identity and disadvantage which may perpetuate social division.[142] Their examples provide a simplistic and misleading indication as to the potential consequences of institutionalising interrogational torture which fails to account for why and how torture occurs.[143] Further, they neglect the fact that the use of torture by democracies and dictatorships is fundamentally different. In an interview, Rejali noted that comparisons between the use of torture by the Nazis and its use as part of the CIA's HVD programme are problematic: '[d]emocracies have a history of torture, but there is no way their history is comparable to the history of authoritarian regimes ... Doing those kinds of comparisons isn't helpful because it muddies up the actual historical record.'[144]

The example of Guatemala is instructive. Following the overthrow of the democratically elected government of Jacobo Árbenz in 1954 by a CIA-backed military coup,[145] there followed large-scale human rights violations carried out by state security forces and their allies, which peaked in the early 1980s.[146] Political assassination, torture, genocide, massacres and the use of 'death squads' characterised the behaviour of the Guatemalan state during this period in its war on supposed communists and anyone else opposed to its activities.[147] During this time, there was widespread political repression, no effective rule of law and an attempt by the state to 'provoke terror in the population'.[148] Torture was used as a tool of oppression and terror, but did not cause the Guatemalan state to become oppressive. It was a symptom, not a cause and can only be responsibly examined in light of this wider context.[149] The use of torture in Guatemala, and other non-democratic states, is a poor indicator of what may occur if torture were legalised in a liberal democracy. An attempt to use such inappropriate comparators falls into a class of SSA described by van der Burg, thus, 'the cogency of the argument—insofar as it exists—depends more upon the horror than upon the likelihood'.[150]

There is a further problem with this type of comparative analysis. No two countries respond to crises in identical ways. They have their own legal and political traditions and observance of the rule of law can vary significantly between nation states. Such differences may have a significant impact on the way in which legalised torture is used by the state. In addition, it is important to make distinctions between democracies and dictatorships, not least because dictatorships have a deserved reputation for 'greater violence and cruelty', though it should be acknowledged that democratic states do torture, but in different ways from dictatorships.[151] While we cannot know the exact consequences of the introduction of legalised torture in any democracy it is likely to differ from the consequences of legalisation in a dictatorship. For those unconvinced of the strength of this argument, it is worth considering the following example. Would the introduction of a torture statute in North Korea have the same societal impact as the same statute introduced in the United Kingdom? North Korea, is a country with a record of widespread and 'systematic human rights violations'.[152] The state has no respect for fundamental human rights. It conducts extra-judicial killing, torture and has no independent judiciary or free press, no freedom of speech or association and no organised political opposition or elections.[153] These are all mechanisms that exist in the United Kingdom (however imperfectly) by which state actions may be controlled, abuses highlighted and wrongdoers held to account.[154] It is simply inconceivable that a torture law would be implemented and interpreted similarly in these two nations. Of course, it can be argued that North Korea has no need of a torture statute since it tortures freely. That, however, is not the point. It is simply the case that comparisons require some level of equivalence at the state and institutional level. The tendency of opponents of torture to cite random dictatorships in this regard, is not helpful when it goes beyond the individual experience of torture victims and perpetrators.

3. An empirical-based argument for an SSA in the context of interrogational torture

This section will endeavour to set out the evidence which suggests that legalisation will result in a variety of undesirable consequences and in so doing addresses one of the core objections to SSAs, that is, the claim such arguments are often made without 'necessary compelling evidence'[155] or involve mistaken empirical assessments.[156] This section will develop an SSA that is based on evidence from a range of counter-terrorism campaigns, military conflicts and abuses, and thus sets out an *empirical* SSA.[157] However, it must be acknowledged that in drawing on such a wide body of evidence there is a danger that some of the examples may be significantly different from a situation that would exist under a tightly controlled torture law. Of course, every conflict or counter-terrorism campaign is unique in terms of the use of regulations and prohibitions. The point of this analysis is to show that in various counter-terrorism contexts where there have been limitations imposed on the actions of state officials, there have still been numerous examples of slippage and it is often the same types of slippage and related-mechanisms that are in evidence across conflicts.

a. Identity

In order to operate successfully any legalised system of torture would have to accurately identify those people who possess ticking bomb intelligence. A torture law may appear specific in terms of those it seeks to target, but the reality is more problematic because 'categories that are at the same time selective and distinctive, [are also] broad and vague'.[158] A situation where a person is wrongly identified as possessing ticking bomb intelligence is perhaps the best example of 'acute slippage' (AS) discussed earlier.[159] The historic and contemporary literature suggests that identifying terrorists and, in particular, identifying those who possess knowledge of an *imminent attack* is very problematic. Similar problems abound in other areas of preventive powers such as public order law.[160] There is a crucial difference between state officials *knowing* something based on solid evidence and *believing* something based on conjecture and circumstantial evidence. It is at times of national emergency, of course, where such distinctions can become blurred and indeed, where procedural safeguards, evidence and human rights are offset by the pressures of exigent circumstances and the need to prevent future terrorist outrages. However, as a matter of determining legal policy distinguishing actual terrorists from sympathisers, family members, colleagues or friends is a crucial concern and requires a careful examination of empirical evidence.

Bagaric and Clarke identify five variables that they claim are 'relevant in determining whether torture is permissible'.[161] One of the variables is the 'likelihood' that the detainee possesses the required information. They admit that 'it will be rare that conclusive proof is available that an individual does, in fact, possess the required knowledge [and] potential torturees will not have been through a trial process in which their guilt has been established'.[162] They claim that this is not a 'decisive objection to the use of torture' because trials do 'not seem to be a particularly effective process'.[163] It is worth noting, of course, that Bagaric and Clarke are prepared to allow the use of 'all forms of harm' on an evidential basis that is significantly lower than that required to convict a person for the most minor criminal offence. Their casual dismissal of basic evidentiary requirements raises the likelihood that some, perhaps many, completely innocent people would be caught up within their torture variables. This problem is likely to be exacerbated in circumstances where it is believed that a terrorist attack is imminent. It is evident that where interrogational torture or other coercive methods have been permitted there are pressures to act against individuals without guilt or knowledge being 'patently obvious'.[164] State authorities can and do make serious mistakes, as did the Metropolitan Police in London when they shot dead Jean Charles de Menezes who they wrongly believed to be a terrorist.[165] The problem of identification is made more complex by the tactics adopted by some terrorist groups. For example, Pedahzur notes that in the 1970s, Palestinian groups 'forged alliances' with terrorist groups in

Europe and Japan as '[t]hey knew that these connections would present intelligence organizations with major obstacles in their attempts to foil attacks perpetrated by foreign nationals who did not seem to have anything to do with the Israeli-Palestinian conflict'.[166]

A further difficulty associated with the notion of identity is that the actual object of a belief, such as an imminent terrorist attack, may not *actually* exist irrespective of the knowledge or belief relating to such a plot. This is illustrated by reference to Operation GIRD. In September 2010, the Metropolitan Police arrested six men who worked as street cleaners in the Borough of Westminster under the Terrorism Act 2000.[167] Their arrest was prompted by intelligence they had received which indicated that the men had been overheard discussing a visit by Pope Benedict XVI to London at the time of the arrests. The intelligence source claimed that five of the men were overheard saying *inter alia* that Christians should be killed following a recent incident of Koran burning, that 'whilst the Pope's vehicle was protected, it could be stopped and that even if he survived, those around him would die', and that 'it would be wonderful if the Pope was killed and that there were virgins waiting for them', and 'they could all be working on the day of the Pope's visit'.[168] In addition, a number of new work uniforms had recently been stolen which presumably could have been used by terrorists.[169] Further, it was initially thought that one of the suspects may have been 'arrested and released in connection with the Madrid [train] bombings'[170] and a 'close associate' of one of the suspects was 'believed' to have been arrested and questioned under the Terrorism Act several months earlier.[171] While these suspects were subsequently released without charge, in his review of the actions of the police, the Independent Reviewer of Terrorism Legislation concluded that the police used 'the powers of arrest, search, seizure and detention … appropriately'[172] and the police's suspicions were reasonable.[173]

On its face, this set of circumstances would appear to resemble the ticking bomb-type scenario depicted by the proponents of legalised torture. There was an apparently credible threat which was imminent (the Pope would be travelling the streets of London within a few hours).[174] The police had questioned the suspects and they had denied ever making the statements of which they were accused.[175] If one applies the variables proposed by Bagaric and Clarke discussed earlier it would appear that these suspects would score highly on all five variables (identity, imminence, alternative means, scale of harm, knowledge possession), thus justifying the infliction of 'all harm' in order to gain life-saving intelligence.[176] Further, the rule-based draft statute discussed earlier might also have been applicable given the short amount of time available to make an assessment. It raises the question of whether circumstantial evidence, at a time of urgency, would be seen as providing proof beyond a reasonable doubt, that a plot existed and those detained possessed relevant intelligence. The GIRD investigation illustrates the way in which an entirely unrelated event (theft of work uniforms), a mistaken belief (a supposed link to the Milan bombings) and an alleged conversation created sufficient suspicion to arrest the suspects for involvement in a non-existent plot. There are also implications for the regulatory framework suggested by Posner and Vermeule which they argue could empower the state to torture those who it is 'reasonably certain' possess the requisite knowledge.[177] As noted earlier, the officers in the GIRD investigation acted in good faith and had reasonable suspicion yet the men were not terrorists and there was no plot. This provides an example of how a reasonableness standard could lead to serious error in the use of a torture law based on such a standard.

Evidence linking individuals to terrorist plots can seem very strong, but still be mistaken. The fingerprint of Brandon Mayfield was wrongly believed to have been found on an item linked to the Madrid train bombings in 2004 that killed 191 and injured 1,841 others.[178] Three different experts employed by the FBI concluded that the fingerprint belonged to Mayfield. It was only after this conclusion was challenged by Spanish authorities that the FBI eventually accepted that a mistake had been made.[179] The Mayfield case has resulted in litigation[180] as well as an FBI review of the events that led to him being wrongly identified as the source of the fingerprint.[181] The case is an important reminder that even widely accepted methods of identification can be found wanting in terrorism cases. In circumstances of urgency when state authorities are considering the use of torture there would be no time for such a detailed reconsideration of key evidence.

Even with greater time for analysis mistakes can still be made. In a 2009 interview, former US Vice President Dick Cheney argued that the detainees who remained at Guantánamo Bay were the 'worst of the worst'.[182] Leaving aside the rhetorical flourish it would appear that this claim is inaccurate. People were detained at Guantánamo as a result of a range of factors, including: the selling of supposed 'terrorists' to US forces,[183] along with poor quality assessment of individuals when they were first screened by inexperienced military intelligence officers.[184] Indeed, early internal intelligence assessments at Guantánamo Bay suggested that 59 detainees (nearly 10% of the total number of detainees at the time) did not meet screening criteria and should not have been sent there.[185] A report in the *Los Angeles Times* noted that an operational commander at Guantánamo Bay had gone to Afghanistan and complained 'that too many "Mickey Mouse" detainees were being sent to the already overcrowded facility'.[186] In an interview for CBS news Sergeant Erik Saar, a US Army linguist who worked at Guantánamo for three months, echoed these problems: '[s]ome of them were conscripts who actually were forced to fight for the Taliban … Some of them were individuals who were picked up by the Northern Alliance, and we have no idea why they were there, and we didn't know exactly what their connections were to terrorism.'[187]

The status of the remaining Guantánamo detainees was the subject of an executive order issued by President Barack Obama in 2009 that created a task force empowered to review the status of Guantánamo detainees.[188] The task force's final report indicated that of those detainees reviewed '[r]oughly 10 percent of the detainees … appear to have played a direct role in plotting, executing, or facilitating … attacks [against US targets]'.[189] Another 20% 'played significant organizational roles within al-Qaida or associated terrorist organizations'.[190] Less than 10% were Taliban leaders and those who were involved in the Afghan insurgency.[191]

Most other detainees were 'low level fighters' with some connection to terrorist groups or the Taliban.[192] This is very much in keeping with earlier analysis by scholars[193] and journalists.[194] In addition, a chief of staff to former Secretary of State Colin Powell has stated in a sworn declaration that while senior Bush Administration officials such as Vice President Cheney were declaring all Guantánamo detainees to be terrorists, they knew this was very unlikely.[195] Of course, this example of slippage is in a military context, as are a number of others discussed in this chapter. This may not provide an ideal comparator with state responses to domestic terrorism and how a torture law may operate. However, these examples tend to show that there are consistent trends in the use of interrogational torture across differing agencies and conflicts. This suggests that the mechanisms that lead to slippage are quite strong and difficult to negate.

Much of the media attention given to the events at Abu Ghraib prison have concerned prisoner abuse, but there is also significant evidence of slippage in terms of the identity of those who were detained.[196] Interviews with some of those who worked at the prison suggests that there was little evidence to link a significant number of those detained at the prison with involvement in the Iraq insurgency. There were detainees who were described by one captain in the US army as '"low-value detainees" who had been picked up for petty offences'.[197] Some of those detained were referred to as 'fifty meter detainees' because 'they had been in the general vicinity of the target of a US raid and had been picked up essentially for being in close proximity.'[198] An officer commented on the 'overpopulation' of the prison and the 'mission creep from *bona fide* security detainees to others who probably really didn't need to be detained for a long period'.[199] While the prison did have a procedure to review the continued detention of inmates, the procedure was limited and subject to a pressure to not release a prisoner who may have turned out to possess actionable intelligence. A captain noted: 'People were on edge and under pressure.'[200] General Janice Karpinski has claimed that when she sat on the prison review board she rarely saw strong evidence that a detainee was linked to the insurgency: 'Military intelligence called the shots, and nobody wanted to find out later that a terrorist had been set free.'[201] Similarly, Colonel Marc Warren described the intelligence in detainee files as 'thin': 'We did not want to take a chance based on what we didn't know. Unfortunately, we didn't know much from an intelligence standpoint.'[202] In a Human Rights Watch report concerning abuse of Iraqi detainees, a sergeant recounted: 'We were told by [military intelligence] that these guys were bad, but they could be wrong, sometimes they were wrong.'[203]

This problem of misidentification has also been acknowledged in the Israeli experience of torture and other forms of coercion. In a newspaper interview cited by the Public Committee Against Torture in Israel, a GSS interrogator admitted: 'To say that [shaking and beating] always succeeds? – it doesn't. I also had a case when we thought mistakenly that someone was a bomb [sic], and only afterwards it became clear that he was an activist, but not related to that specific terrorist attack.'[204] Further, it has been claimed by the Israeli human rights group B'Tselem that coercive techniques have been used against an increasing range of people and well beyond situations involving ticking bombs as stipulated by the Israeli HCJ:[205]

> In practice, not only was torture not limited to 'persons who planted ticking bombs', it was not even limited to persons suspected of membership in terrorist organizations, or to persons suspected of criminal offenses. The GSS regularly tortured political activists of Islamic movements, students suspected of being pro-Islamic, religious sages, sheiks and religious leaders, and persons active in Islamic charitable organizations, the brothers and other relatives of persons listed as 'wanted' (in an attempt to obtain information about them), and Palestinians in professions liable to be involved in preparing explosives – an almost infinite list. In a number of cases, wives of detainees were arrested during their husbands' detention, and the interrogators even ill-treated them to further pressure their husbands. Also, GSS agents used torture to recruit collaborators.[206]

In the context of Northern Ireland, collusion between security forces and Loyalist paramilitaries led to the murder of a number of people who were labelled as being in some way involved in Republican terrorism, but were, in fact, innocent.[207] The targeting of these individuals resulted from the flow of 'targeting material' from the security forces to the loyalist paramilitary group the Ulster Defence Association[208] and is further evidence of flawed intelligence held by state authorities, as well as its misuse. Indeed, when internment was introduced in 1971 it was claimed that every person detained was a 'terrorist or a member of the IRA.[209] McGuffin has argued that some of the detainees were 'political opponents of the Unionists' including 'old retired IRA ex-internees, militant trade unionists, pubic speakers, and, in some cases, people held on mistaken identity'.[210] Indeed, as the numbers of detainees grew, fewer terrorists were identified and increasing numbers of detainees were released from custody.[211] Similar identification problems existed in relation to detainees who were brutalised or subject to the five techniques.[212]

The question of identity as a potentially expansive concept is further emphasised by the proposals of some legalisation proponents. For example, Posner and Vermeule have suggested that if the cost of not using interrogational torture is too high then other types of criminals might also be subject to torture.[213] They make specific reference to 'kidnappers with a violent history who have been captured and refuse to disclose the location of the kidnapping victim'.[214] This suggestion is an illustration of the way in which the consequentialist reasoning that applies to torture as a tool of counter-terrorism can become a normalised response to criminal activity in which the police require urgent information and is potentially a 'rational grounds SSA'.[215] That is, because the proponents rely so heavily on consequentialist reasoning it is difficult to find rational grounds on which to argue it is acceptable to torture in terrorism cases, but not in kidnap cases. It is also an example of what van der Burg describes as a logical version of an SSA: 'the justification for A also applies to B, and therefore acceptance of A will logically imply acceptance of B'.[216] In this way, it could be seen as an example of the application of utilitarian reasoning which 'create[s] a precedent with disastrous long-term effects'.[217] Indeed, it is illustrative of the difficulties of ensuring emergency powers are not applied in times of normalcy. By enshrining an exception within the absolute prohibition there are demonstrable risks that the reasoning underpinning the exception will be applied to other (non-terrorism) cases.[218] This reasoning may also have application well *beyond* terrorism and kidnap cases. Thus torture may slip from a means of saving large numbers of lives threatened by weapons of mass destruction and possibly the existence of the state itself to rooting out criminal conduct that is commonplace.[219]

Posner and Vermeule's suggestion could form part of what Volokh describes as an 'enforcement need' slippery slope which leads to the extension of the powers of law enforcement.[220] This might occur where it is argued that law enforcement needs a torture power in order to find kidnap victims and without it innocent people will die. The number of victims in a kidnap case is likely to be less than in a terrorism case. Thus the benefit to be derived is less. However, applying the torture power to a kidnap case, particularly involving a child, may be 'logically and emotionally appealing' to decision-makers.[221] If, as Posner and Vermeule suggest, a convincing case might be made for the use of torture against kidnappers it is likely that arguments can be made to allow for its use in other types of kidnap cases, such as those involving an offender with no previous history of violence. Further, what should the position be if the police arrest someone who is part of an orga-nised gang that has used deadly force in the past and is planning an imminent armed robbery? If the gang members have a history of violent offending and the suspect is unwilling to provide information that may lead to the capture of other members, then the benefit to be derived from torture could be similar or even greater than in cases of kidnap or terrorism.[222] Similarly, a case might also be made for the use of torture to gain confessions. For example, if the police have arrested someone they believe to be a serial killer or serial child abuser, but have insufficient evidence to charge the suspect, then without a confession he would have to be released. If so he may pose a serious threat to the community. As discussed in previous chapters, the logic of consequentialism leads to a case being made for an expansive torture power.

The legalisation of torture would require the professionalisation of torture, with people trained to administer and supervise its use with the attendant dangers associated with institutionalisation and slippage.[223] Indeed, Posner and Vermeule have sug-gested that all police officers be trained to use coercive interrogation, but they note that this risks 'lead[ing] them to use it in routine cases'.[224] As an alternative they suggest, on the assumption that such techniques would be rarely used, that 'it might make sense to have a special squad of officers who are trained in coercive interrogation'.[225] Further, they have also argued that use of coercive techniques would need to be reviewed and be the subject of analysis for the purpose of guiding future practice.[226] In response to this suggestion one should note that if torture is to be used in true emergencies then it would require trained officers to be located throughout the nation. A small cadre of officers travelling vast distances is likely to lead to significant delays. Instead, training might need to be offered to several thousand officers. At this point, one has to acknowledge that any such officer is not an 'independent moral agent'.[227] Instead, they would form part of a torture bureaucracy in which *inter alia* training, supervision, and the creation of professional standards would be required. This, of course, raises further well-known risks as regards the conduct and motives of those inflicting torture within regulated and democratic systems.[228] The normalisation of this torture power would further take the use of torture into regular policing. Scheppele argues that evidence from the War on Terror suggests that 'specialized knowledge' will spread from one context to another.[229] Further, its use is likely to antagonise particular communities and cause a strain between community members and the state[230] and be exploited by terrorist groups to gain support.[231] As noted in Chapter 1, this can lead to a break down in the relationship of trust necessary for the police to gain co-operation and intelligence.

This discussion suggests two things. First, identifying terrorists, including those who may hold critical intelligence, can be deeply problematic. This does not mean the state gets it wrong all the time, but it is still crucial to understand the phenomenon and the mechanisms by which it occurs. Second, as noted in earlier chapters, the consequentialist theory underpinning the case for legalisation is inherently expansive. The suggestion that kidnap suspects could be tortured is clear evidence of the consequentialist-led spread of torture from its proposed use against terrorist suspects. It is simply a logical extension of consequentialist theory. It may also be an example of what Volokh refers to as a 'legal slippery slope': 'the justification underlying A is vague enough that it could justify B ... '[232] The influence of this type of reasoning appears to place interrogational torture as a permanent part of the criminal justice system with potential applicability to an increasing range of criminal offences. One of the consistent criticisms of anti-terrorism laws enacted in response to a particular emergency situation is that they do become a permanent feature of powers available to the state. Thus the power becomes normalised in the sense that the power spreads beyond terrorism cases.[233] Given the focus of consequentialism and its potential application to a range of similar-type cases without an obvious cut-off or limiting principle, slippage appears inevitable. This is further evidenced in a series of counter-terrorism campaigns that will be discussed next.

b. The CIA's High Value Detainee Interrogation programme

In 2009, the Obama Administration released a number of documents pertaining to the Central Intelligence Agency's 'High Value Detainee' interrogational programme (hereafter HVD programme), including memos drafted by the US Department of Justice, Office of Legal Counsel (hereafter OLC).[234] On a surface reading, these memos appear to suggest the existence of a reasonably clear set of rules governing interrogation, with an evaluation of legally appropriate conduct. An initial reaction to the release of the memos suggested that there existed 'tight control' over the HVD programme.[235] Indeed, one OLC memo stressed that the programme involved 'careful screening procedures' and was 'carefully designed to minimize the risk of suffering or injury and avoid inflicting any serious or lasting physical or psychological harm'.[236] The same memo also stated: '[t]he fact that enhanced techniques have been used to date in the interrogations of only 28 high value detainees out of the 94 detainees in CIA custody demonstrates this selectivity.'[237] When analysing the extent to which the HVD programme can be said to have operated in a controlled manner several issues require consideration. The question of control requires an examination of against whom so-called 'Enhanced Interrogation Techniques' (hereafter EITs), including waterboarding, stress positions, cramped confinement and sleep deprivation, could be used. Further, in judging the problem of slippage the relevant interrogation rules, along with their interpretation and implementation in practice must be considered.[238]

First, there is the notion of the 'high value detainee'. It is evident that HVDs were defined quite widely in the sense that the intelligence being sought involved both ticking bomb intelligence (imminent terrorist threats) and infrastructure intelligence (assisting, planning and preparing terrorist actions). The CIA defined an HVD, thus, 'A detainee who, at time of capture, we have reason to believe:

★ is a senior member of al-Qaeda or an al-Qaida associated terrorist group (Jemaah Islamiya, Egyptian Islamic Jihad, al-Zarqawi Group, etc.)

★ has knowledge of imminent terrorist threats against the USA, its military forces, its citizens and organizations, or its allies, or that has/had direct involvement in planning and preparing terrorist actions against the USA or its allies, or assisting the al-Qaeda leadership in planning and preparing such terrorist actions;

★ and if released, constitutes a clear and continuing threat to the USA or its allies.'[239]

The CIA's own evaluation of the results of the HVD programme suggests that it did uncover from senior al Qaeda operatives, as well as lower functionaries, considerable infrastructure intelligence.[240] Thus, it might be argued that EITs were used in a targeted manner. It has been argued that 'it is safe to assume that if someone is being interrogated by the CIA he is actually significant'.[241] This is a dangerous assumption as it is evident that the CIA has mistakenly identified some detainees as terrorists as part of its 'rendition' programme.[242] Evidence of slippage exists in the case of Khalid El-Masri who was mistaken for an al Qaeda terrorist, abducted by the CIA, held in Macedonia and Afghanistan, tortured and then 'dumped' in Albania.[243] During his captivity, El-Masri was the subject of treatment which went well beyond what was legally permitted in the OLC memos. Indeed, the ECtHR determined that he was assaulted, anally penetrated with an object and subject to a number of other abuses.[244]

In a 2004 Special Review of the CIA's interrogation programme, the CIA's Office of Inspector General (hereafter CIA-OIG) found that despite the rules governing the treatment of detainees there were clear rule breaches as well as the use of a range of techniques that had not been authorised.[245] However, one of the problems with assessing the nature and occurrence of rule breaking is that large sections of the report were redacted in almost their entirety.[246] Give the redactions what follows can only be a partial discussion. Similarly, the report's section under the heading of 'unauthorised or undocumented techniques' were also heavily redacted.[247] However, despite these limitations, the report provides important information about the way in which the CIA's interrogation programme operated in practice and raises doubts about the extent to which the programme was carefully limited.

The report noted that concerns about the use of certain techniques and the actions of interrogators were raised by staff working within the CIA's Counter Terrorism Center programme.[248] The CIA-OIG report observed that many allegations of misconduct by interrogators 'were disputed or too ambiguous to reach any authoritative determination regarding the facts'.[249] However, it is clear that at least some of the allegations regarding the use of unauthorised techniques had a factual basis given the CIA-OIG review interviewed CIA personnel who justified the use of such techniques.[250] For example, in relation to one HVD detainee, Abd al-Rahim Al-Nashiri, who was deemed to be withholding intelligence, a debriefer 'used an unloaded semi-automatic handgun as a prop to frighten Al-Nashiri ... [o]n what was probably the same day, the debriefer used a power drill to frighten Al-Nashiri'.[251] The same debriefer, it was alleged, also made comments about Al-Nashiri's family members which could be viewed as threatening. The debriefer denied this specific allegation.[252] Other allegations included claims that smoke was blown into Al-Nashiri's face during interrogation, that he was placed in 'potentially injurious stress positions' and that he was rubbed with a stiff brush 'intended to induce pain' and interrogators stood on his shackles which 'resulted in cuts and bruises'.[253] The CIA-OIG report also reported that interrogators told Khalid Sheikh Mohammed that if there were further attacks on American soil that '[w]e're going to kill your children'.[254] Given the report's redactions it is unclear whether this rule breaking was part of a wider pattern of incremental abuses. However, whether or not these abuses amount to the acute version of slippage is not important, they clearly form part of an empirical SSA. The allegations are further bolstered by the report's reference to numerous unauthorised techniques, including the use of a pressure point techniques intended to 'restrict the detainee's carotid artery',[255] mock executions[256] and the use of what was termed the 'hard takedown', which appears to have been used to intimidate detainees and resulted in detainee injury.[257] A heavily redacted section referred to detainee treatment at other facilities, including a 'severe beating' leading to the death of one detainee and the beating of another.[258]

Another area of potential slippage related to the use of waterboarding. A 2002 OLC memo declared that waterboarding 'constitutes a threat of imminent death'[259] but did not constitute a breach of the legal prohibition on torture because its effects did not cross the torture threshold as defined by the OLC lawyers.[260] This judgement was based on a particular set of assumptions derived from statements made by the CIA concerning the use of the waterboard.[261] Further, one memo was informed by a view that 'repetition will not be substantial' because the techniques lose their effectiveness over time.[262] Yet this does not accord with the actual use of waterboarding. Khalid Sheikh Mohammed was waterboarded 183 times[263] and Abu Zubaydah 'at least' 83 times,[264] which does raise concerns regarding the risk of mental harm and how the use of the waterboard could be said to have been used on a 'limited' basis. It is also worth noting the view of Gardner Peckham, who co-authored an internal CIA review of the HVD programme, when he referred to the detainee's understanding that 'this was not going to stop, ever, unless they cooperated'.[265] However, the CIA-OIG report reported that the 'Attorney General acknowledged he is fully aware of the repetitive use of the waterboard and that the CIA is well within the scope of the DoJ opinion and the authority given to CIA by that opinion'.[266] This would appear to deprive words of meaning and one wonders what level of repetition would go beyond the scope of the legal opinion.

In 2005, videotapes of CIA interrogations, including the waterboarding of Abu Zubaydah, which are alleged to have shown him 'vomiting and screaming',[267] were destroyed by a senior CIA official.[268] Some of these tapes were examined as part of the CIA-OIG report and 'revealed that the waterboard technique employed at [redacted] was different from the technique as described in the DoJ opinion and used in the SERE training'.[269] In the CIA interrogations, large volumes of water were used to obstruct breathing, in contrast to SERE training and the technique set out in the legal opinions. This was justified by a CIA 'psychologist/interrogator' on the grounds that it is '"for real" and is more poignant and convincing'.[270] This seems a poor explanation for modifying approved methods – after all a victim of waterboarding is being drowned, just how much more real can that be?

Finally, there is evidence that the techniques spread to other locations, in the same way other techniques 'migrated' within the US military from Guantánamo Bay to other areas of conflict.[271] US army personnel have also been accused of 'force feeding water into [a detainee's] mouth, choking him'.[272] Interviews with two former prisoners who were detained by Libyan authorities after being 'rendered' back to Libya by the US prior to the collapse of the Gaddafi regime, have made 'credible'[273] claims that while they were in US custody in Afghanistan, they were repeatedly waterboarded.[274] It has also been claimed that a Senate Intelligence Committee report, which has yet to be released, discusses the CIA's use of a drowning technique against Ammar al-Baluchia, who was held in Kabul, was beaten and had his head 'smash[ed] … against a wall'.[275] This is in direct contradiction to repeated claims made by US officials that the only detainees who were waterboarded in US custody were the three detainees as part of the CIA's HVD programme.[276]

c. Three case studies

Posner and Vermeule argue that democracies have used coercive interrogation techniques 'as temporary measures to deal with a particular emergency—France in Algeria, Britain against the Irish Republican Army—and then abandoning them when the emergency is over'.[277] There is a good reason to question such an assessment not least because both conflicts provide compelling evidence of slippage.

For example, techniques continued to be used by interrogators after they had been officially withdrawn and torture and other illegal interrogation methods were used against innocents and for reasons unconnected to the prevention of acts of terrorism. These findings provide further support for an empirical SSA. This section will proceed by examining the use of torture and other forms of coercion in Algeria, Northern Ireland and Israel.

i. Algeria

In 1957, the use of torture by the French military and police to destroy the terrorist campaign of the Algerian *Front de Libèration Nationale* (FLN)[278] was characterised by several examples of slippage. The use of torture was accompanied by the killing of many detainees by the police and army.[279] It is claimed that murder was used to silence detainees who complained of torture and that '[c]hildren were known to have been murdered because their brothers or fathers had laid a complaint of torture'.[280] McCoy states that 'the systematic French torture of thousands from the Casbah of Algiers in 1957 also entailed over three thousand "summary executions" as "an inseparable part" of this campaign, largely, as one French general put it, to insure that "the machine of justice" not be "clogged with cases" and free terror suspects to launch other attacks'.[281] There are also allegations that some of those who were tortured had no link to terrorism, but were seen as a danger to French rule in Algeria for other reasons. For example, Vidal-Naquet refers to a young woman, Saadia Mebarek, who was arrested and then tortured to death by members of the French army. She had allegedly encouraged Algerians not to take part in local elections.[282] Further, an earlier official French government report by Civil Inspector-General Wuillaume in 1955 (hereafter the Wuillaume Report)[283] suggested other motives for brutality: some people were detained and whipped 'to satisfy some personal grudge'.[284]

The Wuillaume Report listed a range of interrogation techniques that were 'long-established'[285] and 'more or less in general use', including: beatings, holding detainees under water or the use of a hose to force water into the mouth with hands tied and nose blocked, use of electricity applied via needles to the body, being forced to stand for extended periods, being strung up by the arms and having feet burnt by a torch.[286] The report suggested that the techniques were targeted: 'the methods used are old-established; in normal times they are only employed on persons against whom there is considerable weight of evidence of guilt and for whom there are therefore no great feelings of pity.'[287] The problem with this assertion is that it is contradicted by another passage in the report: 'arrests were very numerous and were frequently made without due consideration; as a result a considerable proportion of those arrested were able to proclaim their innocence, either because no charge against them could be proved or because they were in fact innocent.'[288] Further, the techniques were not necessarily used in a controlled manner. Wuillaume made reference to 'amateur police' such as the reservist gendarmes, 'who were unable to distinguish between brutality and true police methods'.[289] This report provides crucial evidence in support of an empirical SSA.

In addition to the stronger slippage claims, the use of torture by the French has also been the subject of two other claims that fail for lack of empirical support. First, it is claimed that techniques used in Algeria appear to have spread to France itself, with police officers in France shooting, beating and drowning Algerians who took part in peaceful demonstrations.[290] At this point it should be acknowledged that if the use of torture in Algeria is to be linked to the abuse of Algerians in France, a causal link between the two must be explained. While historians such as Horne have referred to specific torture techniques spreading from Algeria to France, we do not know how this occurred.[291] If it did occur, perhaps it did so in a similar fashion to the 'migration' of techniques within the US military discussed elsewhere in this chapter.[292] However, the French police already engaged in abuse directed at minorities who lived in France.[293] This may provide an alternative explanation for such practices. The second slippage claim that is open to doubt has been made by Kassimeris who claims: 'Numerous recent studies on the Algerian war show that French violence in Algeria was designed to terrify, subdue and exhibit power rather than to extract information.'[294] If true, then this is slippage in terms of the motives behind the use of torture. There can be little doubt that the French used brutal methods in suppressing terrorist violence. However, from one of the sources that Kassimeris cites, it is clear that torture was used for the purpose of intelligence gathering. When discussing the so-called 'Battle of Algiers', Wall states: ' … the elite paratroops under General Massu, who entered the Casbah, routinely applied torture in order to break the terrorist infrastructure … '[295] This is supported by other scholars[296] and the testimony of some victims of the French use of torture.[297] In his memoir detailing his month-long detention and torture by French authorities in Algeria, Henri Alleg makes clear that in detaining and subjecting him to horrific acts of torture – his captors were seeking information about his activities and associates.[298]

ii. Northern Ireland

The background to the use of the 'five techniques'[299] by state authorities in Northern Ireland in the early 1970s was discussed in Chapter 3. However, it is important to understand these techniques from the point of view of an empirical SSA. The use of the 'five techniques' formed part of a history of repressive practices in the Province[300] and drew upon the use of similar techniques during colonial rule in countries such as Kenya,[301] India[302] and following the end of the Second World War.[303] They were used against detainees who were believed to have links to the IRA.[304] Newbery has analysed UK government documents concerning the 'five techniques' and notes that there was a wish to depict three of the techniques (hooding, wall standing and noise) as security measures used to prevent communication between detainees and protect interrogators.[305] It is also clear, however, that these techniques were also used to 'soften up' detainees for interrogation.[306]

These interrogations were governed by the *Joint Directive on Military Interrogation in Internal Security Operations Overseas*, 17 February 1965 (as amended 10 February

1967)[307] which prohibited physical coercion, torture, along with humiliating and degrading treatment. The Directive impliedly endorsed sleep deprivation when it made reference to continuous interrogation lasting day and night and involving 'disruption of the normal routine of living'. It did not specifically prohibit any of the five techniques.[308] During the 1970s many allegations were made of mistreatment by the armed forces and during interrogations carried out by the Royal Ulster Constabulary. A subsequent inquiry chaired by Sir Edmund Compton concluded that many of these allegations of brutality could not be substantiated.[309] However, this report was very limited in that it only involved investigation of abuse on *one* single day[310] and can be viewed as flawed on a number of other grounds.[311] In March 1972, Prime Minister Edward Heath announced to Parliament that the techniques had been withdrawn.[312] However, there is compelling evidence that the use of physical coercion and brutality, as well as the use of techniques such as sleep deprivation, continued.[313] The continued use of some of the five techniques and other coercion was confirmed by the findings of an Amnesty International Mission to Northern Ireland[314] and recent interviews with former interrogators.[315] In his study of interrogations in Northern Ireland, Taylor notes that the police and army were subject to rules on the conduct of interrogations, but '[t]hey made little difference'.[316] Further, recent evidence suggests that the army may have also used water boarding against certain terror suspects, which further emphasises the way in which interrogations departed from formal restrictions.[317]

The significance of these findings is not that they are based solely on the allegations of detainees, whom, it must be acknowledged, at times gave entirely false or exaggerated accounts of brutal treatment.[318] The compelling evidence comes from doctors in the interrogation centres who examined the detainees.[319] This medical evidence strongly suggests that some detainees were beaten with fists, burnt with cigarettes, slapped and choked. They suffered a range of injuries including, cuts, bruising, broken bones, perforated eardrums and concussion.[320] These allegations are supported by the Bennett Committee which reported some injuries suffered by detainees 'were not self-inflicted and were sustained during the period of detention at a police office'.[321] Recently, crucial corroboration for allegations of brutality is provided by interviews conducted by journalist Ian Cobain with some of those who interrogated terrorist suspects in the 1970s. In these interviews, former interrogators admitted *inter alia* using torture, developing 'specialities' involving the twisting of limbs and punching detainees in such a way as to leave few marks of violence.[322] Cobain argues that the beating of detainees was used in a 'random, even haphazard' manner to gain intelligence and developed in order to gain confessions and 'ensure that they were convicted of serious criminal offences'.[323]

iii. Israel

There is clear evidence that Israeli security forces have used torture and other forms of coercion against Palestinian detainees. This evidence also suggests that the existence of rules has not necessarily prevented abuse. An internal Israeli government report in 2000 acknowledged that between 1988 and 1992 the Israeli internal security service Shin Bet (also known as the General Security Service (GSS)) engaged in 'grave and systematic' violations of rules that permitted the use of 'moderate physical pressure' against detainees.[324] In 1999, the Israeli High Court of Justice (hereafter *PCATI* decision) held that the GSS did not have lawful authority to use techniques such as shaking detainees or the use of stress positions. It did decide however that the defence of necessity might be available where such techniques are used in cases involving ticking bombs where 'there exists a concrete level of imminent danger of the explosion's occurrence'.[325] The *PCATI* decision states that the Israeli Attorney General can 'instruct himself regarding the circumstances in which investigators shall not stand trial, if they claim they acted from a feeling of "necessity"'.[326] The use of language here is revealing. As noted in Chapter 2, the court defined an imminent need to act as involving attacks that may take place within days or even weeks.[327] The reference to 'instruct himself' provides the Attorney General with a broad discretion and the use of the word 'feeling' in the context of necessity introduces language that is so vague that it is inappropriate for a regulatory framework.

The *PCATI* decision was made within the context of a pre-existing situation in which the use of coercion and torture was widespread and institutionalised.[328] Following the decision it appears that GSS interrogations have suffered from several different forms of slippage. In its report on the treatment of detainees between September 2001 and April 2003 the Public Committee Against Torture in Israel noted a 'rapid deterioration in the ethics of GSS interrogations'.[329] In a report it stated:

> The achievements of the HCJ ruling of 1999 have been ground to dust. The HCJ's attempt to allow torture 'only' in extreme conditions as the improvisation of an interrogator in an 'isolated case' that can be recognized as legal 'only' retroactively, has failed completely. Today, dozens and maybe hundreds of Palestinian detainees are tortured monthly, with torture and ill treatment being the rule, and what the HCJ termed 'reasonable interrogation' being the exception.[330]

There is evidence that coercion has not only been used to gain ticking bomb intelligence, but also to gain confessions, which, of course, do not in themselves prevent imminent terrorist attacks.[331] This appears to mirror the experience of other jurisdictions where coercion has been used in order to secure confessions.[332] Indeed, it has been noted that the Israeli military court system relies heavily on confession evidence as a means of gaining convictions.[333] It is also reported that detainee relatives are used as a means of coercing confessions or intelligence from detainees.[334] In 2011, a West Bank military tribunal acquitted a defendant because 'harsh and problematic measures', including threats directed at relatives, were used to gain a confession.[335] More recently, a West Bank military tribunal censured the GSS for using this technique to coerce a confession from a detainee.[336]

Another form of slippage relates to the use of prohibited techniques and their use in the context of criminal behaviour that falls short of a ticking bomb situation.

In a report concerning the treatment of children arrested for stone throwing by the Israeli authorities, B'Tselem detailed allegations that they were subject to sleep deprivation, threats and even violence.[337] Sleep deprivation is a technique to which the court in *PCATI* referred, thus: 'If the suspect is intentionally deprived of sleep for a prolonged period of time, for the purpose of tiring him out or "breaking" him, it is not part of the scope of a fair and reasonable investigation. Such means harm the rights and dignity of the suspect in a manner beyond what is necessary.'[338] The use of threats, violence, the use of painful stress positions have also been regularly reported in detainee testimony.[339] This suggests that torture and other abuses are institutionalised within the Israeli state response to terrorism and are not limited to cases involving 'ticking time bombs'. Criminal investigations into the conduct of GSS interrogators are reported to be extremely rare which may help to explain some of the examples of slippage discussed here.[340] This is contrary to a reported trend elsewhere within the Israeli state in which the Supreme Court has shown increasing willingness in recent years to review the actions of Israeli military commanders in the Occupied Territories.[341]

The HVD programme and case studies discussed in this section provides important evidence in support of an empirical SSA. It also illustrates the many different types of slippage that can occur across differing counter-terrorism campaigns, forms of regulation and prohibition. However, this provides only limited evidence of the mechanisms by which slippage can occur. This issue will be dealt with in the next section.

4. Explaining slippage

In order for an empirical SSA to have credibility it is important that the mechanisms (or causes) that lead to slippage are understood. This will assist in explaining the difficulties in regulating interrogational torture and offers a direct refutation to the proponents of legalisation who claim that there is little or no slippage risk.[342] In addressing this issue it is necessary to consider a wide range of factors including a 'complex array of psychological and social considerations'.[343] It is evident from this analysis that similar to the types of slippage that are in evidence, there are many mechanisms that lead to slippage.

a. Mechanisms

The first mechanism that leads to slippage concerns rules that are drafted with insufficient clarity which may hinder state officials in recognising impermissible conduct. Schauer has noted that slippage can occur where decision-makers fail to fully comprehend the principle being interpreted thereby potentially widening its scope.[344] He goes on to note that slippage may occur because 'future decision makers do not fully comprehend where the line drawn by their predecessors lies'.[345] Clarity in the drafting of rules may help to minimise this cause of slippage in day-to-day decision making. Clear rules may also lessen the possibility of confusion and unintended rule breaking. The problem is illustrated by reference to the CIA's HVD programme. The CIA-OIG report observed that some of the rule breaking in this programme resulted from 'the lack of clear guidance at that time and the Agency's insufficient attention to interrogations'.[346] It also noted that 'no formal mechanisms' existed for ensuring personnel were aware of legal and policy constraints.[347] Further evidence of Schauer's notion of 'limited comprehension'[348] appears in a report that examined interrogations in Iraq, Afghanistan and Guantánamo Bay where it was found that some interrogation techniques continued to be used after they were officially withdrawn:

> some of the techniques approved in the September 2003 memorandum continued even until July 2004, despite the fact that many were retracted by the October 2003 memorandum, and some were prohibited by the May 2004 memorandum. However, the use of the retracted and prohibited techniques was by no means universal. Some units we interviewed ... appeared to have received and strictly interpreted the May 13, 2004 policy. Nevertheless, the relatively widespread use of these techniques supports our finding that the policy documents were not always received or thoroughly understood.[349]

Another mechanism is the impact of group psychology and situational factors. In their famous analysis of interpersonal dynamics in a simulated prison environment (commonly referred to as the 'Stanford Prison Experiment'[350]) Haney and colleagues divided students into prisoners and guards. They found a number of troubling findings which might help to explain the existence of rule breaking and the use of unauthorised techniques in the context of interrogational torture. Despite an 'explicit and categorical prohibition against the use of physical punishment or physical aggression'[351] various forms of 'less direct aggressive behaviour' especially by guards 'were observed frequently',[352] including threats and harassment.[353] Further, the researchers found that harassment of prisoners 'escalated'[354] with guards appearing to enjoy the power and control they had over prisoners.[355] The situational environment, the power held by the guards, lack of control and enjoyment in exercising power appeared to lead to abuses against prisoners. It is worth noting that in the context of the HVD programme concerns regarding the behaviour of the abusive debriefer discussed earlier[356] were actually raised by 'newly arrived' personnel.[357] This may suggest that the newer personnel were not inculcated in a situational culture where rule breaking and a failure to report such conduct was, to some degree, tolerated.

The tolerance of abuse by superiors is another mechanism by which wrongdoing is either hidden or not subject to sanction. In the internal Israeli government report discussed earlier it was observed that: 'Most of the violations were not caused by lack of knowledge of the line between what was permitted and what was forbidden, but were committed knowingly.'[358] In a 2009 report, *PCATI* argued that there existed 'an organizational culture based on the systemic use of torture and abuse, false reports, the elimination of evidence, and failure to accept responsibility.

The organizational culture that permits the torture and abuse of detainees is combined with a culture of concealing the truth, avoiding investigation, and preventing
punishment of those responsible.'[359] This description is particularly relevant in that
many examples of slippage do not involve a single cause. Instead, slippage occurs
and in some instances is sustained through multiple mechanisms. This will pose
particular problems for a regulatory regime that is based on standards and is likely
to challenge a rule-based approach, too.

The multiplicity of mechanisms leading to slippage in specific cases is further
evidenced by reference to Northern Ireland where abuses resulted from lack of
training, ill-discipline, perhaps inflamed by sectarian hatred,[360] encouragement by
superiors,[361] institutional denial that abuses were taking place, obstruction of
investigations,[362] as well as the institutional narrative that coercion produced
results.[363] The use of physical coercion may also have been motivated by a wish to
gain confessions that were admissible in the Northern Ireland courts,[364] including
cases involving child suspects.[365] This led to a number of miscarriages of justice.[366]
Indeed, Conroy has identified nine stages in which the use of coercion in Northern
Ireland was denied, excused or justified.[367] Research on the internal working culture of corporations might also be of relevance in explaining how a particular
culture of coercive interrogation is sustained. It suggests that that the retelling of
particular stories contributes to a shared memory within an organisation.[368] This
institutional memory involves efforts to 'preserve aspects of their past ... and to use
them in the present to influence the future'.[369] In this context, Newbery's reference to 'historical narratives' within government suggesting that torture works[370]
and normal techniques are ineffective is an excellent example of institutional
memory and may have contributed to rule breaking by leading personnel to
believe that abuse was a useful and permissible interrogation method.

The activities of the US military in Afghanistan, Iraq and in Guantánamo Bay[371]
provide further evidence of abuse, torture and the failure of rules to control behaviour.[372] As noted by Human Rights Watch, allegations of abusive conduct against
detainees during interrogation by the US military began in December 2001 and
continued following deaths in custody, including the use of beatings and other
violence, mock executions, sexual assault and humiliation of detainees.[373] A number
of military inquiries have examined allegations of abuse and certain trends are
apparent which may help to explain some of rule breaking.[374] These reasons
include: confusion over rules,[375] non-existent, vague or poorly understood rules,[376]
inadequate training and inspection,[377] failure to enforce rules and punish wrongdoers,[378] failure to report abuse appropriately,[379] failures of leadership[380] and in the
supervision of personnel.[381] Furthermore, the 'stress and emotion'[382] caused by the
conditions of battle has long been recognised as a potential factor in detainee abuse.
The US Army Field Manual notes: '[i]f torture to gain information or to intimidate is
allowed, even tacitly, it can become an all-too-easy outlet for combat stress-related
tension and frustration, with steadily worsening consequences.'[383] Sometimes
stress, combined with other factors, may also lead to abusive conduct: 'potential for
abuse increases when interrogations are conducted in an emotionally charged field

environment by personnel unfamiliar with approved techniques.'[384] A report authored by Army Brigadier General Charles Jacoby observed how lack of clarity in applicable standards may lead to abuse and undermine military objectives:

> While humane treatment of detainees is in fact the understood and practiced standard in the theatre, lack of clarity regarding authorities, standards of detention, and standards of interrogation, provides for sufficient friction in the process to create opportunities for detainee abuse and impede effective intelligence collection and dissemination.[385]

Battlefield stress may lead to actions or decisions that begin the slide towards unintended consequences. It is worth noting too, that stress is not only felt by military personnel, but also by police officers[386] and lawyers.[387] In his discussion of decisions made by OLC lawyers, Zelikow notes that 'anxiety mixed with hubris [was] a stimulant to action [that] loosened inhibitions about experiments with new ideas'.[388] A similar point was observed by the ECtHR in a case involving a police officer, who on the order of a superior, threatened a kidnapper with torture: '[t]he threat took place in an atmosphere of heightened tension and emotions in circumstances where the police officers were under intense pressure, believing that J.'s life was in considerable danger'.[389] This evidence that stress can lead to rule breaking, as well as decisions by lawyers and government officials that enable abuse to take place.

The Abu Ghraib prisoner abuse scandal combined many factors previously identified, including failures to 'properly ... supervise ... interrogation operations' and 'to react appropriately to those instances where detainee abuse was reported ... '[390] Further, personnel were inadequately trained, there was a 'lack of clear interrogation policy' and there existed 'intense pressure felt by the personnel on the ground to produce actionable intelligence from detainees'.[391] In his report, Major General Antonio M. Taguba, noted that between October and November 2003 'numerous incidents of sadistic, blatant, and wanton criminal abuses were inflicted on several detainees'.[392] This included 'punching slapping and kicking', using military dogs to 'intimidate and frighten', forcing detainees to engage in involuntary sexual behaviour.[393] Other allegations which were found to be 'credible' included detainees being threatened with rape, beatings with a broom handle and chair, and 'sodomising a detainee with a chemical light and perhaps a broom stick'.[394] Military intelligence interrogators and other agencies 'actively requested that MP guards set physical and mental conditions for favourable interrogation of witnesses'.[395] Senior officers were unprepared to accept that there existed 'poor leadership' and attempted to shift blame.[396] There was also a lack of supervision and failure to take action in relation to MPs that were viewed as 'dysfunctional', as well as *inter alia* failure to ensure compliance with the Geneva Convention.[397] Zimbardo analysed the Abu Ghraib abuses and concluded that a multiplicity of factors, also identified in the military inquiry reports, constituted 'situational forces' which 'created *freedom* from the usual social and moral constraints on abusive actions'[398] (emphasis in original).

Further, slippage can and does occur when coercion is used for means other than for the purposes of intelligence gathering. Evidence of this problem was provided by three serving members of the US military, who in disclosures to Human Rights Watch, pointed to the 'systematic' abuse of Iraqi detainees by US forces. The report noted that military intelligence officers encouraged the abuse of detainees so as to force compliance with interrogators.[399] However, even if one accepts such techniques as a legitimate means of gaining cooperation, coercion spread beyond that used for the purpose of intelligence gathering. One sergeant of the 82nd Airborne Division reported that detainees would be abused because 'we would just get bored', '[w]e did that for amusement', '[e]veryone in camp knew if you wanted to work out your frustration you show up at the [detainee] tent. In a way it was sport.'[400] Thus, it can be argued that encouragement, combined with other situational factors formed an attitude changing slippery slope in which abuse became an acceptable norm amongst certain personnel.[401]

This section has identified a range of mechanisms that lead to slippage and is an important element in the case for developing an empirical SSA and in refuting inaccurate factual claims within the torture debate. One objection to this analysis is that it can be argued that some of the examples given, such as those involving conduct by the military, is unlike a domestic context in which a torture law would operate. This is true. However, the strength of this analysis is that the mechanisms are in evidence across counter-terrorism campaigns and can be seen in the actions of the police, as well as military. Thus, there appear to be common mechanisms that require recognition. It is also helpful to examine the potential of these mechanisms to operate in a specific institutional context. In the context of a law that requires judicial authorisation of interrogational torture, then it is sensible to examine how slippage may operate within the judicial domain.

b. The judiciary and slippery slopes

Explaining the influences on judicial decision-making is a complex task which has to take account of group dynamics, attitudes, psychology and competing viewpoints.[402] It is essential that there is an examination of what might influence the judiciary in its interpretation of a torture law if it were ever to be enacted. Such an analysis, however, is further complicated by the fact that across national and international jurisdictions the judiciary has not addressed the issue of torture in a consistent manner. It is not unknown for judges to be tolerant of lesser forms of coercion and abuse that may fall short of the torture threshold.[403] Similarly, in some countries torture victims are 'often failed by justice systems that did not hold those responsible to account',[404] while elsewhere judges have shown themselves largely intolerant of interrogational torture and other lesser forms of abuse in terrorism and general criminal cases.[405]

In the context of judicial interpretation it is possible to identify several possible areas of slippage. First, there is the possibility of psychological pressure or fear influencing judicial decision-making. If judges do not accede to a request for a warrant where it is claimed lives can be saved, judges may face public outrage if a terrorist attack occurs. Another cause of slippage could be the time-limited nature of the judicial role when considering the authorisation of torture in either a standards or rule-based system. Time would be short and only a cursory examination of the strength of evidence would be possible. These types of pressure may lead to the use of the 'is-ought fallacy' whereby people assume 'that just because the law allows some government action … actions of this sort must be proper'.[406] The acceptability of granting torture warrants in circumstances that come close, but do not meet the type of exacting standards set out in the draft rule-based statute discussed earlier, may result in slippage being viewed as 'less extreme and thus more acceptable'.[407] Further, some scholars have argued that there is a greater scope of slippage in judicial reasoning as the attitudes of judges may change over time and, indeed, a torture law might be interpreted differently by individual judges.[408]

Volokh's notion of an 'attitude altering slippery slope'[409] also has utility as an explanation of possible slippage in judicial decision-making. In essence, the argument is that if torture were legalised and permitted in a narrow set of circumstances pressure may grow on Parliament or the judiciary to create a wider exception. The single exception might 'undermine the rule's attitude shaping force'[410] and the strength of the general prohibition on torture. When considering cases that fall within the exception judges might consider utilitarian reasoning and the balancing of the interests of the terrorist suspect with the potential victims of a terrorist attack. The role of deference may also encourage a judicial approach to decision-making that defers to the factual claims of the state as a matter of national security.[411] Unless carefully drafted, judges may find themselves balancing the right to life with the prohibition against torture in other contexts because the original exception to the absolute prohibition invites such a form of analysis. While judges might well reject such an application, it will not necessarily prevent desperate police officers from applying for authorisation, which in itself would represent a shift in attitude by state officials.[412]

Some proponents of legalisation regard the judicial role as limited. Posner and Vermeule propose a 'deference thesis [which] holds that the executive branch, not Congress or the judicial branch, should make the tradeoff between security and liberty'.[413] They argue that at times of emergency what is required is 'secrecy, speed and flexibility' and thus the executive is best suited to decision-making during emergencies because the courts have 'less to contribute'.[414] In emergencies they argue a judicially sanctioned torture warrant would be an 'empty formality'[415] and 'if a government is intent on engaging in coercive interrogation to protect national security, there is little that judges can do about it anyway'.[416] This is surely a self-defeating argument. If state officials will ignore an absolute prohibition, then on what basis are they going to observe a regulatory regime which at any given moment could be seen to be obstructing the collection of vital life-saving intelligence? This would appear an approach wide open to the slippery slope mechanisms already identified. It is an illustration of the weakness of an approach to the rule of law influenced by the writings of Carl Schmitt[417] who argued that it is desirable for state power to be exercised outside the normal constitutional and legal order in circumstances of 'extreme peril, a danger to the existence of the state, or the like'.[418] It encourages state officials to act without restraint and is likely to result in unintended consequences.

Posner and Vermeule's approach also has potential implications for the rule of law. The liberal democratic state as a form of government constrained by law is viewed as 'the essence of modern, constitutional government'.[419] Allowing the state license to torture 'anyway' whether through excessive judicial deference or some other means[420] grants it a wide power devoid of meaningful legal constraint. It undermines any notion of judicial or legal authority. This may lead to uncertainty as to the nature of the state's power, when it could or should be used and in what circumstances conduct might be the subject of subsequent sanction. In this sense, Posner and Vermeule's proposal is characterised by the disadvantages of the standards approach discussed earlier. They attempt to add weight to their argument by suggesting that interrogational torture can be regulated in a similar way to the use of lethal force by police officer.[421] The use of lethal force in the context of terrorism should also encourage caution. The Northern Ireland[422] and Spanish[423] experience suggests that the state has sometimes used lethal force in dubious circumstances that appear to have little legitimacy in fact or law.[424] Criticism of state actions in Northern Ireland resulted from the killing of unarmed individuals and the failure of the state to hold to account police officers or military personnel who acted unlawfully and without restraint.[425] As noted in Chapter 1, this resulted in a violent backlash.[426]

Adherence to the rule of law may, of course, be inhibited by poor legal drafting. Fuller has argued that 'it is obvious that obscure and incoherent legislation can make legality unattainable by anyone, or at least unattainable without an unauthorized revision which itself impairs legality'.[427] Indeed, the domestic judiciary has shown itself reluctant to override rights on the basis of ambiguity, as Lord Hoffmann observed: 'Fundamental rights cannot be overridden by general or ambiguous words.'[428] Any statutory enactment that allows the state to torture violates a fundamental right and any statutory language would have to define the limits of this power clearly. Further, ambiguous language may increase the likelihood of slippage. Van der Burg notes that a vaguely worded law which intends to permit (A) may actually allow for (B).[429] This would pose particular challenges for the judiciary who would be acting in time-limited circumstances and under considerable pressure.

This analysis is necessarily speculative, but empirical and historic evidence provides some insight into possible judicial approaches to interpretation. Evidence from case law suggests that there is judicial deference to the executive on questions of national security.[430] In the context of English law, Griffith notes the pressure on the criminal justice system to produce results in terrorism cases: '[t]he police are under great pressure to show that they can make arrests and obtain convictions. Ministers want results. And the judicial system is not expected to impede the process.'[431] Despite evidence of judicial deference, there is also a well-established body of case law that has long recognised that any 'coercive action' carried out by the state must be 'justified in law'.[432] Indeed, domestic courts are also prepared to engage in 'intense scrutiny' of state actions to ensure legality.[433] While there is judicial *dictum* to suggest that certain acts of illegality might be permissible on behalf of the state 'there must be stringent limits to what breaches of the law can [be] considered excusable ... I cannot conceive of physical violence ever coming within this category'.[434] In the last decade the judiciary has also been prepared to challenge the use of terrorism powers in a range of areas, including detention without trial,[435] control orders,[436] deportation of terror suspects,[437] the use of evidence gained from the use of torture[438] and terrorist financing.[439] Indeed, such decisions have resulted in public criticism of the judiciary by politicians concerned about judicial blocking of state responses to terrorism.[440] Some senior members of the judiciary have publicly responded to this criticism. For example, in 2005, former Master of the Rolls Lord Donaldson reacted to comments by Prime Minister Tony Blair concerning judicial interpretation of anti-terrorism legislation, thus: 'It is the job of governments to put forward measures which make the work of the police and security services easier – and it is the job of judges to resist that where necessary [in order to uphold the rule of law].'[441]

This survey does not provide definitive answers as to how a torture law might be interpreted, but it does identify mechanisms by which slippage could occur. Any scholar or state official who proposes the introduction of a counter-terrorism measure has a responsibility to explore whether it is possible to construct a law that could prevent or minimise slippage.[442] General options that have been suggested to reduce slippage in the application of legal rules include the creation of 'arbitrary stopping rules' that would provide clear stipulations for future state officials as to what conduct is permissible and what is not.[443] Volokh argues that 'a slope that contains no non-arbitrary stopping place is slipperier than one that does'.[444] In reality of course, any slope without stopping places, arbitrary or otherwise, is slipperier. Another option is the creation of legal presumptions that make the conditions for permitting torture more demanding thus reducing the likelihood of error.[445] This may well have some beneficial effect from a regulatory point of view, but of course, this is subject to consequentialist pressures and the mechanisms of slippage. It remains a matter for speculation as to how effective such a presumption would be.

5. Conclusion

This chapter has detailed the risks of slippage associated with the use of interrogational torture. The analysis suggests that there is significant empirical support for the various mechanisms by which slippage can occur. Some caution must always be shown when using SSAs in the context of the torture debate because they are predictive. While it is not possible to know for certain how a torture statute might operate in practice, it would be reckless to ignore the dangers of slippage. There is a good reason to endorse Volokh's view that 'slippery slopes present a real risk— not always, but often enough that we cannot lightly ignore the possibilities of such slippage'.[446] This chapter has identified a significant body of empirical evidence to support an empirical SSA which pointedly contradicts factual claims made by proponents of legalisation. Further, this analysis makes clear that slippage in the context of interrogational torture can occur and the mechanisms can operate independently of any regulatory system. That is not to argue that the type of regulation is irrelevant, only that the forces of slippage can be powerful, if not inevitable. Indeed, there are multiple types of slippage and associated mechanisms that are in evidence in many differing counter-terrorism campaigns involving the police and military. Thus, Bagaric and Clarke's claim that there is 'no evidence to suggest that an institutionalised practice of inflicting pain on one person to save another or for the common good will lead to abuses',[447] is simply untrue. It is the product of a failure to engage with the relevant theoretical and empirical literature[448] and to consider the logic of their own consequentialist reasoning.

At the same time, the more extreme slippage claims made by critics of legalisation which link the actions of brutal, military regimes with the potential consequences of legalisation in democracies seem wide of the mark. There are examples of slippage in democracies, but comparative analysis must acknowledge the differences in the use of interrogational torture between societies that are fundamentally different from one another. To properly understand the phenomenon of slippage it is crucial to acknowledge that there are a variety of mechanisms that influence the problem of unintended consequences. It is these mechanisms that require analysis, including how they might exist even where there are legal efforts to control the use of interrogational torture. These mechanisms exist in a range of circumstances and can act in combination. On the basis of evidence from the democratic use of torture and coercive interrogation it is clear that slippage will occur, and that there is a good chance it will become commonplace. This may seem counter-intuitive to those who focus on the police use of lethal force as a comparator or amongst those who neglect the historic record. However, this is the lesson from other conflicts.

Finally, this chapter shows that the theoretical underpinning of the case for legalisation is deeply problematic. This is illustrated by how far interrogational torture could extend into the daily workings of the criminal justice system, by being used in non-terrorism cases. This is a product of the consequentialist reasoning utilised by proponents of legalisation. In his work, Volokh poses a crucial question, thus: will 'citizens, judges, and legislators' be able to draw the line in future decision making between (A) and (B)?[449] This chapter shows that there exist theoretical, as well as empirical grounds for believing that such a distinction would be difficult to maintain. It is the case that there clearly exist numerous examples of slippage in the contemporary and historic literature. Thus slippage undoubtedly increases the cost of legalisation. Further, since no regulatory framework appears to exist that would negate many of the slippage mechanisms identified in this chapter, it would be wise to refrain from legalisation on this ground alone. It is for the proponents of legalisation to recognise this reality and explain how law could negate the risks of slippage. Even supporters of legalisation, such as Bentham, have pointed to this problem: '[a]s to the Cases in which [torture] has been applied, in most of them it has been applied to no purpose or a bad one'.[450]

Notes

1 Some small and occasional sections of text in this chapter were also published as part of a previous publication: P. Rumney, 'The Torture Debate: A Perspective from the United Kingdom', in J. Moran and M. Phythian (eds.), *Intelligence Security and Policing: the UK Response to the War on Terror* (2008). The author expresses his thanks to Palgrave Macmillan for permission to reuse this material.

2 R. Hutchinson, *Elizabeth's Spy Master* (2006) 78.

3 Memorandum for John Rizzo Acting General Counsel of the Central Intelligence Agency, *Interrogation of al Qaeda Operative* 1 August 2002, 3.

4 See, for example, Office of Legal Counsel, *Memorandum for William J. Haynes IT, General Counsel of the Department of Defense, Re: Military Interrogation of Alien Unlawful Combatants Held Outside the United States* 14 March 2003. See also. P. Gaeta, 'May Necessity be Available as a Defence for Torture in the Interrogation of Suspected Terrorists?' (2004) 2 J. *Int'l Criminal Justice* 785 (arguing the necessity defence is not available under international law for the use of torture).

5 OLC memoranda, *id.* See also D. Hill, 'Ticking Bombs, Torture and the Analogy with Self-Defence', (2007) 44 *American Philosophical Quarterly* 395 (arguing against the self-defence analogy in the context of torture).

6 O. Gross and F. Ní Aoláin, *Law in Times of Crisis: Emergency Powers in Theory and Practice* (2006) 134–7 (arguing that the presumption that public officials show 'obedience' to the law might be rebuttable where it is outweighed by the harm caused by obeying the law).

7 See CIA memorandum, *supra* n. 3. For critical discussion, see D. Cole, *The Torture Memos: Rationalizing the Unthinkable* (2009) 9–35.

8 E.A. Posner and A. Vermeule, 'Should Coercive Interrogation be Legal?' (2006) 104 *Mich. L. Rev.* 671, 673 (making the slightly different point, that: '[a]mong legal academics, a near consensus has emerged: coercive interrogation must be kept "illegal", but nonetheless permitted in certain circumstances').

9 See, for example, E.A. Posner and A. Vermeule, *Terror in the Balance: Security, Liberty, and the Courts* (2007) ch. 6; P.B. Heymann and J.N. Kayyem, *Protecting Liberty in an Age of Terror* (2005) ch. 1. See also: Parker Report, *infra* n. 54. There has also been discussion of the appropriate rules and safeguards for the detention and interrogation of foreign nationals held in third countries: A.N. Guiora, *Constitutional Limits on Coercive Interrogation* (2008).

10 For discussion of some of these issues, see J.T. Parry, *Understanding Torture: Law, Violence and Political Identity* (2010).

11 A.M. Dershowitz, *Why Terrorism Works: Understanding the Threat, Responding to the Challenge* (2002) 147.

12 E. Lode, 'Slippery Slope Arguments and Legal Reasoning', (1999) 87 *Calif. L. Rev.* 1469.

13 F. Schauer, 'Slippery Slopes', (1985) 99 *Harv. L. Rev.* 361.

14 E. Volokh, 'The Mechanisms of the Slippery Slope', (2003) 116 *Harv. L. Rev.* 1026.

15 See, for example, W.L. Twining and P.E. Twining, 'Bentham on Torture', (1973) 24 *N.I.L.Q.* 305 (discussing the writings of Jeremy Bentham). Most recently see S. Greer, 'Should Police Threats to Torture Suspects Always be Severely Punished? Reflections on the *Gäfgen* Case', (2011) 11 *Human Rights Law Review* 67.

16 Dershowitz, *supra* n. 11, Ch 4.

17 B. Brecher, *Torture and the Ticking Bomb* (2007) 39.

18 For discussion of how judges deal with the challenges of statutory interpretation, see: M. Zander, *The Law-Making Process* (2004) ch. 3 (noting the ambiguities of language and interpretive approaches of judges).

19 For discussion of Posner and Vermeule's proposal for the use of interrogational torture in kidnapping cases, see: *infra* nn. 213–9 and accompanying text.

20 B. Morgan and K. Yeung, *An Introduction to Law and Regulation* (2007) 17–8.

21 J.H. Langbein, *Torture and the Law of Proof: Europe and England in the Ancien Régime* (2006).

22 *Id.* 6–7.
23 *Id.* 7–8.
24 *Id.* 5.
25 *Id.* 12–7.
26 *Id.* 14.
27 *Id.* 5.
28 *Id.* 57.
29 *Id.* 9.
30 *Id.*
31 *Id.* 14.
32 *Id.* 16–7.
33 *Id.* 16.
34 See also: D. Jardine, *A Reading on the Use of Torture in the Criminal Law of England Previously to the Commonwealth* (1836) (includes analysis of many of the warrants used by Langbein in his later analysis).
35 Langbein, *supra* n. 21, ch. 6.
36 *Id.* 78.
37 *Id.* 80.
38 *Id.* 82.
39 *Id.* 88.
40 *Id.* Xi.
41 It also contradicts the claim made by Shue, *infra* n. 124–5 and accompanying text.
42 Langbein, *supra* n. 21, 136–7.
43 *Id.* ch. 6.
44 Dershowitz, *supra* n. 11, 155.
45 Langbein, *supra* n. 21, 139 (discussing the case of William Monke who had 'been framed and was in fact innocent of the suspicion of treason cast upon him').
46 M. Bagaric and J. Clarke, *Torture: When the Unthinkable is Morally Permissible* (2007) 34.
47 *Id.* 35.
48 *Id.* 34.
49 Id. 38.
50 *Id.*
51 L. Kaplow, 'Rules Versus Standards: An Economic Analysis', (1992) 42 *Duke L.J.* 557, 560. Kaplow notes that many laws combine rules and standards (at 561–2). However, in this chapter they will be treated as distinct for the purpose of clarity.
52 *Id.* 560.
53 O. Gross, 'Chaos and Rules: Should Responses to Violent Crises Always be Constitutional?' (2003) 112 *Yale L.J.* 1011, 1021.
54 Lord Parker of Waddington, *Report of the Committee of Privy Counsellors appointed to consider authorised procedures for the interrogation of persons suspected of terrorism* (1972) para. 36.
55 Schauer, *supra* n. 13, 370–3.
56 Kaplow, *supra* n. 51, 580.
57 Indeed, litigation has already arisen concerning rules that govern the reporting of torture by intelligence officials operating abroad: *R v. Prime Minister and others* [2011] EWHC 2401 (Admin). Judicial reaction to allegations of abuse have also given rise to litigation: *R v. Secretary of State for Foreign and Commonwealth Affairs (No. 2)* [2010] EWCA Civ 65 (concerning redactions in a court judgment discussing allegations of abuse reported to the UK intelligence services by US officials).
58 S.V. Shiffrin, 'Inducing Moral Deliberation: On the Occasional Virtues of Fog', (2010) 123 *Harv. L. Rev.* 1215, 1217, 1222–9.
59 P.J. Schlag, 'Rules and Standards', (1985) 33 *U.C.L.A.L. Rev.* 379.
60 For an excellent discussion of the respective benefits and drawbacks of rules and standards, see *id.*
61 Bagaric and Clarke, *supra* n. 46, 2.

62 *Id.* 3–4.
63 P. Gill and M. Phythian, *Intelligence in an Insecure World* (2006) 104.
64 Bagaric and Clarke, *supra* n. 46, 38.
65 *Id.* 37.
66 For discussion, see: Chapter 3.
67 J.H. Langbein, 'The Legal History of Torture', in S. Levinson (ed.), *Torture: A Collection* (2004) 97.
68 Bagaric and Clarke, *supra* n. 46, 38.
69 M. Bagaric and J. Clarke, 'Not Enough Official Torture in the World? The Circumstances in which Torture is Morally Justifiable', (2005) 39 *U.S.F.L. Rev.* 581, 614.
70 For example, Lotfi Raissi, an Algerian pilot living in the United Kingdom was wrongly accused and then detained without trial for five months for allegedly being part of the 9/11 plot: *Lotfi Raissi* v. *The Secretary of State for Justice* [2010] EWCA Civ 337.
71 Gill and Phythian, *supra* n. 63, 116–9.
72 D. Omand, 'The Dilemmas of Using Secret Intelligence for Public Security', in P. Hennessy (ed.), *The New Protective State: Government, Intelligence and Terrorism* (2007) 153–4.
73 Bagaric and Clarke, *supra* n. 46, 39.
74 In the context of Israel's use of 'secret guidelines' see: L. Hajjar, *Courting Conflict: The Israeli Military Court System in the West Bank and Gaza* (2005) 72–3.
75 The importance of accountability and transparency is emphasised by Dershowitz, *supra* n. 11, 158–9.
76 Similar omissions are evident in the Bagaric and Clarke proposal.
77 There are clear examples of unethical behaviour by doctors in the use of torture or other coercive interrogation methods, see: Public Committee Against Torture in Israel, *Doctoring the Evidence, Abandoning the Victim: The Involvement of Medical Professionals in Torture and Ill Treatment in Israel* (2011).
78 The infliction of torture could have fatal results on suspects with particular vulnerabilities and so such checks would appear essential and follow the approach of some intelligence agencies prior to interrogation: Central Intelligence Agency, *Background Paper on CIA's Combined Use of Interrogation Techniques* (2004) 3. There is another issue that arises in the context of the vulnerable. A question arises as to how a detainee who suffers from a learning disability or severe mental health problem should be treated. This is a real world problem because there is evidence of terrorist groups deliberately recruiting people with such problems. See, for example, M. al-Qaisa, 'Al-Qaeda Recruiting Mentally Challenged Individuals for Suicide Attacks', www.Al-Shorfa.com 20 August 2012; 'Nail-bomber given Life Sentence', www.bbc.co.uk/news 30 January 2009.
79 Some scholars have suggested that special detention/interrogation rules should adopt particular definitions of terrorism. Radsan suggests a definition of terrorism involving an act 'that has caused or reasonably may cause the deaths of three or more United States citizens': J. Radsan, 'A Better Model for Interrogating High-Level Terrorists', (2006) 79 *Temp. L. Rev.* 1227, 1235. Such specific definitions do raise problems of predicting the harm inflicted by a terror attack. Section 1(1)(b) and reference to 'substantial risk of harm' faces similar interpretative difficulties as the Radsan model.
80 See, for example, Brecher, *supra* n. 17.
81 For discussion, see Posner and Vermeule, *supra* n. 9, 212.
82 Article 15 of the ECHR does not permit abrogation from Article 3 even in times of emergency so Parliament would have to legislate without regard for this limitation. Section 3 of the HRA requires the judiciary 'So far as it is possible to do so, primary legislation and secondary legalisation must be read and given effect in a way that is compatible with Convention rights'. Given the unambiguous approach of the ECtHR to the interpretation of Article 3's prohibition on torture, as was discussed in Chapter 1, it is evident that unless the judiciary were prevented from considering the ECHR and

related case law, a torture statute would be inoperable. This, however, raises another issue: while judges would be required to ignore the ECtHR in terms of its absolute rejection of torture in all circumstances, would they be able to take account of ECtHR case law on the meaning of torture?

83 Dershowitz, *supra* n. 11, 144, 148.
84 Posner and Vermeule, *supra* n. 9, 211.
85 Brecher *supra* n. 17, 28.
86 The use of torture is often divided between intelligence analysts, those who administer techniques and interrogators or debriefers who question the detainee. Such a practice was used as part of the CIA's HVD programme discussed below and is hardly designed for swift disclosures.
87 B. Anderson, 'We not only have a Right to use Torture. We have a Duty', *The Independent* 15 February 2010.
88 Dershowitz, *supra* n. 11, 146.
89 E. Bakker, *Jihadi terrorists in Europe: their characteristics and the circumstances in which they joined the jihad: an exploratory study* (2006) 41.
90 See, for example, Dershowitz, *supra* n. 11, 147–8; Posner and Vermeule, *supra* n. 9, ch. 6.
91 For two recent examples of teenagers aged 16 years or younger being shot dead by police officers, see 'Texas Police Shoot Dead 15-Year-Old Boy Carrying Air Pistol', www.guardian.co.uk 5 January 2012; C. Wells, 'Parents of Suicidal Boy Shot by Police Sniper Speak Out for First Time', *New York Daily News* 28 October 2012.
92 Posner and Vermeule, *supra* n. 9, 39.
93 For a detailed discussion, see Chapter 3, nn. 71–84 and accompanying text.
94 See, for example, interviews Khalid Sheikh Mohammed gave to a journalist prior to his capture in Pakistan: Y. Fouda and N. Fielding, *Mastermind of Terror: The Truth Behind the Most Devastating Terrorist Attack the World Has Ever Seen* (2003). Mohammed was the subject of extremely harsh interrogation methods as part of the CIA's HVD programme. It did not result in the disclosure of any intelligence pertaining to imminent attacks, see Chapter 3, nn. 180–1, 184 and accompanying text.
95 Central Intelligence Agency Office of Inspector General, *Counterterrorism Detention and Interrogation Activities (September 2001–October 2003)* 7 May 2004, para. 205–6 (hereinafter CIA-OIG-CIA Report).
96 This could be further bolstered by a provision that confession evidence gained through torture would not be admissible in legal proceedings.
97 See Chapter 2, nn. 115–41 and accompanying text.
98 Threats of torture were judged inhuman treatment and a violation of Article 3 ECHR in *Gäfgen* v. *Germany* (application no. 22978/05) para 108.
99 L. Roper, *Witch Craze: Terror and Fantasy in Baroque Germany* (2006) 65–6.
100 Posner and Vermeule, *supra* n. 9, 202.
101 Bagaric and Clarke, *supra* n. 46, 41–2.
102 Posner and Vermeule, *supra* n. 9, 200.
103 H. Lafollette, 'Living on a Slippery Slope', (2005) 9 *The Journal of Ethics* 475, 478.
104 This section draws on the analysis of Lode, *supra* n. 12, 1477.
105 E. Volokh and D. Newman, 'In Defense of the Slippery Slope', *Legal Affairs* March/April 2003, 21.
106 Lode, *supra* n. 12, 1472.
107 Schauer, *supra* n. 13, 364.
108 Lode, *supra* n. 12, 1477, Lafollette, supra n. 103, 481.
109 G. Spielthenner, 'A Logical Analysis of Slippery Slope Arguments', (2010) 18 *Health Care Anal.* 148, 151–2.
110 Lafollette argues that such arguments differ from classic SSAs because it is 'causal argument' that does not involve analogous steps from (A) to (B): *supra* n. 103, 481.
111 D. Enoch, 'Once You Start using Slippery Slope Arguments, You're on a Very Slippery Slope', (2001) 21 *O.J.L.S.* 629, 633.

112 Lode, *supra* n. 12, 1482.
113 R.E. Sternglantz argues that SSAs are 'a rhetorical technique designed to combine rational argument with emotional appeal': 'Raining on the Parade of Horribles: Of Slippery Slopes, Faux Slopes, and Justice Scalia's Dissent in Lawrence v. Texas', (2005) 153 *U. Penn. L. Rev.* 1097, 1100.
114 Lafollette, *supra* n. 103, 497–9.
115 Lode, *supra* n. 12, 1522.
116 Volokh, *supra* n. 14, 1032.
117 *Id.*
118 J. Oakley and D. Cocking, 'Consequentialism, Complacency, and Slippery Slope Arguments', (2005) 26 *Theoretical Medicine and Bioethics* 227, 232–3.
119 Spielthenner, *supra* n. 109, 158.
120 This argument should not be overstated. In many countries the execution of the innocent has not led to a rejection of the death penalty.
121 Matthews takes the view that the nature of the institutional and social harms of torture lead to its rejection: R. Matthews, *The Absolute Prohibition: Why Torture Must be Prohibited* (2008) ch. 3.
122 *Id.* 132–7.
123 Amnesty International, *Torture and Ill-treatment: the Arguments* cited in P. Rumney, 'Is Coercive Interrogation of Terrorist Suspects Effective? A Response to Bagaric and Clarke', (2006) 40 *U.S.F.L. Rev.* 479, 502, n. 105. However, see Langbein, *supra* nn. 38–42 and accompanying text.
124 H. Shue, 'Torture in Dreamland: Disposing of the Ticking Bomb', (2005) 37 *Case W. Res. J. Int'l. L.* 231, 234.
125 *Id.* 234, n. 16. See Langbein, *supra* n. 124–5 (suggesting such an example).
126 Brecher, *supra* n. 17, ch. 3; A. O'Rourke *et al*, 'Torture, Slippery Slopes, Intellectual Apologists, and Ticking Bombs: An Australian Response to Bagaric and Clarke' (2006) 40 *U.S.F.L. Rev.* 85; Matthews, *supra* n. 121, 133 (arguing torture will make 'additional violence' such as murder and rape 'inevitable' because it is not 'controllable').
127 S. Lukes, 'Liberal Democratic Torture', (2005) 36 *B.J.Pol.S.* 1, 13–4.
128 Matthews, *supra* n. 121, 132.
129 *Id.* ch 3.
130 G. Williams, 'Euthanasia Legislation: A Rejoinder to the Nonreligious Objections' (1958) 43 *Minn. L. Rev.* cited in W. van der Burg, 'The Slippery Slope Argument', (1991) 102 *Ethics* 42, 42, n. 1.
131 J.S. Mill, *On Liberty and Other Essays* (1998) 106.
132 Bagaric and Clarke, *supra* n. 46, 47–8.
133 *Id.* ch. 4.
134 *Id.* 48.
135 Posner and Vermeule, *supra* n. 9, 200.
136 Brecher, *supra* n. 17, 59.
137 *Id.* 65.
138 For discussion of these issues, see: R.J. Evans, *The Third Reich in Power* (2005); G. Aly and S. Heim, *Architects of Annihilation: Auschwitz and the Logic of Destruction* (2003).
139 Matthews, *supra* n. 121, 133.
140 V. Bufacchi and J.M. Arrigo, 'Torture, Terrorism and the State: A Refutation of the Ticking-Bomb Argument', (2006) 23 *Journal of Applied Philosophy* 355, 367.
141 Significantly, these factors *are* acknowledged by the source they cite in support of their argument: L.E. Fletcher and H. Weinstein, 'Violence and Social Repair: Rethinking the Contribution of Justice to Reconciliation', (2002) 24 *Human Rights Quarterly* 573.
142 J.W. McAuley *et al*, 'Conflict, Transformation, and Former Loyalist Paramilitary Prisoners in Northern Ireland', (2010) 40 *Terrorism and Political Violence* 22.
143 Darius Rejali has noted that explanations of torture sometimes fail to properly explain how and why torture occurs: *Torture and Democracy* (2007) 21.

144 M.A. Thiessen, *Counting Disaster: How the CIA Kept America Safe and How Barack Obama is Inviting the Next Attack* (2010) 157.
145 For discussion of this aspect, see: N. Cullather, *Secret History: The CIA's Classified Account of its Operations in Guatemala 1952–1954* (1999).
146 Historical Clarification Commission, *Guatemala: Memory of Silence, Report of the Commission for Historical Clarification: Conclusions and Recommendations* (1999).
147 *Id.* See also: S. Schlesinger and S. Kinzer, *Bitter Fruit: The Story of the American Coup in Guatemala* (1999) (noting *inter alia* that in the eyes of military leaders '[a]nyone not supporting the regime was almost by definition a leftist, and therefore an enemy').
148 Historical Clarification Commission, *supra* n. 146, paras. 10–1, 44.
149 In repressive states, torture is often accompanied by other human rights abuses: T. Landman and E. Carvalho, *Measuring Human Rights* (2009) ch. 5.
150 van der Burg, *supra* n. 130, 43.
151 D. Rejali, *Torture and Democracy* (2007) 405.
152 *Amnesty International Report 2013 – State of the World's Human Rights* (2013) 149.
153 *Id.* Human Rights Watch, North Korea Country Summary (2012).
154 For a discussion of the limitations of some of these methods of control, see Matthews, *supra* n. 121, 171–6.
155 *Id.* 232.
156 Volokh, *supra* n. 14, 1101.
157 For excellent discussion of empirical SSAs and their potential defects, see T. Douglas, 'Intertemporal Disagreement and Empirical Slippery Slope Arguments', (2010) 22 *Utilitas* 184.
158 J.M. Eckert, 'Laws for Enemies', in J.M. Eckert (ed.), *The Social Life of Anti-Terrorism Laws: The War on Terror and the Classifications of the Dangerous Other* (2008) 15.
159 *Supra* 108–10 and accompanying text. It is possible that misidentification may be a result of other incremental failures, so it not necessarily the case that these types of cases are always the product of a single, acute failure.
160 The domestic common law power of anticipatory breach of the peace allows police officers to take necessary measures, including arrest, where they have reasonable grounds to anticipate that an imminent breach of the peace will occur. For a detailed discussion, see *Laporte* v. *Chief Constable of Gloucestershire Constabulary* (2006) UKHL 55. The use of anticipatory powers risk being used inappropriately because of the factors a police officer may take into account when judging the risk of an imminent breach of the peace. For example, these powers have been used by police officers to target peaceful protestors on a 'false assumption' that they were 'violent troublemakers': *Id.* paras. 87–9 *per* Lord Bingham of Cornhill. Further, their use has been upheld when invoked against individuals where there was no specific evidence that they would engage in future unlawful activity. This has included situations where small groups of pickets were linked with a much larger group, a proportion of whom had previously engaged in public disorder: *Moss* v. *McLachlan* (1985) IRLR 76.
161 Bagaric and Clarke, *supra* n. 46, 34.
162 *Id.* 37.
163 *Id.* In doubting the efficacy of the normal trial process Bagaric and Clarke state 'research carried out in the United Kingdom for the Royal Commission on Criminal Justice suggests that up to eleven percent of people who plead guilty claim innocence': *id.* This of course undermines their argument: if significant numbers of people are being wrongly convicted of criminal offences with a high standard of proof, how many mistakes are going to be made in the context of a system with a lower standard of proof?
164 *Id.*
165 For discussion, see: Independent Police Complaints Commission, *Stockwell One: Investigation into the Shooting of Jean Charles de Menezes at Stockwell Underground Station on 22 July 2005* (2006) (pointing to the errors that that led to the shooting of de Menezes).

166 A. Pedahzur, *The Israeli Secret Services and the Struggle Against Terrorism* (2009) 38.
167 D. Anderson Q.C., *Operation GIRD – Report Following Review* (2011).
168 *Id*. para. 30.
169 *Id*.
170 *Id*. para. 32.
171 *Id*. para. 31.
172 *Id*. para. 90.
173 *Id*. paras. 97, 100.
174 *Id*. para. 99.
175 *Id*. paras. 52, 58.
176 Bagaric and Clarke, *supra* n. 46, 34–7.
177 Posner and Vermeule, *supra* n. 9, 211. Their discussion here involves several options.
178 BBC, 'Madrid Train Attacks', http://news.bbc.co.uk/1/shared/spl/hi/guides/457000/457031/html (accessed 1 February 2014).
179 *Id*.
180 *Mayfield* v. *United States of America* 599 F.3d 964 (2010).
181 Department of Justice-Office of the Inspector General, *A Review of the FBI's Handling of the Brandon Mayfield Case – Unclassified Executive Summary* (2006) 1–3.
182 'Cheney: Gitmo Holds "Worst of the Worst"', www.NBCNews.com 1 June 2009.
183 The Guantánamo files that have been disclosed by Wikileaks suggest that some detainees captured by Afghan forces may have been detained for inappropriate reasons. For example, one file suggests that a detainee may have been held by Afghan forces for personal motivations and they 'falsely portrayed the detainee as a former Taliban commander': ISN 001117.
184 D. Rose, *Guantánamo: America's War on Human Rights* (2004) 46–7. See also 'Gitmo Detainees Say They Were Sold', *Associated Press* 31 May 2005.
185 G. Miller, 'Many Held at Guantánamo Not Likely Terrorists', *Los Angeles Times* 22 December 2002. An Amnesty International report noted that: 'scores of people have been released from Guantánamo without charge or trial. They, too, had been labelled by the administration as "enemy combatants" and "terrorists". On return to their countries, the vast majority have been released. Their home governments evidently either believed that there was no evidence against the detainees, or that any evidence was inadequate, unreliable or inadmissible': *Guantánamo and Beyond: The Continuing Pursuit of Unchecked Executive Power* (2005) 11.
186 *Id*.
187 CBS News, 'Torture, Cover Up at Gitmo?' 1 May 2005.
188 Executive Order 13492 – Review and Disposition of Individuals Detained at the Guantánamo Bay Naval Base and Closure of Detention Facilities, 22 January 2009.
189 Guantánamo Review Task Force, *Final Report* (2010) 13.
190 *Id*. 13.
191 *Id*. 14.
192 *Id*. 14.
193 Research has noted that the US government defined association with or membership of al Qaeda very broadly and could apply to 'anyone who the Government believed ever spoke to an al-Qaeda member. Even under this broad framework, the Government concluded that a full 60% of the detainees do not have even that minimum level of contact with an al Qaeda member': M. Denbeaux and J. Denbeaux, *Report on Guantánamo Detainees: A Profile of 517 Detainees through Analysis of Department of Defense Data* (2006) 9.
194 In an analysis of 132 prisoner files, along with a review of 'heavily censored' Combatant Status Review Tribunals transcripts for 314 Guantánamo detainees. Corine Hegland found:

   Most, when captured, were innocent of any terrorist activity, were Taliban foot soldiers at worst, and were often far less than that. And some, perhaps many, are guilty only of being foreigners in

Afghanistan or Pakistan at the wrong time. And much of the evidence – even the classified evidence – gathered by the Defense Department against these men is flimsy, second-, third-, fourth- or 12th hand. It's based largely on admissions by the detainees themselves or on coerced, or worse, interrogations of their fellow inmates, some of whom have been proved to be liars.

C. Hegland, 'Empty Evidence', *National Journal* 3 February 2006.

195 *Declaration of Colonel Lawrence B. Wilkerson (Ret.)* CV 05–1009 JDB, 24 March 2010, paras. 9, 11 ('I soon realized from my conversations with military colleagues as well as foreign service officers in the field that many of the detainees were, in fact, victims of incompetent battlefield vetting. There was no meaningful way to determine whether they were terrorists, Taliban, or simply innocent civilians picked up on a very confused battlefield or in the territory of another state such as Pakistan … [the view of senior officials] was that innocent people languishing in Guantánamo for years was justified by the broader war on terror and the capture of the small number of terrorists who were responsible for the September 11 attacks, or other acts of terrorism').

196 P. Gourevitch and E. Morris, *Standard Operating Procedure: A War Story* (2008).

197 *Id.* 35.

198 *Id.*

199 *Id.* 39.

200 *Id.* 55.

201 *Id.* 42.

202 *Id.* 43.

203 Human Rights Watch, *Leadership Failure: Firsthand Accounts of Torture of Iraqi Detainees by the U.S. Army's 82nd Airborne Division* (2005) 10.

204 Public Committee Against Torture in Israel, *Back to a Routine of Torture* (2003) 48.

205 *Public Committee Against Torture in Israel v. The State of Israel* (1999) 38 ILM 1471.

206 B'Tselem, *Legalisation Allowing the Use of Physical Force and Mental Coercion in Interrogations by the General Security Service* (2000) 32.

207 For discussion, see: Sir J. Stevens, *Stevens Enquiry 3* (2003) (investigating security force collusion in the murders of Pat Finucane and Brian Adam Lambert).

208 For discussion see: Rt. Hon. Sir Desmond de Silva, *Pat Finucane Review: An Independent Review into any State Involvement in the Murder of Pat Finucane* (2012).

209 J. McGuffin, *Internment* (1973) 87.

210 *Id.*

211 *Id.* 86–9.

212 For discussion of this issue in the context of Northern Ireland, see: T.P. Coogan, *The Troubles: Ireland's Ordeal 1996–1996 and the Search for Peace* (1996) 150–1.

213 Posner and Vermeule, *supra* n. 9, 212.

214 *Id.* 212–3.

215 Lode, *supra* n. 12, 1483–9.

216 van der Burg, *supra* n. 130, 44.

217 T. Nagel, 'War and Massacre', in S. Scheffler (ed.), *Consequentialism and its Critics* (1988) 53.

218 Gross and Ní Aoláin, *supra* n. 6, ch 4.

219 N. Ben-Asher, 'Legal Holes', (2009) 5 *Unbound: Harvard Journal of the Legal Left* 1, 18.

220 Volokh, *supra* n. 14, 1051.

221 *Id.* 1061.

222 This is similar to the scenario sketched out by Jeremy Bentham discussed in Chapter 2, nn. 10–5 and accompanying text.

223 Matthews, *supra* n. 121, 95–6, 122–5.

224 *Id.* 212.

225 *Id.*

226 Posner and Vermeule, *supra* n. 9, 211–2.

227 K.L. Scheppele, 'Hypothetical Torture in the "War on Terrorism"', (2005) 1 *J. Nat'l Security L.& Pol'y* 285, 307.

228 For discussion, see Roper, *supra* n. 99 (discussing the observations of Jesuit Friedrich Spee who in his 1631 writings on the torture of witches observed that many 'find such pleasure in the cruelty'); J. Conroy, *Unspeakable Acts, Ordinary People: The Dynamics of Torture* (2000). The behaviour of torturers in dictatorships is not dissimilar: M.K. Huggins, *Violence Workers: Police Torturers and Murderers Reconstruct Brazilian Atrocities* (2002).

229 Scheppele, *supra* n. 227, 318.

230 G. Mythen *et al*, '"I'm a Muslim, but I'm not a Terrorist": Victimization, Risky Identities and the Performance of Safety', (2009) 49 *B.J. Crim.* 736.

231 C. Campbell, 'Beyond Radicalization-Towards an Integrated Anti-Violence Rule of Law Strategy', in A.M. Salinas de Frías *et al*, (eds.), *Counter-Terrorism: International Law and Practice* (2012) 258.

232 Volokh, *supra* n. 14, 1065.

233 Gross and Ní Aoláin, *supra* n. 6, ch. 4. See also S. Rainey, 'Man Questioned for Taking Photos of Daughter', www.telegraph.co.uk 10 October 2011 (father told by police that his camera could be seized under anti-terrorism laws after he used it to take a picture of his four-year old daughter in a shopping centre which had a no-photograph rule); 'Hero's Return for Labour Heckler', www.bbc.ac.uk/news 29 September 2005 (Labour Party delegate removed from auditorium for heckling a speech and then arrested under counter-terrorism legislation).

234 These documents can be viewed on the American Civil Liberties Union website: www.aclu.org/human-rights_national-security/aclu-obtains-detailed-official-record-cia-torture-program (accessed 1 February 2014).

235 S. Shane and M. Mazzetti, 'Report Shows Tight C.I.A. Control on Interrogations', *New York Times* 25 August 2009 (claiming '[the] program operated under strict rules, and the rules were dictated from Washington with the painstaking, eye-glazing detail beloved by any bureaucracy').

236 S.G. Bradbury, *Re: Application of United States Obligations Under Article 16 of the Convention Against Torture to Certain Techniques that May Be Used in the Interrogation of High Value al Qaeda Detainees* 30 May 2005, 3.

237 *Id.* 29.

238 It is worth noting that not all the CIA's actions pertaining to HVDs were the subject of OLC memoranda. In an interview conducted as part of a House of Representatives Judiciary Committee investigation, former Assistant Attorney General Jay Bybee, acknowledged that various aspects of the treatment of HVDs, such as the conditions of their transportation, had not been formally considered as part of OLC memoranda: House Judiciary Committee, *Transcript of May 26, 2010 House Judiciary Committee Interview of Former Assistant Attorney General Jay Bybee* (2010) 20, 78–115.

239 Fax for Daniel Levin, Assistant Attorney General, Office of Legal Counsel, from [name redacted] Assistant General Counsel, CIA; January 4, 2005 cited in Bradbury, *supra* n. 236, 5.

240 Central Intelligence Agency Directorate of Intelligence, *Detainee Reporting Pivotal for the War Against Al Qa'ida* (2005).

241 Radsan, *supra* n. 79, 1241.

242 For respective discussion of the cases of Maher Arar and Khaled Masri, see *Commission of Inquiry into the Actions of Canadian Officials in Relation to Maher Arar* (2006); Human Rights Watch, *Getting Away with Torture: The Bush Administration and Mistreatment of Detainees* (2011) 33–4; D. Priest, 'Wrongful Imprisonment: Anatomy of a CIA Mistake', *Washington Post* 4 December 2005.

243 *El-Masri* v. *Former Yugoslav Republic of Macedonia* Application no. 39630/09 (2012) paras. 17–33.

244 *Id.* paras. 169–70. For detailed discussion of the allegations, see paras. 17–27.

245 Central Intelligence Agency Office of Inspector General, *Counterterrorism Detention and Interrogation Activities (September 2001-October 2003)* 7 May 2004 (hereinafter CIA-OIG Report).

246 *Id.* paras. 100–63.
247 *Id.* paras. 164–210.
248 *Id.* para. 2.
249 *Id.* para. 90.
250 *Id* para. 70.
251 *Id.* para. 92.
252 *Id.* para. 94.
253 *Id.* paras. 96–8. In one instance an interviewee said he had to 'intercede after [redacted] expressed concern that Al-Nashiri's arms might be dislocated' (para. 97). Other allegations were disputed by interrogators.
254 *Id.* para. 95. According to a CIA manager interviewed by Ron Suskind, Khalid Sheikh Mohammed is reputed to have responded to this threat by saying 'so, fine, they'll join Allah in a better place': *The One Percent Doctrine: Deep Inside America's Pursuit of its Enemies Since 9/11* (2006) 230.
255 CIA-OIG, *supra* n. 245, para. 166
256 *Id.* paras. 169–74.
257 *Id.* paras. 187–92. The report found that this resulted from poor understanding of the limitations placed on the use of the technique.
258 *Id.* 193–203.
259 J.S. Bybee, Assistant Attorney General, U.S. Department of Justice, Office of Legal Counsel, Memorandum for J. Rizzo, Acting General Counsel of the Central Intelligence Agency, *Interrogation of al Qaeda Operative*, 1 August 2002, 15.
260 *Id.*
261 The memo states: 'Our advice is based upon the following facts, which you have provided to us', *id.* 1.
262 *Id.* 2.
263 CIA-OIG, *supra* n. 245, para. 100.
264 *Id.* paras. 223, 225. For discussion, see S. Shane, 'Waterboarding Used 266 Times on 2 Suspects,' *The New York Times* 19 April 2009.
265 Thiessen, *supra* n. 144, 116.
266 CIA-OIG, *supra* n. 245, para. 99.
267 P. Taylor, '"Vomiting and Screaming" in Destroyed Waterboarding Tapes', www.news.bbc.co.uk 9 May 2012.
268 M. Mazzetti and C. Savage, 'No Criminal Charges Sought Over CIA Tapes', *The New York Times* 9 November 2010.
269 CIA-OIG, *supra* n. 245, para. 79.
270 *Id.* para. 70.
271 Army Major Gen. George Fay and Lt. Gen. Anthony R. Jones, *AR 15–6 Investigation of the Abu Ghraib Prison and 205th Military Intelligence Brigade* (2004) 37 (hereafter: Fay and Jones Report); Hon. James R. Schlesinger, *The Report of the Independent Panel to Review DoD Detention Operations* (2004) 68 (hereafter: Schlesinger Report).
272 Department of the Army, 'General Court-Martial Order Number 20', 26 July 2006, 10, 12, 18.
273 Human Rights Watch, *Delivered into Enemy Hands: US-Led Abuse and Rendition of Opponents to Gaddafi's Libya* (2012) 2, 4. It is only very recently that there appears to be some corroboration for the suggestion that the use of drowning techniques by the CIA were used beyond the three HVDs that have been officially acknowledged: G. Miller *et al*, 'CIA Misled on Interrogation Program, Senate Report Says', www.washingtonpost.com 3 April 2014.
274 Human Rights Watch, *id.*, 47–51. The report contains a single allegation of the use of water from a hose to prevent breathing by guards at Guantánamo Bay (at 119).
275 Miller, *supra* n. 273.
276 Human Rights Watch, *supra* n. 274, 5.
277 Posner and Vermeule, *supra* n. 9, 202.

278 For discussion of this campaign of terrorism and the French response, see A. Horne, *A Savage War of Peace: Algeria 1954–1962* (2006) ch. 9; P. Vidal-Naquet, *Torture: Cancer of Democracy* (1963).

279 Vidal-Naquet, *id.* ch. 6 and 137.

280 *Id.* 77.

281 A.W. McCoy, *A Question of Torture: CIA Interrogation, from the Cold War to the War on Terror* (2006) 195–6.

282 Vidal-Naquet, *supra* n. 278, 130–1.

283 Office of the Governor-General, Civil Inspectorate-General in Algeria, Algiers, 2 March 1955, in Vidal-Naquet, *id.*

284 *Id.* 176. The report states that this was followed by 'legal action'.

285 *Id.* 178.

286 *Id.* 172–3.

287 *Id.* 175.

288 *Id.*

289 *Id.* 179.

290 *Id.* ch. 7.

291 Horne, *supra* n. 278, 500.

292 *Supra* nn. 271–6 and accompanying text.

293 Wuillaume noted that in the context of Algeria the French abuses were 'long established': *supra* n. 283 and Horne, *supra* n. 278, 196 (noting that abuses had 'long existed as a police institution in France').

294 G. Kassimeris, 'The Warrior's Dishonour', in G. Kassimeris (ed.), *Warrior's Dishonour: Barbarity, Morality and Torture in Modern Warfare* (2006) 15.

295 I.M. Wall, *France, the United States and the Algerian War* (2001) 68.

296 Horne, *supra* n. 278, 204–7.

297 H. Alleg, *The Question* (1958).

298 *Id.* 39, 59, 83–4.

299 The five 'disorientation' techniques: wall standing, hooding, subjection to noise, sleep deprivation and deprivation of food and drink: *Ireland v United Kingdom* [1978] 2 EHRR 25, para. 96.

300 This included collusion between elements within the British security forces and Loyalist terrorists. See, for example, Sir John Stevens, *Stevens Inquiry 3 – Overview and Recommendations* (2003).

301 H. Bennett, *Fighting the Mau Mau: The British Army and Counter-Insurgency in the Kenya Emergency* (2012). In recent legal proceedings brought by three victims of abuse, counsel for the government acknowledged that during the Mau Mau rebellion there had been 'torture and other ill-treatment at the hands of the colonial administration': 'Kenyans were Tortured during Mau Mau Rebellion, High Court Hears', *The Telegraph* 31 July 2012. See also *Mutua v Foreign and Commonwealth Office* [2012] EWHC 2678 (QB); C. Elkins, *Imperial Reckoning: the Untold Story of Britain's Gulag in Kenya* (2005); D. Anderson, *Histories of the Hanged: Britain's Dirty War in Kenya and the End of Empire* (2005).

302 J. Lokaneeta, *Transnational Torture: Law, Violence, and State Power in the United States and India* (2011) ch. 4.

303 I. Cobain, *Cruel Britannia: A Secret History of Torture* (2012) ch. 2.

304 Sir Edmund Compton, *Report of the Enquiry into Allegations against the Security Forces of Physical Brutality in Northern Ireland Arising out of Events on the 9th August, 1971* (1971) Introduction (hereafter Compton Report).

305 S. Newbery, 'Intelligence and Controversial British Interrogation Techniques: The Northern Ireland Case, 1971–72', (2009) 20 *Irish Studies in International Affairs* 103, 110–2.

306 *Id.* 111. Newbery notes the 'dual-purpose nature' of the three techniques (at 113). It is worth noting that if the techniques were to be justified on security grounds alone, then the purpose behind their use clearly slipped to one involving 'softening up' and intelligence gathering.

307 For the text, see Lord Parker of Waddington, *Report of the Committee of Privy Counsellors Appointed to Consider Authorised Procedures for the Interrogation of Persons Suspected of Terrorism* (1972) 23–4 (hereafter Parker Report).

308 *Id.* 24.

309 Compton Report, *supra* n. 304, ch. 8.

310 The Compton investigation only examined allegations of 'physical brutality' that occurred on 9 August 1971: *id.* para. 19.

311 For discussion, see H. Bennett, 'Detention and Interrogation in Northern Ireland, 1969–75', in S. Scheipers (ed.), *Prisoners in War* (2010).

312 Hansard HC vol. 832, 2 March 1972, col. 744.

313 P. Taylor, *Beating the Terrorists? Interrogation in Omagh, Gough and Castlereagh* (1980). See also Fr. Denis Faul and Fr. Raymond Murray, *The Castlereagh File: Allegations of RUC Brutality 1976–1977* (1978) (featuring statements by numerous male and female detainees claiming to be victims of violence, sexual assault, threats and some of the 'five techniques' that a had been officially withdrawn).

314 Amnesty International, *Report of an Amnesty International Mission to Northern Ireland (28 November–6 December 1977)* (1978).

315 Cobain, *supra* n. 303, ch. 6.

316 Taylor, *supra* n. 313, 26–8.

317 The allegation of waterboarding by members of the British Army has been recently made in legal proceedings: *R* v. *Holden* [2012] NICA 26 (the 1973 conviction of the appellant was overturned after evidence that had not been disclosed at the time of the appellant's trial had been uncovered that might undermine the credibility of two prosecution witnesses). A former police officer has also admitted to the use of drowning to force confessions from suspected terrorists: I. Cobain, 'Inside Castlereagh: "We Got Confessions by Torture"' www.guardian.co.uk (accessed 11 October 2010).

318 Taylor, *supra* n. 313, 11; His Honour Judge H.G. Bennett, Q.C, *Report of the Committee of Inquiry into Police Interrogation Procedures in Northern Ireland* (1979) ch. 8. (hereafter Bennett Report); Amnesty International, *supra* n. 314, 20 (finding limited evidence of self-inflicted injuries intended to embarrass the RUC).

319 Taylor *supra* n. 313, ch. 3.

320 For a detailed discussion of medical evidence, see Taylor, *supra* n. 313.

321 Bennett Report, *supra* n. 318, para. 163.

322 Cobain, *supra* n. 303, 316.

323 *Id.* 170.

324 BBC, 'Israel Admits Torture', www.bbc.co.uk/news 9 February 2000.

325 *Public Committee Against Torture in Israel* v. *The State of Israel* (1999) 38 ILM 1471, paras. 35, 34.

326 *Id.* para. 38. For excellent analysis of what they term the 'necessity procedure', see: I. Mann and O. Shatz, 'The Necessity Procedure: Laws of Torture in Israel and Beyond, 1987–2009,' (2010) 59 *Unbound: Harvard Journal of the Legal Left* 59, 71.

327 PCATI, *supra* n. 325, para. 34.

328 In the past, B'Tselem estimate that coercive techniques have been used against up to 85% of detainees, with the General Security Service annually interrogating 1,000–1,500 Palestinians: *Routine Torture: Interrogation Methods of the General Security Service* (1998) 5.

329 PCATI, *supra* n. 204, 48.

330 *Id.* 89. Byman quotes GSS officials who, in 2007, claimed one in six interrogated detainees were the subject of 'extraordinary measures': D. Byman, *A High Price: The Triumphs & Failures of Israeli Counterterrorism* (2011) 305.

331 For a recent example of a West Bank military tribunal rejecting a confession and acquitting a detainee because of violence, abuse and threats to family members by Israeli security forces, see: C. Levinson, 'IDF Dismisses Palestinian Confession over Physical Shin Bet Interrogation', www.Haaretz.com 7 December 2011.

332 R.W. Thurston, 'The Rise and Fall of Judicial Torture: Why It Was Used in Early Modern Europe and the Soviet Union', (2000) *Human Rights Review* 26.
333 Hajjar, *supra* n. 74, 69.
334 Public Committee Against Torture in Israel, *Family Matter: Using Family Members to Pressure Detainees Under GSS Interrogation* (2008). A security official has admitted that Shin Bet has used this method on one occasion: 'Shin Bet Admits using Relatives to Pressure Jailed Palestinians', www.Haaretz.com 13 April 2008.
335 C. Levinson, 'IDF Dismisses Palestinian Confession over Physical Shin Bet Interrogation', www.Haaretz.com 7 December 2011.
336 A. Hass, 'Sleeping with the Enemy: Shin Bet Censured for "Exhausting" Interrogation' www.Haaretz.com 7 January 2013.
337 B'Tselem, *No Minor Matter: Violation of the Rights of Palestinian Minors Arrested by Israel on Suspicion of Stone-Throwing* (2011).
338 *PCATI, supra* n. 325, para. 31.
339 See, for example, Public Committee Against Torture in Israel, *Ticking Bombs: Testimonies of Torture Victims in Israel* (2007).
340 M. Ginsburg, 'Despite 750 Abuse Claims against Shin Bet, State has yet to Launch a Criminal Probe in Over a Decade', *The Times of Israel* 11 July 2012 (noting that there has been no criminal investigation in 11 years).
341 G. Davidov and A. Reichman, 'Prolonged Armed Conflict and Diminished Deference to the Military: Lessons from Israel', (2010) 35 *Law & Social Inquiry* 919.
342 *Supra* nn. 132–5 and accompanying text.
343 Volokh, *supra* n. 14, 1479.
344 Schauer, *supra* n. 13, 375.
345 *Id.* 380.
346 CIA-OIG, *supra* n. 245, para. 164.
347 *Id.* para. 89.
348 Schauer, *supra* n. 13, 380
349 Vice Admiral A.T. Church III USN, *Review of Department of Defense Detention Operations and Detainee Interrogation Techniques* (2005) 281.
350 C. Haney *et al*, 'Interpersonal Dynamics in a Simulated Prison', (1973) 1 *International Journal of Criminology and Penology* 69. The prison experiment lasted for six days before it was abandoned (at 88).
351 *Id.* 75.
352 *Id.* 81.
353 *Id.* 85.
354 *Id.*
355 *Id.*
356 *Infra* nn. 365–6 and accompanying text.
357 *Supra* n. 245, para. 93.
358 'Israel Admits Torture', www.bbc.co.uk/news 9 February 2000.
359 Public Committee Against Torture in Israel, *Accountability Denied: The Absence of Investigation and Punishment of Torture in Israel* (2009) 30.
360 J. Conroy, *Unspeakable Acts, Ordinary People: The Dynamics of Torture* (2000) 5.
361 One former interrogator told Ian Cobain how 'Detective Chief Superintendent Bill Mooney, the RUC's most senior detective, would fire up his interrogators before they entered the interview rooms, demanding: "What are you, men or mice – get in there!" If they failed to quickly break a suspect, Mooney would ask them: "Have I got to get in there and do it myself?"' I. Cobain, 'Inside Castlereagh: "We Got Confessions by Torture"', www.Guardian.co.uk October 2010.
362 Conroy, *supra* n. 360, ch. 5, 136.
363 For discussion, see Newbery, *supra* n. 305, 105–8.
364 Cobain, *supra* n. 303, 173–5.
365 *Id.* 186–7.

366 See, for example, *R* v. *Mulholland* (2006) NICA 32; *R* v. *Brown et al* (2012) NICA 14; I.
Cobain, 'Northern Ireland Teenagers who Told of Beatings Before Murder Confessions',
www.guardian.co.uk 11 October 2010.

367 Conroy, *supra* n. 360, 244–7.

368 C. Linde, *Working the Past: Narrative and Institutional* Memory (2009) ch. 4.

369 *Id.* 11.

370 Newbery, *supra* n. 305, 106.

371 For several first-hand accounts, see J. Sharrock, *Tortured: When Good Soldiers Do Bad Things* (2010).

372 For an excellent overview of these problems up until 2008, see: Committee on Armed
Services United States Senate, *Inquiry into the Treatment of Detainees in US Custody*
(2008).

373 Human Rights Watch, *Getting Away with Torture: The Bush Administration and Mistreatment of Detainees* (2011) 39.

374 This section will focus on report findings which suggest reasons for the existence of
abuse. It is worth noting however, that military investigations have varied in their
findings with some reporting systematic abuse and others finding only limited abuse,
while other reports cleared individuals of wrongdoing. For examples of the latter, see
Lt. Gen. Stanley E. Green, *Report on Abu Graihb* (2005) (hereafter Green Report); Lt.
Gen. Randall M. Schmidt, *Investigation into FBI Allegations of Detainee Abuse at Guantánamo Bay, Cuba Detention Facility* (2005) (hereafter Schmidt Report).

375 Schlesinger Report, *supra* n. 271, 68.

376 Army Brig. Gen. Charles Jacoby, *CFC-A Detainee Operations: Report of Inspection* (2004)
para. 19 (referring to 'lack [of] cohesive direction' and 'lack of comprehensive
detention guidance') (hereafter Jacoby Report); *id.* 29–30, 37–8.

377 Jacoby Report *id.* ('Current theatre guidance is drafted clearly, but is not comprehensive or well known outside of the task force headquarters … a comprehensive means of
disseminating guidance, training, and inspecting detention operations needs to be
developed'). See also Schlesinger Report, *supra* n. 271, 67.

378 Major General Antonio M. Taguba, *Article 15–6 Investigation of the 800th Military Police
Brigade* (2004).

379 Schlesinger Report, *supra* n. 271, 51 ('failure to report abuses … in a timely manner').

380 Taguba Report, *supra* n. 378.

381 Jacoby Report, *supra* n. 376.

382 *Id.* para. 19g.

383 United States Army, *Field Manual 22–51 – Leaders' Manual for Combat Stress Control*
(1994) 4–7.

384 Schlesinger, *supra* n. 271, 67.

385 Jacoby, *supra* n. 376, para. 23.

386 H. Keeble and K. Hollington, *Terror Cops: Fighting Terrorism on Britain's Streets* (2010)
(discussing the work and experiences of a police officer who was a member of a
counter-terrorism unit).

387 Former Bush-era OLC lawyer, Jack Goldsmith has noted: 'Everyone in the administration with access to highly classified intelligence on threats to the homeland was
scared of another deadly attack, and of not knowing how to prevent it. This fear created
enormous pressure to stretch the law to its limits in order to give the President the
powers he though necessary to prevent a second 9/11': *The Terror Presidency: Law and
Judgment Inside the Bush Administration* (2007) 11.

388 P. Zelikow, 'Codes of Conduct for a Twilight War', (2012) 49 *Hous. L. Rev.* 1, 11.

389 *Gäfgen* v. *Germany* (application no. 22978/05) paras. 106, 47.

390 Fay and Jones Report, *supra* n. 271, para. 2(a)(3). See also the Schlesinger report which
noted 'lapses of leadership', 'weak and ineffectual leadership' and a 'lack of supervision',
supra n. 271, 43, 45.

391 Fay and Jones Report, *id.* para. 2(a)(4).

392 Major General Antonio M. Taguba, *Article 15–6 Investigation of the 800th Military Police Brigade* (2004) para. 5.

393 *Id.* para. 6.

394 *Id.* para. 8.

395 *Id.* para. 10.

396 *Id.* part III, 14–6.

397 *Id.* para. 17. See also Part III Recommendations.

398 P. Zimbardo, *The Lucifer Effect: How Good People Turn Evil* (2007) 352.

399 Human Rights Watch, *supra* n. 203, 1–2, 12.

400 *Id.* 9, 11. Similarly, as a result of an Israeli security crackdown in 2002, Amnesty International reported the physical abuse of detainees during interrogation and also questioned the motives behind the treatment of thousands of detainees, suggesting it was a form of 'collective punishment': Amnesty International, *Mass Detention in Cruel, Inhuman and Degrading Conditions* (2002).

401 Volokh, *supra* n. 14, 1084.

402 See, for example, A. Vermeule, *Law and the Limits of Reason* (2009) ch. 4.

403 J. Hodgson, 'The Police, the Prosecutor and the Juge D'Instruction: Judicial Supervision in France, Theory and Practice,' (2001) *Brit. J. Crim* 342, 352–6 (discussing the use of physical coercion by French police officers and the response of the judiciary which suggests tolerance of brutality during interrogation).

404 Amnesty International, *The State of the World's Human Rights* (2012) (discussing Europe and Central Asia).

405 For discussion, see Chapter 1 nn. 30–43 and accompanying text.

406 Volokh, *supra* n. 14, 1080.

407 *Id.* 1100.

408 van der Burg, *supra* n. 130, 50.

409 Volokh, *supra* n. 14, 1094.

410 *Id.*

411 Hajjar has noted that in 1970, the Israeli military courts were officially urged not to interfere in the activities of the General Security Service and in decades since, the courts not hindered the widespread use of torture and other forms of coercion: Hajjar, *supra* n. 74, 69.

412 Such an approach was taken in a brief before the US Supreme Court in *Chavez* v *Martinez* 538 U.S. 760 (2003), citing the work of Alan Dershowitz, the petitioner referred to a hypothetical situation in which a police officer 'threatens, cajoles, and pressures [the suspect] into confessing to [a] kidnaping and disclosing the whereabouts of the child [whom he is believed to have kidnapped]'. The petitioner argued that the suspect should not be able to bring action under the Fourteenth amendment because: 'He has no liberty interest in inhibiting the investigation of a serious crime and, even if he did, that interest is outweighed by the government's interest in solving the crime and saving the victim': *Brief for the Petitioner* No. 01–1444 (2002) 27. For discussion, see S. Kreimer, 'Too Close to the Rack and the Screw', (2003) 6 U. Penn. J. Con. L. 278.

413 Power and Vermeule, *supra* n. 9, 5.

414 *Id.*

415 *Id.* 209.

416 *Id.* 208.

417 *Id.* 38–9.

418 C. Schmitt, *Political Theology: Four Chapters on the Concept of Sovereignty* 2nd edn (1934) 6. This view is perhaps better understood by reference to Schmitt's negative views on democracy, fundamental freedoms and his willingness to support dictatorship. For discussion, see: C. Koonz, *The Nazi Conscience* (2003) 58–9; M. Lilla, *The Reckless Mind: Intellectuals in Politics* (2006) ch. II.

419 V.V. Ramraj, *Emergencies and the Limits of Legality* (2008) 4.

420 *Supra* nn. 3–7 and accompanying text.

421 Posner and Vermeule, *supra* n. 9, ch. 6.

422 A. Jennings, 'Shoot to Kill: The Final Courts of Justice', in A. Jennings (ed.), *Justice Under Fire: Abuse of Civil Liberties in Northern Ireland* 2nd ed. (1990). For a detailed discussion of the regulatory framework of law, policy and procedures in which the police's use of lethal force is regulated, see: M. Punch, *Shoot to Kill: Police Accountability, Firearms and Fatal Force* (2011).

423 O.G. Encarnación, 'Democracy and Dirty Wars in Spain', (2007) 29 *Human Rights Quarterly* 950.

424 This might also have the effect of mobilising a violent terrorist response as discussed in Chapter 1.

425 Jennings, *supra* n. 422.

426 Chapter 1, nn. 108–47 and accompanying text.

427 L.L. Fuller, *The Morality of Law* rev. ed. (1970) 63.

428 *R* v. *Home Secretary ex parte Simms* [2000] 2 AC 115, 131 (referring to judicial interpretation of legislation).

429 van der Burg, *supra* n. 130, 48.

430 See, for example, *Secretary of State for the Home Department* v. *Rehman* [2003] AC 153 para. 31, 49; *Secretary of State for the Home Department* v. *MB* [2007] QB 415 para. 64–65; cited with approval in *CF* v. *The Secretary of State for the Home Department* [2013] EWHC 843 (Admin).

431 J.A.G. Griffith, *The Politics of the Judiciary* 5th edn (1997) 308. Deference is also in evidence in the US courts: 'federal judges have been showing a high rate of deference to the executive branch [but not] nearly as high as it might be expected to be. Judges have not adopted anything like an irrebuttable presumption in government's favour': C.R. Sunstein, 'Judging National Security Post-9/11: An Empirical Investigation', (2008) *Supreme Court Review* 269.

432 *Liversidge* v. *Anderson* [1942] AC 206.

433 MB, *supra* n. 430, para. 97.

434 *per* Sir John Donaldson MR, *Attorney General* v. *Guardian Newspapers Ltd (No. 2)* [1988] 3 WLR 776 (questioning whether the 'secret search of the premises' of a spy by the security services be deemed as wrongdoing).

435 *A (FC) and others* v. *Secretary of State for the Home Department* [2004] UKHL 56 (House of Lords holding that detaining foreign terror suspects indefinitely without charge or trial was a breach of Article 14 ECHR as the provision only applied to foreign nationals).

436 For a recent example, see: *AT* v. *Secretary of State for the Home Department* [2012] EWCA Civ 42 (declaring the imposition of a control order in breach of the right to a fair trial).

437 *W (Algeria) (FC) and BB (Algeria) (FC) and Others* v. *Secretary of State for the Home Department* [2012] UKSC 8 (court endorsing an order granting anonymity and confidentiality to a witness giving evidence in support of a foreign terrorist suspect subject to deportation proceedings).

438 *A (FC) and others* v. *Secretary of State for the Home Department* [2005] UKHL 71.

439 *A* v. *HM Treasury* [2010] UKSC 2.

440 M. White, 'Public Mood has Hardened Over Terror Cases, Blair Tells Judges', *The Guardian* 27 July 2005; S. Knight, 'Blair Turns on Judges Over Escaped Terror Suspects', *Times Online* 17 October 2006. In 2005, Conservative Party leader criticized what he described as 'activist' judges in 'thwarting the wishes of Parliament': M. Howard, 'Judges Must Bow to the Will of Parliament', *The Daily Telegraph* 10 August 2005.

441 F. Gibb and P. Webster, 'We Won't Heed Blair, Say Judges', *The Times* 28 July 2005.

442 M. Rizzo and G. Whitman, 'The Camel's Nose is in the Tent: Rules, Theories and Slippery Slopes', (2003) 51 *U.C.L.A Law Rev.* 539, 578–90 (discussing slippage and mechanisms to reduce its occurrence generally).

443 *Id.* 579.

444 Lode, *supra* n. 13, 1484.
445 Rizzo and Whitman, *supra* n. 442, 588–9.
446 Volokh, *supra* n. 14, 1038.
447 Bagaric and Clarke, *supra* n. 46, 47–8.
448 This is a point made by Rejali, Chapter 1, n and accompanying text.
449 Volokh, supra n. 14, 1035.
450 W.L. Twining and P.E. Twining, 'Bentham *on* Torture', (1973) 24 *N.I.L.Q.* 305, 315.

5

DEBATING TORTURE AND THE BENEFITS OF DISSENT

'Respectable arguments can be made on all sides of this debate.'[1]

'There would be little to say on this subject, were it not for the nonsense that has been talked about it.'[2]

The idea that interrogational torture should be legalised is undoubtedly controversial. The controversy sometimes masks the fact that, as Luban notes in the quotation above, respectable arguments exist on both sides of the torture debate. This chapter examines the various means by which discussion of this topic has been discouraged and obstructed, and proponents of legalisation vilified. It may seem a departure from the rest of the book to focus on the manner in which scholars have debated the question of interrogational torture. The focus of this chapter, however, is consistent with earlier chapters because it makes a consequentialist argument that debate and discussion will strengthen the absolute prohibition. It does so by enabling scholars and others to identify weak ideas and assist in the discovery of truth. Suppression of ideas is also counter-productive because stifling discussion or debate ignores the need to develop and refine existing arguments against the use of interrogational torture. This chapter challenges those who wish to silence ideas which they claim are dangerous with a strong defence of free speech. It is argued that discussion will be of benefit to scholars, government and the wider community. Indeed, lessons should be learned from the War on Terror when decisions regarding the use of torture and other coercive techniques were accompanied by a lack of debate within government and the silencing of dissent.[3]

Given the widespread use of torture and other ill-treatment in the world, it is essential that the case for legalisation is clearly refuted. The calls for legalisation will continue and in the future a major terrorist attack may place torture as a strongly favoured policy option within government. This would demand a strong, factually supported case against the use of interrogational torture, particularly where there is support for its use amongst the general public or in government. It is irrational to suggest discussion will legitimise the use of torture when state officials in many countries already see its use as legitimate. In such circumstances, discussion and debate is not only desirable, but essential. As noted by Namier at the beginning of this chapter, where nonsensical beliefs are widely held it is important to respond. Finally, this chapter critically analyses attempts to vilify proponents of legalisation and argues that such tactics are damaging in that they can only serve to entrench attitudes. By contrast, dialogue provides an opportunity to persuade proponents of legalisation by the use of argument and evidence. It also enables those who defend the prohibition to identify weak ideas and develop more convincing arguments. As such, this chapter will argue that attempts to silence or vilify will only damage the prohibition.

1. Freedom to debate torture in a democracy?

Nietzsche once argued that in relation to '[a] prohibition whose reason we do not understand ... let us put it to the test, so as to learn *why* this prohibition exists'[4] (emphasis in original). Since the terrorist attacks on 9/11, the absolute legal prohibition against the use of torture has come under sustained attack from scholars and state officials who have, in essence, questioned whether 'there are times when the rights-based model of democracy is supplanted by ... a siege mode of democracy'.[5] The suggestion that interrogational torture should be legally regulated has tested the rationale underpinning the absolute prohibition, as well as the arguments for reform. To the critics of such an idea, the proponents of legislation favour the reversal of internationally-recognised legal norms on the basis of flawed moral reasoning, false empirical claims and a failure to acknowledge the harms of torture.[6] Those who have questioned the absolute prohibition have been met with detailed refutations of their viewpoint.[7] Some opponents of legalisation have engaged in abuse, name calling and have even attempted to prevent the publication of certain viewpoints, while others have suggested that the legalisation of torture is an illegitimate topic for discussion and potentially dangerous. This section argues that the legalisation of interrogational torture is a legitimate topic for discussion and debate. Indeed, on the basis of free speech theory reiterated over many centuries it can be argued that the benefits of debate far outweigh the potential risks. If the reasoning underpinning the prohibition is sound, then a reaffirmation of these reasons will assist in educating those who doubt the need to retain it. Discussion and debate also allows for the development of new insights and stronger arguments in defence of the prohibition.

The scholarly debate over the legalisation of interrogational torture takes place within a specific context. Debate over contentious subject matter is an inherent part of academic life. In its 1940 statement concerning academic freedom, the American Association of University Professors stated that controversy is 'at the heart of ... free academic inquiry'.[8] The idea of 'free academic inquiry' is seen as a crucial means by which truth can emerge. Hamilton observes: 'In a liberal intellectual system, the primacy of evidence, reason, and fair argument in pursuing knowledge and free speech in rectifying error is widely accepted.'[9] Similarly, writing in 1927, Newman described a university as a place 'where inquiry is pushed forward, and discoveries verified and perfected, and rashness rendered innocuous, and error exposed, by the collision of mind with mind, and knowledge with knowledge'.[10] It is through this 'collision of minds' that error is identified and knowledge furthered. Benson and Stangroom emphasise that the furtherance of truth is a central part of scholarly life: 'If researchers aren't after the truth, surely they might as well hand in their badges and try another line of work. In fact, to put it bluntly, surely it's not so much that they might as well, as that they ought to. If they're not after the truth they have no business being researchers at all.'[11] In the form of a free expression right, academic freedom affords scholars the liberty to discover new truths, challenge the existing order and 'is designed to create the liberty necessary to facilitate the advancement of knowledge, understood as the unimpeded application of professional norms of inquiry'.[12] In other words, academic freedom includes the liberty to express views and engage in research within the confines of recognised disciplinary standards.[13]

This bounded liberty makes inevitable the fact that scholars will, on occasion, express views or come to conclusions which other scholars and members of the wider community find objectionable, offensive or even dangerous. However, academic freedom affords scholars the opportunity to express such viewpoints and for other scholars to challenge them and highlight any errors that lie within. While academic freedom encompasses the right to dissent and to challenge accepted truths, it is not necessarily the case that all scholars are prepared to accept the right of others to dissent. In such circumstances a number of tactics are used in an attempt to suppress dissenting perspectives. This section will proceed by analysing the ways in which scholarly opponents of legalisation have attempted to silence discussion or depict proponents in the most negative and personalised terms.

a. Silencing dissent

Attempts to suppress scholarly ideas that challenge accepted truths are not uncommon and occur in several ways. First, there is a long history of university administrators punishing or dismissing those who express dissenting viewpoints.[14] The second means by which dissent can be silenced is through attempts to prevent the publication or expression of controversial or dissenting viewpoints.[15] The third way in which ideas can be suppressed is where scholars engage in self-censorship resulting from the fear of how others will react to their ideas.[16] Certain ideas may attract public criticism, as well as insults and abuse from other scholars, students, employers and pressure groups.[17] This may lead scholars to engage in 'preference falsification' which is defined as 'the act of misrepresenting one's genuine wants under perceived social pressures'.[18] For other scholars, they may simply avoid certain areas of inquiry. Empirical research involving scholars with a scientific background suggests that 'the mere threat of social sanction deterred particular types of inquiry'.[19] In this way, pressures that fall far short of formal government or administrator intervention can 'eliminate speech at the margins'.[20]

The problem of ideas being met by ostracism or other forms of social sanction, as well as attempts to prevent or inhibit the expression of dissenting viewpoints has occurred in many, if not all academic fields of study, including: education,[21] race,[22] women's studies,[23] health physics,[24] theoretical physics,[25] climate science,[26] medicine[27] and ancient history.[28] While many scholars enthuse about new discoveries, theories or ideas,[29] there are some who attempt to silence those who offer challenges to accepted truths. Indeed, in commenting on the state of free speech in universities in the United States of America, Downs observes that freedom of expression has been undermined by 'progressive social censorship'.[30] Some scholars have even advocated the suppression of 'policies, opinions and movements' that undermine progressive social and economic ideas.[31] Suppression of new ideas is a reminder that the discovery of 'new truths' can be 'shackled by the requirement that [a scholar's] conclusions shall never seriously deviate from other generally accepted beliefs ... '.[32] Clearly, when an existing consensus is challenged there will be resistance – sometimes for good reason. Not every new idea is a good idea and the onus is on those who propose new ideas to use argument and evidence in order to convince others of their merit.[33] However, even truth does not guarantee acceptance of an idea as it has long been acknowledged that '[t]ruth ... just by being truth, runs always a sufficiently great risk of being rejected'.[34] Indeed, recent empirical research suggests that it can be very difficult to correct false beliefs amongst people who hold strong opinions and the correction of such beliefs may actually 'backfire' by reinforcing them.[35]

Given the volume of work that exists concerning the legalisation of interrogational torture, it is tempting to view questions of suppression as fanciful. However, evidence of efforts to silence dissent do exist, albeit to a limited extent. There have been attempts to prevent the publication of certain viewpoints.[36] When it became known that Bagaric and Clarke had written an article justifying the use of interrogational torture in the *University of San Francisco Law Review* 'letters were sent to the editors of the ... Review ... urging it not to publish'.[37] There have also been attempts to silence scholars through the threat of social isolation. When discussing an edited book concerning the alleged use of torture by US authorities as part of the 'War on Terror',[38] Greenberg has described 'big pressure' relating to the use of the word 'torture' in the book title and said 'there were a number of colleagues of mine ... [who] told me I wasn't going to publish this book or if I did, they didn't want to be associated with me'.[39] Scholars who have argued that the use of interrogational torture is legally or morally justifiable have been subject to calls that they should be sacked[40] as well as suggestions that in one case, a scholar is unfit to teach.[41] In this way, dissenting scholars are treated as 'outsiders' and 'separated from a place in the legitimate order'.[42] Such pressures may also chill free expression and lead to self-censorship.

Ironically, the intolerance of dissent within parts of the scholarly community is mirrored by efforts to silence dissent within government and the armed forces. In his memoir, Jack Goldsmith, a former lawyer in the US Department of Justice, Office of Legal Counsel (OLC) refers to conversations he had with John Yoo, formerly of the OLC, in which Yoo characterised the actions of David Addington, who was counsel to Vice President Dick Cheney, as: 'slaying the legal wimps in the administration who stood as an obstacle to the President's aggressive antiterrorism policies.'[43] Similarly, a former chief legal advisor to the British army in Iraq has claimed that he was 'gagged' following his criticism of British army commanders and Ministry of Defence officials after the death of an Iraqi prisoner while being detained by British troops.[44] An official inquiry examining the development of policy towards detainees in US military custody noted that errors could have been avoided had there been 'more robust debate' within government.[45] Other state officials have encountered hostility when raising concerns about the use of torture by strategic allies.[46] These examples illustrate the pressure that can be placed on dissenters to conform and contribute to the phenomenon of 'groupthink', where dissent is discouraged and poor decisions are the result.[47] As noted by Woodruff, governmental decisions that are made without open discussion and debate tend to magnify error.[48] As such, scholarly opponents of torture should take note that the case for legalised torture needs to be met with 'more speech, not enforced silence'.[49]

b. Demonising opponents

Scholarly discussion of interrogational torture and the War on Terror has sometimes included highly emotive characterisations and *ad hominem* attacks. In his study of incivility, Carter has identified an assumption within political discourse that 'all truly moral people agree on the issue; there is no reasonable alternative. Those on the other side then become monsters, and demonizing them is not incivility, it is simply description.'[50] In the torture debate, demonisation has taken several forms. The torture and counter-terrorism literature is littered with attacks on American morality, its citizenry and the value of American culture.[51] More specifically, Manderson, for example, appears to suggest that proponents of torture or its legalisation suffer from psychopathy.[52] Scholars who have argued for legalisation have been accused of dishonesty,[53] been the recipients of hate mail[54] or have been compared to Hitler.[55] Dershowitz has complained about the repeated misrepresentation of his views, as well as some of the personal attacks to which he has been subject.[56] In this vein, Gearty has authored a stinging attack on those he terms 'Rumsfeldians', who in his view, attempt to normalise the use of torture. The tone and content of his article personalises the issues and includes sweeping assertions regarding the views of those with whom he disagrees. As an illustration of the tone of this piece, Gearty writes:

> These individuals are distinguished by their determination to permit, indeed to encourage, the holding of suspected 'terrorists' or 'unlawful combatants' … in

conditions which make torture, inhuman and degrading treatment well-nigh situationally inevitable. No ethic drives their policy, not even one of self or national interest, since torture is inefficient as well as (in post-post-modern terms) plain wrong. The brutality to which they commit themselves is that of the stupid playground bully, lashing out just because it is possible ... they push back the barriers of the unsayable, thereby opening the door to the hitherto undoable. To succeed in transforming the liberal discourse, however, [they] need a great trauma on which to feed; 11 September is an obvious example though not in itself sufficient. They also require an ideological super-structure that fits with the democratic times in which they still (perhaps reluctantly) find themselves.[57]

Elsewhere, Gearty goes so far as to suggest that the details of the arguments in favour of legalised torture are relatively unimportant.[58] Instead, in his view the crucial factor is that these 'supposed "human rights" experts ... allegedly well versed in the requirements of their subject', are discussing torture at all.[59] The questionable tone of the work in this area extends to those who challenge opponents of legalisation. Seidman characterised academics as having 'little desire to talk seriously about torture', and accuses some of 'evasion' in failing to deal with the 'hardest issues'.[60] Those whom he terms 'moralists', he claims are guilty of 'wilful blindness' involving a 'readiness to substitute pious denunciation for practical measures that might limit the amount and severity of torture'.[61] Later, he states: 'It should come as no surprise that people are most comfortable with a stance of moral purity when they do not have to pay the price.'[62] Finally, the personalisation of issues often takes place with little regard for the implications of a particular line of reasoning. For example, Dratel, when discussing policy makers who favour the use of interrogational torture, states: 'they should be compelled to watch the application of "aggressive interrogation" techniques or "counter resistance" measures on a human subject, or, better yet, perform such techniques themselves – or, even better still, be subjected to them.'[63] Of course, this analysis begins to unravel when one raises the question of whether Dratel would apply similar reasoning to himself in the context of lethal force used by the police or the military. If he would approve of the use of such force in at least some circumstances, it gets us nowhere to suggest that he should witness, or indeed be subject, to such measures.

Of course, ostracism may have little or no impact on scholarly activity, however, it may serve to chill free inquiry. The discussion of controversial subject areas are unlikely to be encouraged when scholars who express the 'wrong' point of view are accused of being Nazis or mentally ill, or whose work is the subject of criticism laced with sarcasm – none of which are likely to convince the proponents of legalisation of the wrongness of their view.[64] The scholars who engage in such behaviour clearly assume the correctness of their own ideas. The problem with such an approach is highlighted by Paine, who argued: 'He who denies to another [the right to an opinion], makes a slave of himself to his present opinion, because he precludes himself the right of changing it.'[65] While it can be argued that a commitment to the absolute prohibition reflects empirical reality and that there are significant dangers in the legalisation of torture, it cannot be assumed that this is a position without potential cost. Even if that were not the case, the arguments cited in opposition to legalisation are not equally convincing. Ironically, the consequences of ostracism may serve to undermine the very case for the absolute prohibition which opponents of legalisation seek to promote. Silence hinders the identification of weak ideas and the debate necessary to develop resilient arguments in defence of the absolute prohibition.

Finally, another analytical technique in evidence within the torture debate is the use of guilt by association. Žižek, for example, has argued that Alan Dershowitz's style of argumentation in favour of the use of torture warrants is akin to the arguments used at the Wannsee Conference in 1942 where senior Nazis planned the Final Solution.[66] Leaving aside Žižek's reliance on a BBC docudrama for his insight into the conference,[67] one assumes that Žižek's comparison is based on the fact that parts of the protocol resulting from the conference setting out the 'Final Solution of the European Jewish Question', stipulated that some questions, such as establishing who was Jewish and to be subject to 'evacuation' to the East, would be settled within the 'general framework' of the Nuremberg Laws.[68] In other words, the decision of who would be included within the Nazi's policy of genocide involved a veneer of legality. Dershowitz has argued that if states are going to use torture it would be preferable to allow for judicial authorisation of torture in 'grave' circumstances in order to provide some control over its use.[69] By contrast, the Wannsee Conference discussions were animated by a desire to destroy an entire race of people and were thus of an entirely different order of magnitude in terms of their underlying motive, intention and effect. Indeed, Dershowitz argues that his proposals would 'decrease the amount of physical violence directed against suspects'.[70] There is good reason to doubt that conclusion,[71] but this illustrates the importance of engaging with the arguments and the weakness of Žižek's simplistic approach.

c. Torture as an undiscussable topic

It has been suggested that until the aftermath of the 9/11 terror attacks, the use of torture to gain intelligence from terrorist suspects was 'undiscussable'.[72] Such a suggestion shows a poor awareness of history. The use of interrogational torture and coercion as an intelligence gathering technique has, for decades, been considered by state officials in many democracies, including: France,[73] Israel,[74] the United States of America[75] and the United Kingdom.[76] In some instances these discussions have gone back centuries with many European states incorporating torture within their respective legal systems.[77] The suggestion that torture was once 'undiscussable' is a milder version of attempts by opponents to cordon off the legalisation of interrogational torture as a topic of discussion. For some scholars interrogational torture is not a topic appropriate for policy discussions. Gearty observes that '[t]he unspeakable is no longer unspoken'[78] and refers to torture, and other controversial counter-terrorism measures, as solutions 'to supposed ethical dilemmas that need now to be considered and debated, as you might consider and debate any other kind of policy proposal'.[79] This is a classic example of the 'cordon[ing] off [of] certain sets of ideas, to declare them special, inviolate, taboo, sacred: different from ordinary, mundane sets of ideas ... '[80] The problem with cordoning off is that it leaves the absolute prohibition without a defence or a means by which the case for legalised torture can be challenged. Rather than seeing the use of interrogational torture as undiscussable, one of the few UK-based academics to consider this specific issue has argued that:

> It is a lack of debate which would be more worrisome since this would threaten to condemn the prohibition to obscurity. The idea that serious discussion of the legal questions surrounding the realisation of the absolute prohibition of torture as a matter of international law somehow has the effect of weakening the normative force of that prohibition is difficult to fathom.[81]

Indeed, silence would prevent an articulation of the absolute prohibition's value and the consequences of its loss. This would render the prohibition unimportant and the creation of an exception to it inconsequential.

d. Debate as a dangerous legitimisation of torture?

Some commentators have suggested that it is wrong and dangerous to discuss the legalisation of interrogational torture. Kassimeris claims that '[a]t the start of the twenty-first century we should not be debating the use of torture'[82] and Spicer claims that '[t]here ... should not be any such debate'.[83] Žižek goes further by arguing that to introduce torture 'as a legitimate topic of debate, [is] even more dangerous than an explicit endorsement of torture: while – for the moment, at least – an explicit endorsement would be too shocking and therefore rejected, the mere introduction of torture as a legitimate topic allows us to entertain the idea while retaining a pure conscience'.[84] Despite Žižek's claim that discussing the legalisation of torture is 'dangerous', he and others who have sympathy for this view[85] appear to have no difficulty discussing, often repeatedly, their own views on the question of legalisation.[86] Indeed, in later work Žižek argues against the recognition of a 'universal principle' that allows for the use of torture. Yet, he also states: 'I can well imagine that, in a very specific situation, I would resort to torture ... '[87] However, by retaining the absolute legal prohibition, Žižek argues 'I retain the proper sense of the horror of what I did'.[88] It is a curious position for a scholar to argue on the one hand, that it is dangerous to view torture as a legitimate topic of debate, while at the same time lending some legitimacy to its use by suggesting he himself would torture in certain, undisclosed circumstances.

An issue that arises is whether the case for legalised torture represents a dangerous idea. Some scholars emphasise the potential danger of ideas: '[i]deas are the most powerful forces we can unleash on the world, and they should not be let loose without careful consideration of their consequences.'[89] By contrast, others suggest that no knowledge or idea is 'evil in and of itself ... [e]vil and destruction lie only in the mode of acquisition and application of knowledge'.[90] A similar view was shared by Milton who, writing in 1644, observed that 'knowledge cannot defile, nor consequently the books, if the will and conscience be not defiled'.[91] To describe the torture debate as dangerous assumes that people will learn nothing from the ideas and arguments of those opposed to interrogational torture. Ideas can be dangerous because they can lead to actions which have negative consequences. For example, it has been suggested that the idea that HIV is not a cause of AIDS has resulted in changes in government policy in countries such as South Africa and has had a 'devastating' impact on the prevention and treatment of HIV.[92] In the context of interrogational torture, it is evident that scholarly works advocating the legalisation of torture were judged favourably by lawyers working within the Bush administration at the time when memoranda were prepared permitting the use of highly coercive interrogation methods.[93] This might add weight to the notion that certain ideas are dangerous. It should be noted, however, that it is not necessarily a straightforward task linking ideas promoted by particular scholars and resultant government action. The significance of the citation of Dershowitz's work in some of the OLC memos should not be overstated. It is evident that there was a strong desire to use highly coercive interrogation methods by the Bush Administration. It can be argued that the use of Dershowitz's work merely gave some supposed authority for views already held by OLC lawyers.[94]

Dershowitz has argued that discussion of legalised torture can be justified on the basis that 'open discussion' is less dangerous than 'secret discussion or no discussion at all'.[95] While Dershowitz uses the idea of an open discourse to propose the use of torture warrants it also allows for his ideas and claims to be challenged and for the reasoning underpinning the absolute prohibition to be reaffirmed rather than being 'condemned to obscurity'.[96] Indeed, Berlin has argued that 'the only real remedy for the evil consequences, whether of ignorance or of knowledge, is more knowledge: clearer understanding of what is involved, of what is worth pursuing, of means and ends, consequences and their value'.[97] Such understanding cannot be achieved through suggestions that torture is undiscussable and so dangerous that that it should be avoided.

There is another reason why discussion of interrogational torture has social utility.[98] Given that a significant proportion of the general public approve of the use of interrogational torture to prevent terrorist attacks[99] it can be argued that an evidence-led case against its use may help inform public views on torture. Further, public discussion and debate of interrogational torture can be defended on the grounds that informed civic engagement on matters of political and social importance is an integral part of a well-functioning democracy.[100] Indeed, public support for what some scholars describe as 'authoritarian' counter-terrorism measures strongly suggests the need for a debate that helps inform the general public.[101] It is a deeply pessimistic view of the case for the absolute prohibition to assume that discussion of legalised torture will inevitably lead to the undermining of the absolute prohibition and is typical of the 'civil libertarian pessimism' that often pervades discussions of counter-terrorism policy.[102]

If the opponents of legalisation are correct in their claims that talk of torture is dangerous, then surely the best they can do is make a convincing case that legalisation would be a bad idea. How else can the case for the absolute prohibition and against legalisation be made? Kant argued that '[t]he public use of one's reason must always be free, and it alone can bring about enlightenment among men'.[103] Enlightenment can only occur with a restatement of the arguments and values underpinning the absolute prohibition. Another relevant consideration is that while the absolute prohibition is widely recognised as a matter of principle, this is certainly not the case in terms of state practice.[104] Reaffirming the reasoning underpinning the absolute prohibition is a crucial task when faced with state authorities who use torture. Further, to remain silent in response to arguments that torture is morally or legally justifiable poses its own dangers.[105] By failing to engage with the arguments of the proponents, the danger will be that those arguments will go unchallenged. Unsurprisingly, those who criticise the discussion of proposals for legalised torture do not explain how the case for the absolute prohibition can be made by silence. In addition, those who refuse to debate do not suffer the inconvenience of having their own assumptions, arguments and ideas challenged. Fish emphasises this particular point when he warns of the 'attractions of premature judgement' and suggests that: '[the individual] must be protected from his own tendency to assume that the opinions he holds now are the right ones.'[106] Whether people need to be 'protected' from the tendency Fish describes is open to question, but scholars certainly need to be aware of the dangers of making unwarranted assumptions and failing to consider 'rival evidence'.[107]

There is a further reason not to shy away from the discussion of controversial subject matter. Through debate, weak arguments can be identified and errors corrected.[108] As argued by Holmes, free speech is important so as to allow for the 'correction' of weak ideas.[109] Failure to debate, or at least engage with the issues by some other means, may therefore result in scholars avoiding any consideration of the weaknesses inherent within their own arguments. By contrast, what is implicit within the argument that torture should never be debated is that those who want to retain the absolute prohibition have little confidence that their arguments will persuade others. In reality, failure to engage also carries with it risks. Not least that poorly supported arguments on either side of this debate will go unchallenged. The reality is that in a 'liberal intellectual system' the discussion and exchange of ideas is essential to testing their resilience.[110] There is no field of academic inquiry where weak ideas cannot be found, in this regard the debate over the legalisation of interrogational torture is no different. Indeed, those who defend the prohibition but reject discussion or debate potentially undermine their own case by depriving themselves of information that could strengthen their own position.[111]

A recent opinion-piece by Vincent Warren, Executive Director of the Centre for Constitutional Rights, provides a case study of the difficulties of the 'don't debate' approach. He suggests that ' … by debating the utility of torture, even its opponents are implicated in the conclusion that if torture does work, it is justified'.[112] Warren may prefer not to engage in such arguments but his approach is problematic because he praises those who have challenged claims regarding the role of torture in locating the hiding place of Osama bin Laden.[113] Given that opponents of torture argue that it is ineffective and should not be used, it makes no sense to implicate them in a suggestion that torture is justified. He wrongly assumes that the case against torture rests on a single argument. He also assumes an unsophisticated measure of torture's effectiveness, which, as noted in Chapter 3, requires careful analysis. His affirmation that 'torture is simply, and always, wrong' is open to the obvious response of 'it's not always wrong to torture because ... '. Affirmative statements against the use of interrogational torture, invite disagreement. Warren is entitled not to engage in such discussions, but by commenting on it, and rightly defending the absolute prohibition, he inevitably involves himself.

There is another facet to the question of whether to engage in discussion on a controversial topic. Support amongst Americans for the use of torture grew between 2005 and 2012.[114] At the end of 2009, 58% of US voters supported 'waterboarding and other aggressive interrogation techniques' in order to gain intelligence from Umar Farouk Abdulmutallab, the so-called 'underwear bomber'.[115] A 2012 YouGov survey found that: '[36%] of Americans support the use of torture; 38% do not. But when it comes to whether torture can produce useful information, 53% say it can, and just 25% say it cannot.'[116] The argument of this book is that in these circumstances such beliefs require more of a response than an effort to silence viewpoints, some of which might be widely held. Warren makes the interesting counter-argument that Americans do not debate the utility of genocide, but *if* 36% of Americans supported genocide or 53% thought genocide was an effective means of treating a particular ethnic or racial group it would be crucial to develop ways of countering the misunderstandings, ignorance, bigotry or other factors that underpin such beliefs. On a societal level, to do anything else would be irresponsible.

Some lessons might be also learned from the phenomenon of Holocaust denial. One response to Holocaust denial is to ignore deniers so as to not give them civic status, time or a platform for their false beliefs and arguments. However, this approach poses its own dangers. It does not allow for engagement with these arguments and an explanation as to why they are incorrect. Some scholars and educators have recognised this problem and have engaged with denial in several different ways. For example, some scholars such as Michael Shermer, have engaged in television debates with hardcore deniers. Elsewhere, the web-based *Nizkor Project* has responded to 66 questions about the Holocaust put to it by the historical 'revisionist' group, the *Institute for Historical Review*.[117] *Nizkor*'s 66 answers provide an excellent refutation of the ideas underpinning denial, as well as providing answers to questions often posed in an effort to cast doubt on the existence of the Holocaust. It might be argued that engaging in dialogue or debate with hardcore deniers will have no impact given the motivations underpinning denial.[118] This is certainly possible, although even amongst hardcore deniers, some have recanted.[119] The objection to engaging in dialogue or debate assumes that all deniers are equally committed to the cause. Some deniers might be confused or ignorant and their denial may result from being exposed to anti-Semitism or other teachings as part of their upbringing. Such views can change when subjected to alternative viewpoints and experiences.[120]

Shermer and Grobman note that the 'Holocaust denial movement remains in a state of relative flux. Yet it is hardly about to disappear.'[121] Research suggests that Holocaust education programmes have a beneficial effect on knowledge, and raise awareness of racism, anti-Semitism, intolerance and scapegoating.[122] Scholars, including historians,[123] social scientists,[124] along with those running websites[125] have highlighted the tactics, motivations and flawed reasoning of deniers.[126] This work provides accurate and reliable information to inform educational projects[127] and provides a resource that can be accessed by those who are confused, naïve or uncertain. In this way, benefit can be derived from engagement with controversial subject matter. While there might be risks, these are exaggerated and serve little purpose other than deter engagement with controversial issues. Shermer and Grobman argue that there is a *duty* on experts to share knowledge in the 'belief that truth will always win out when the evidence is made available for all to see'.[128] It is open to debate as to whether this is a realistic belief. It is the case, however, that silence does not explain, educate or change minds. Here, we are faced with similar dilemmas to the torture debate, but also a more developed notion of public education than exists amongst those who oppose the use and legalisation of interrogational torture. This divergence of approach should be considered and the lessons learned.

2. Conclusion

This chapter has sought to defend the right of scholars to discuss and debate the legalisation of interrogational torture. It has done so on classical free speech grounds – not merely as a way of defending the right of scholars to challenge accepted truths, but as a means of developing stronger arguments in order to undermine the case for legalisation. The purported vulnerability of the prohibition in the post-9/11 security environment requires the best possible defence.[129] This chapter has also taken issue with the demonisation of proponents of legalisation and has challenged attempts to cordon off torture as a topic for discussion and debate. Such attacks fail to address core issues and deprive defenders of the absolute prohibition an opportunity to strengthen their own arguments. In previous chapters, it is hoped that engagement with the arguments of proponents has produced a strong argument against legalisation and illustrates what can be gained by a careful analysis of issues, the identification of error and use of empirical data.

This method is at the core of any credible scholarly examination of a controversial issue and reflects the 'political liberty' of scholars, access to information, academic freedom and scholarly 'training to seek the truth'.[130] To depart from this approach can lead to failure in making a compelling case against the legalisation of interrogational torture. It can also lead to personal abuse or ideologically-motivated attacks that simply ignore the basic demands of scholarship.[131] That is not to deny that anger or passion may motivate scholars, but it serves no purpose to abandon rational, evidence-led argument in favour of name-calling and attempts to silence dissent. Brecher has admitted that he reacted with anger when he became aware of the legalisation argument favoured by Dershowitz and '[m]y initial anger remains'.[132] However, Brecher used his anger as a motivation to craft a detailed and important rebuttal of Dershowitz's torture warrant idea. This should provide an example to all scholars who write in areas that attract controversy.

Notes

1 D. Luban, 'Torture, American-Style', *Washington Post* 27 November 2005.
2 A.J.P. Taylor quoting Sir Lewis Namier, in his introduction to Fritz Tobias's *The Reichstag Fire* (New York: G.P. Putnam's Sons, 1964) 16.
3 See *infra* nn. 43–6 and accompanying text.
4 R.J. Hollingdale (trans.), *A Nietzsche Reader* (1977) 85.
5 D. Kostakopoulou, 'How to do Things with Security Post 9/11', (2008) 28 *OJLS* 317, 321.
6 See, for example, A. O'Rourke *et al*, 'Torture, Slippery Slopes, Intellectual Apologists, and Ticking Bombs: An Australian Response to Bagaric and Clarke', (2005–6) 40 *U.S. F.L. Rev.* 85.
7 See, for example, B. Brecher, *Torture and the Ticking Bomb* (2008) (analysing Alan Dershowitz's 'torture warrant' idea).
8 American Association of University Professors, *1940 Statement of Principles on Academic Freedom and Tenure* (1940) 5. See also the University and College Union's *Statement on Academic Freedom* (2012) para. 3 (noting that academic freedom may 'touch upon sensitive and controversial issues').
9 N. Hamilton, *Zealotry and Academic Freedom* (1998) 3.
10 J.H. Newman, *The Idea of a University* (1927) in R. George Wright, 'The Emergence of First Amendment Academic Freedom', (2007) 85 *Neb. L. Rev.* 793.
11 O. Benson and J. Stangroom, *Why Truth Matters* (2006) 164.
12 R. Post, 'The Structure of Academic Freedom', in B. Doumani (ed.), *Academic Freedom After September 11* (2006) 70.
13 E. Barendt, *Academic Freedom and the Law: A Comparative Study* (2010) 19–21 (noting that 'academic speech, unlike general public or political discourse, is essentially subject to quality controls on the basis of general professional standards of accuracy and coherence').
14 This particular issue is outside the remit of this book. For discussion, see L. Menand, *The Metaphysical Club: A Story of Ideas in America* (2001) ch. 15; M.J. Schueller and A. Dawson, *Dangerous Professors: Academic Freedom and the National Security Campus* (2012).
15 *Infra* nn. 21–39.
16 G.C. Loury, 'Self-Censorship in Public Discourse: A Theory of "Political Correctness" and Related Phenomena', (1994) 6 *Rationality and Society* 428.
17 For examples on the left and right of the political spectrum, see D. Horowitz, *Indoctrination U. The Left's War Against Academic Freedom* (2007); A.J. Nocella II, *et al* (eds.), *Academic Repression: Reflections from the Academic Industrial Complex* (2010).
18 T. Kuran, *Private Truths, Public Lies: The Social Consequences of Preference Falsification* (1995) 3.
19 J. Kempner *et al*, 'Forbidden Knowledge: Mechanisms of Social Control in Science', (2005) 307 *Science* 854. For an early discussion of the fear that may lead to self-censorship, see Nicholas Copernicus who, in a dedication to Pope Paul III, in his *On the Revolutions of the Heavenly Bodies* (1543) stated: 'the contempt which I had to fear because of the novelty and apparent absurdity of my view, nearly induced me to abandon utterly the work I had begun'.
20 K. Roosevelt, 'The Cost of Agencies: *Waters* v. *Churchill* and the First Amendment in the Administrative State', (1997) 106 *Yale L.J.* 1233, 1263.

21 R. Attwood, 'Top Scholars are Kings of "Wishful Thinking"', *Times Higher Education* 20 January 2010 (Bahram Bekhradnia noting: 'The general concern I have ... is to address the question of academics in positions of authority ignoring evidence – making up their evidence, even – engaging in frankly extraordinary personal abuse and attacks ... because they see a body of evidence that is being assembled and presented undermining their zeitgeist and their beliefs').

22 Loury, *supra* n. 16. D. Horowitz, *Uncivil Wars: the Controversy Over Reparations for Slavery* (2002); K.J. Norwood, 'The Virulence of Blackthink and How its Threat of Ostracism Shackles those Deemed not Black Enough', (2004–5) 93 *Ky. L.J.* 143; R. Kennedy, *Sellout: The Politics of Racial Betrayal* (2008) (all discussing the way in which ostracism is used by scholars and others in an attempt to stifle contentious points of views regarding the issue of race in America).

23 A.C. Kors and H.A. Silverglate, *The Shadow University: The Betrayal of Liberty on America's Campuses* (1998); D. Patai and N. Koertge, *Professing Feminism: Education and Indoctrination in Women's Studies* (2003) (noting the narrow ideological leanings of many women's studies departments in the United States of America and attempts to silence or intimidate critical students and colleagues).

24 E. Sternglass, *Secret Fallout: Low Level Radiation from Hiroshima to Three Mile Island* (1981) ch. 6 (discussing attempts to prevent publication of his work suggesting the US government underestimated the health effects of ionising radiation).

25 L. Smolin, *The Trouble with Physics: The Rise of String Theory, and Fall of a Science and What Comes Next* (2008) (noting that within theoretical physics the proponents of dominant theories have stifled dissent and failed to acknowledge weaknesses in their own arguments).

26 A. Revkin, 'Climate Expert Says NASA Tried to Silence Him', *The New York Times* 29 January 2006 (noting attempts to silence a proponent of the view that human activity is a cause of global warming); S. Pincock, 'Australian agency denies gagging researchers', *Nature* 6 November 2009.

27 S. Rustin, 'Edzard Ernst: The Professor at War with the Prince', www.guardian.co. uk 30 July 2011; R. Booth, 'Prince Charles Health Charity Accused of Vendetta against Critic', www.guardian.co.uk 19 March 2010 (discussing hate mail and other attempts at silencing Professor Edzard Ernst who is a staunch critic of complimentary medicine).

28 M. Lefkowitz, *Not Out of Africa: How Afrocentrism Became an Excuse to Teach Myth as History* (1996) (noting accusations of racism directed at those challenging false Afrocentrist claims regarding Egyptian and Greek history).

29 For an example of such a phenomenon, see R. Feynman, *The Pleasure of Finding Things Out* (1999) 396. In a letter published following his death, Feynman wrote: 'It is fun to find things you thought you knew, and then to discover you didn't really understand it after all.' There are also examples in the scientific literature of scholars involved in 'acrimonious disputes' urging others to take their opponent's work 'seriously': G. Farmelo, *The Strangest Man: The Hidden Life of Paul Dirac, Quantum Genius* (2009) 100–1. However, scientific inquiry is also littered with examples of attempts to silence or otherwise punish dissenters. For discussion of this phenomenon, see M. Brooks, *Free Radicals: The Secret Anarchy of Science* (2011).

30 D.A. Downs, *Restoring Free Speech and Liberty on Campus* (2005) 107.

31 For a scholarly defence of this type of suppression, see H. Marcuse, 'Repressive Tolerance', in R.P. Wolff *et al*, *A Critique of Pure Tolerance* (1969) 119. Marcuse called for 'restraining the liberty of the Right' and intolerance of ideas 'destructive of the prospects for peace, justice, and freedom for all' as well as those 'opposing the extension of social legislation to the poor, weak, disabled' (at 133–4). He also proposed to 'do away with the sacred liberalistic principle of equality for "the other side"' arguing that on some issues 'there is no "other side"' (at 134).

32 Post, *supra* n. 12, 68 (quoting A.O. Lovejoy).

33 See K. Miller, *Finding Darwin's God: A Scientist's Search for Common Ground Between God and Evolution* (2002) ch. 2 (discussing the way in which scientific ideas relating to evolution have developed).

34 J. Le Rond D'Alembert, 'The Human Mind Emerged from Barbarism', in I. Kramnick (ed.), *The Portable Enlightenment Reader* (1995) 16.

35 B. Nyhan and J. Reifler, 'When Corrections Fail: The Persistence of Political Misperceptions', (2010) 32 *Polit. Behav.* 303.

36 See the acknowledgements section of this book for an example involving the reaction of one anonymous reviewer to the proposal for this text.

37 M. Bagaric and J. Clarke, *Torture: When the Unthinkable is Morally Permissible* (2007) 78. In his book, *The Pear Tree: Is Torture Ever Justified?* (2006), Eric Stener Carlson refers to the difficulties he had in finding a publisher for his work. He states that for some publishers: 'the topic just wasn't palatable (after all, torture doesn't "sell"). For others, merely discussing our susceptibility to torturing was to mention the unmentionable ... ' (at 95). See also M.S. Moore, 'Torture and the Balance of Evils', (1989) 23 *Isr. L.R.* 280, 344 ('I have been urged by some inside and outside of Israel not to publish this article. One ground for this has been that I am an outsider, one who does not have the direct experience with terrorism to appreciate the moral issues it poses, and for whom, in any event, this is "none of my business". ... A second ground urged by some has been that complex moral discussion like that contained in this article "will only get misused by the wrong people"').

38 K. Greenberg and J. Dratel (eds.), *The Torture Papers* (2005).

39 K. Greenberg and P. Sands, 'Torture and Accountability: Where Does President Obama Go from Here?', 3 November 2009, *London School of Economics*.

40 Bagaric and Clarke, *supra* n. 37, 78.

41 L. Rosenthal, 'Those Who Can't Teach: What the Legal Career of John Yoo Tells us about Who Should be Teaching Law', (2011) 80 *Miss. L.J.* 1563, 1632 (arguing 'individuals who claim to be able to teach students to practice law, but in fact cannot provide their own clients with defensible legal advice ... may well be incapable of teaching their students how to do so ... ').

42 S. Cottee and T. Cushman, 'The Suppression of Open Debate: The Case of Christopher Hitchens', (2008) 45 *Soc.* 397 (quoting the work of Harold Garfinkel).

43 J. Goldsmith, *The Terror Presidency: Law and Judgment Inside the Bush Administration* (2007) 27.

44 R. Norton-Taylor, 'Former Army Lawyer Urges End of "State Torture" to Prevent Future Abuses', www.guardian.co.uk 19 October 2012.

45 Hon. James R. Schlesinger, *The Report of the Independent Panel to Review DoD Detention Operations* (2004) 36.

46 C. Murray, *Murder in Samarkand: A British Ambassador's Controversial Defiance of Tyranny in the War on Terror* (2006) 138.

47 P. 't Hart, *Groupthink in Government: A Study of Small Groups and Policy Failure* (1990) 54–5.

48 P. Woodruff, *First Democracy: The Challenge of an Ancient Idea* (2006) ch. 8.

49 *per* Justice Brandeis in *Whitney* v. *California* 274 US 357 (1927).

50 S.L. Carter, *Civility: Manners, Morals and the Etiquette of Democracy* (1998) 122–3.

51 See, for example, N. MacMaster, 'Torture: from Algiers to Abu Ghraib', (2004) 46 *Race & Class* 1, 4. (reacting to American calls for the legalisation of torture, thus: 'That liberals and civil libertarians could go down such a road is symptomatic of the depth of the moral rot that has set into American society.'). In a review of Richard Posner's book *Not a Suicide Pact* (2006), Richard Mullender describes Posner as making a 'large assumption' that American culture is of 'intrinsic value' and that 'it is a short step from the assumption that a culture is intrinsically valuable to the conclusion that those who pose a threat to it are a "foe"', (2008) 35 *Journal of Law and Society* 422. It is worth reminding the reader that those posing a 'threat' in Mullender's words, are al Qaeda

and its allies. Successive US governments have regarded al Qaeda as a foe, not on the basis of an assumption of intrinsic value, but because of the group's acts of terrorism directed at the US targets and the murder of its citizens. J.K. Puar and A.S. Rai, 'Monster, Terrorist, Fag: The War on Terrorism and the Production of Docile Patriots', (2002) 20 *Social Text* 117, 135 (labelling Americans who supported their government's counter-terrorism policies or were insufficiently critical as 'normalized and docile patriots').

52 D. Manderson, 'Another Modest Proposal: In Defence of the Prohibition against Torture', in M. Gani and P. Mathew, *Fresh Perspectives in the 'War on Terror'* (2008) 53.

53 *Id.* n. 41.

54 G. Maslen, 'Make Torture Legal, Say Law Academics', *Times Higher Education* 27 May 2005 (referring to hate mail and criticism of Bagaric and Clarke's views by former Australian Prime Minister Malcolm Fraser).

55 M. Bagaric and J. Clarke, 'Tortured Responses (a Reply to our Critics): Physically Persuading Suspects is Morally Preferable to Allowing the Innocent to be Murdered', (2006) 40 *U.S.F.L. Rev* 703, 732.

56 A. Dershowitz, 'The Torture Warrant: A Response to Professor Strauss', (2003–4) 48 *N.Y.L. Sch. L. Rev.* 275, 275–6.

57 C. Gearty, 'Legitimising Torture – with a Little Help', *Index on Censorship* (2005).

58 C. Gearty, *Can Human Rights Survive?* (2006) 131 (arguing: 'the details [of the debate] matter less than the fact of the discussions … ').

59 *Id.*

60 L.M Seidman, 'Torture's Truth', (2005) 72 *U. Chi. L. Rev.* 881, 882–3.

61 *Id.* 884–5.

62 *Id.* 891.

63 J. Dratel, 'The Curious Debate' in K.J.Greenberg (ed.), *The Torture Debate in America* (2005) 116.

64 For an example of the latter phenomenon, see: A. Ristroph, 'Professors Strangelove', (2008) 11 *Green Bag* 245.

65 T. Paine, *The Age of Reason* (1794) vii.

66 S. Žižek, *Welcome to the Desert of the Real* (2002) 105–6.

67 British Broadcasting Corporation, *Conspiracy* (2004).

68 M. Roseman, *The Villa, the Lake, the Meeting: Wannsee and the Final Solution* (2003) 114.

69 A.M. Dershowitz, *Why Terrorism Works: Understanding the Threat, Responding to the Challenge* (2003) ch. 4.

70 *Id.* 158.

71 For a detailed analysis of this claim, see Brecher, *supra* n. 7.

72 O'Rourke, *supra* n. 6, 86.

73 P. Vidal-Naquet, *Torture: Cancer of Democracy* (1963); A. Horne, *A Savage War of Peace: Algeria 1954–1962* (2006).

74 See, for example, *Commission of Inquiry into the Methods of Investigation of the General Security Service Regarding Hostile Terrorist Activity* (1987).

75 For the involvement of US government agencies in torture, see A.W. McCoy, *A Question of Torture: CIA Interrogation, From the Cold War to the War on Terror* (2006); J.K. Harbury, *Truth, Torture, and the American Way: The History and Consequences of U.S. Involvement in Torture* (2005).

76 See, for example, *Report of the Committee of Privy Counsellors Appointed to Consider Authorised Procedures for the Interrogation of Persons Suspected of Terrorism* Cmnd. 4901 (1972).

77 See, for example, J. Ross, 'A History of Torture', in K. Roth *et al*, *Torture: Does it Make us Safer? Is it Ever OK? A Human Rights Perspective* (2005).

78 Gearty, *supra* n. 58, 132.

79 *Id.* 131–2. As a point of contradiction, two pages earlier Gearty refers to torture being 'integral to US foreign policy' and so was never unspoken (at 129). On this latter point, see McCoy, *supra* n. 75.

80 Benson and Stangroom, *supra* n. 11, 5.

81 M.D. Evans, 'Torture', (2006) 7 *EHRLR* 101, 105.

82 G. Kassimeris, 'The Warrior's Dishonour', in G. Kassimeris (ed.) *Warrior's Dishonour: Barbarity, Morality and Torture in Modern Warfare* (2006) 14.

83 E. Spicer, 'No Torture; No Debate', *New Law Journal* 14 December 2007, 1761.

84 Žižek, *supra* n. 66, 103–4. For other examples of this type of argument, see P. Rumney, 'Is Coercive Interrogation of Terrorist Suspects Effective? A Response to Bagaric and Clarke', (2006) 40 *U.S.F.L. Rev.* 479, 511, n. 149.

85 Žižek is favourably cited by Thomas P. Crocker, who argues that '[w]e should simply stop talking about torture' and that the types of consequentialist argument cited in the torture debate are not made 'about even selective mass killing' which would be 'beastly': 'Torture, With Apologies', (2008) 86 *Tex. L. Rev.* 569, 609. See also Brecher, *supra* n. 7, 2 (arguing that he 'respects' Žižek's view, but argues that 'present reality demands a direct response, despite [the] danger'); Steven Lukes responds to such arguments by pointing out: 'why should we think the protection of the purity of our consciences to be more important than facing up to hard questions?': 'Liberal Democratic Torture', (2005) 36 *B.J.Pol.S.* 1, 1; Henry Shue also argues that 'Pandora's box is open': 'Torture', in S. Levinson, *Torture: A Collection* (2004) 47.

86 For examples of Žižek's repeated discussion of this 'dangerous' topic, see S. Žižek, 'Are We in a War? Do We Have an Enemy?' *London Review of Books* 23 May 2002; S. Žižek, 'The Depraved Heroes of 24 are the Himmlers of Hollywood', www.guardian. co.uk 10 January 2006; S. Žižek, *Violence: Six Sideways Reflections* (2009) 35–8.

87 S. Žižek, *In Defense of Lost Causes* (2008) 50.

88 *Id.*

89 W. Daniel Hillis, 'The Idea that We Should All Share Our Most Dangerous Ideas', in J. Brockman (ed.), *What is Your Dangerous Idea? Today's Leading Thinkers on the Unthinkable* (2006) 41.

90 R. Shattuck, *Forbidden Knowledge: From Prometheus to Pornography* (1996) 222.

91 J. Milton, *Areopagitica* (1644) 18.

92 J. Cartwright, 'Unconventional Thinkers or Recklessly Dangerous Minds?' *Times Higher Education* 6–12 May 2010, 36.

93 P. Sands, *Torture Team: Uncovering War Crimes in the Land of the Free* (2009) 65 (quoting William Haynes, former General Counsel at the US Department of Defense who may have been referring to the work of Alan Dershowitz at Harvard Law School, thus 'I know there's some very good work going on in academia … highly coercive interrogation is the phrase I've heard up at Harvard'). In drafting memoranda authorising the use of coercive interrogation methods by the Central Intelligence Agency, John Yoo, a lawyer in the US Department of Justice Office of Legal Counsel, cited several scholarly sources, including Alan Dershowitz, as supposed authority for the claim that the doctrine of self-defence might be available to those using torture in the interrogation of terrorist suspects: US Department of Justice, Office of Professional Responsibility, *Investigation into the Office of Legal Counsel's Memoranda Concerning Issues Relating to the Central Intelligence Agency's Use of 'Enhanced Interrogation Techniques' on Suspected Terrorists* (2009) 221–3. The report dismisses the citation as providing no such authority (at 222).

94 For discussion of the flawed nature of this authority, see US Department of Justice *id.*

95 Dershowitz, *supra* n. 69, 163.

96 Evans, *supra* n. 81 and accompanying text.

97 I. Berlin, *The Power of Ideas* (ed. by H. Hardy, 2000) 214.

98 For discussion of the value of dissent and circumstances where it may have little value, see M. Tushnet, 'Why Societies Don't Need Dissent (as Such)', in A. Sarat (ed.), *Dissenting Voices in American Society: The Role of Judges, Lawyers, and Citizens* (2012) ch 5.

99 BBC, 'One-third Support "Some Torture"' www.bbc.co.uk/news 19 October 2006 (in a survey of 27,000 people in 25 countries a significant minority of participants

supported torture as a means of combating terrorism). See also the Introduction to this book n. 1.

100 H. Milner, *Civic Literacy: How Informed Citizens Make Democracy Work* (2002).

101 C. Pantazis and S. Pemberton, 'Reconfiguring Security and Liberty: Public Discourses and Public Opinion in the New Century,' (2012) 52 *B.J. Crim.* 651.

102 P.A.J. Waddington, 'Slippery Slopes and Civil Libertarian Pessimism', (2005) 15 *Policing & Society* 353.

103 I. Kant, 'What is Enlightenment?' in Kramnick, *supra* n. 34, 3.

104 *The Amnesty International Report 2010 The State of the World's Human Rights* (reporting that individuals suffered either torture or ill-treatment in 111 countries across the globe). The 2013 State of the World's Human Rights report lists several dozen states involved in torture and other forms of ill-treatment.

105 Of course, debating legalisation may result in false or weak ideas being repeated and reinforced in the minds of some people but in the view of this author, these are risks worth taking. The case for legalisation is already in the public domain and scholars have a particular responsibility to challenge false or weak ideas.

106 S. Fish, *The Trouble With Principle* (2001) 85.

107 Benson and Stangroom, *supra* n. 11, 10.

108 Of course, there is no guarantee of this, but unless arguments are put forward there is no basis upon which people of differing opinions can be convinced to change their minds.

109 For discussion, see G.E. White, 'Justice Holmes and the Modernization of Free Speech Jurisprudence: The Human Dimension', (1992) 80 *California Law Review* 391, 440. See also Menand, *supra* n. 14, 431.

110 For discussion, see P. Rumney and M. O'Boyle, 'A Tortured Debate', *New Law Journal* 25 January 2008, 121.

111 C.R. Sunstein, *Why Societies Need Dissent* (2003) 209.

112 V. Warren, 'Does Torture Work? Wrong Question!' *HuffPoliticsBlog* 21 December 2012.

113 *Id.*

114 G.W. Shulz, 'More Americans Support Torture to Fight Terrorism, Poll Finds', *Salon* 2 October 2012 (noting a 14% increase in support for the use of torture between 2005 and 2012).

115 Rasmussen, '58% Favor Waterboarding of Plane Terrorist To Get Information', 31 December 2009, http://www.rasmussenreports.com/public_content/politics/general_politics/december_2009/58_favor_waterboarding_of_plane_terrorist_to_get_information.

116 YouGov, '36% Favor, 38% Oppose Using Torture on Terror Suspects', (2012), http://today.yougov.com/news/2011/05/13/36-favor-38-oppose-using-torture-terror-suspects/.

117 For a detailed discussion of the Institute for Historical Review, see D. Lipstadt, *Denying the Holocaust: The Growing Assault on Truth and Memory* (1994) ch. 8.

118 This view is challenged: M. Shermer and A. Grobman, *Denying History: Who Says the Holocaust Never Happened and Why Do They Say It?* (2000) chs. 2 and 4.

119 *Id.* 69–74 (discussing the case of David Cole).

120 See, for example, the online article 'Confessions of a Former Holocaust Denier', http://skepchick.org/2013/07/holocaust (accessed 1 February 2014).

121 Shermer and Grobman, *supra* n. 118, 74.

122 J. Jedwab, 'Measuring Holocaust Knowledge and its Impact: A Canadian Case Study', (2010) 40 *Prospects* 273; P. Cowan and H. Maitles, 'Policy and Practice of Holocaust education in Scotland', (2010) 40 *Prospects* 257.

123 R.J. Evans, *Telling Lies About Hitler: The Holocaust, History and the David Irving Trial* (2002).

124 Shermer and Grobman, *supra* n. 118.

125 See, for example, *The Nizkor Project*: www.nizkor.org (accessed 1 February 2014).

126 Lipstadt, *supra* n. 117.
127 P. Duncan, '"Accurate and Irrefutable" Information Essential in Countering Holocaust Denial', *The Irish Times* 10 August 2013.
128 Shermer and Grobman, *supra* n. 118, 17.
129 M.S.-A. Wattad, 'The Torturing Debate on Torture', (2008) 29 *N.Ill.U.L. Rev.* 1, 2.
130 N. Chomsky, 'The Responsibility of Intellectuals', in T. Roszak (ed.), *The Dissenting Academy: Critical Essays on the American Intellectual Establishment* (1969) 255. See also R. Falk, 'Responsible Scholarship in "Dark Times"', (2008–9) 7 *U.C.L.A. J. Islamic & Near E. L. 1, 15* (suggesting that in a liberal society 'silence [in the face of dark times] is tantamount to acquiecence').
131 The role of political ideology in determining truth is becoming an increasing problem, particularly within the sciences: 'Decline and Fall', *New Scientist* 29 October 2011, 38 (discussing the impact of political ideology on scientific questions, such as the causes of climate change).
132 Brecher, *supra* n. 7, 3.

CONCLUSION

This book has set out a consequentialist argument against the legalisation of interrogational torture. The case against legalisation does not rest on a single argument or evidential claim. Instead, it is cumulative and involves a convergence of evidence. In times of crisis, it might be seen as superficially attractive to balance the absolute prohibition against the use of torture with security interests. However, this approach fails to consider a wealth of empirical evidence that suggests legalised interrogational torture would, in fact, grant state officials an expansive power which would be difficult to control and provide little discernable benefit. Leaving aside the tremendous difficulties that balancing presents, it seems likely that the costs of legalisation would be significant. There might, of course, be individual instances where torture provides such benefit that it would outweigh the harm caused to the tortured detainee in *that* case. However, this does not count the wider harms that legalised torture may cause, including social and institutional harms, along with the mobilisation of a violent backlash. Such consequences are particularly problematic because the proponents of legalisation make a legal policy argument that would create a torture power applicable beyond a single, never-to-be-repeated event.

In making the case that the legalisation of interrogational torture would grant the state an expansive power, this book has examined three core arguments used to justify legalisation. The first argument is based on the ticking bomb hypothetical in which it is suggested that if the police arrest a suspect who is deemed to have planted a ticking bomb, and refuses to disclose the location of the device, then the use of torture is justified to force compliance. Here, the various component parts of the hypothetical have all been expansively defined by proponents of legalisation and in the real world use of interrogational torture. The significance of the hypothetical, other than its use by proponents, is that all of these component parts (imminence, intelligence, nature of the threat and identity) would require incorporation into a statute-based torture law. Far from providing components that are narrowly focused on securing ticking bomb intelligence, the case for legalising interrogational torture rests on a flexible definition of these terms which gives state officials significant discretion. Hence the creation of an expansive power to torture.

The second argument is that torture is an effective means of gaining ticking bomb intelligence. The problem with this claim is that there is very little evidence that torture or other coercive methods can produce timely and accurate information in an emergency. Instead, there is a body of evidence suggesting that torture may produce infrastructure intelligence. This intelligence is very unlikely to prevent an imminent attack because it is more concerned with the organisational structure and the inner workings of terrorist groups. Infrastructure disclosures can help to undermine the ability of terrorist groups to operate effectively, so it may save lives in the longer term, but it has nothing to do with ticking bomb-type situations. If the use of interrogational torture were permitted in this wider context it would mean *every* terrorist suspect could be tortured – because all terrorists possess at least some knowledge of infrastructure. Indeed, an emphasis on consequences has already led to the use of torture and other coercive methods to gain infrastructure disclosures in various counter-terrorism operations including the CIA's HVD programme, Northern Ireland and Algeria. The fact that some proponents rely on these examples as supporting the case for the use or legalisation of interrogational torture is an indication of their overriding concern with a narrow range of consequences, rather than the creation of a tightly controlled torture power.

The third argument put forward by proponents is that interrogational torture can be targeted and controlled within a law-based regulatory regime. The actual use of interrogational torture and other forms of coercion, even when subject to legal restrictions and prohibitions, supports the view that it is an expansive power. This book has demonstrated that variables and narrowly drafted legal rules can be undermined by the mechanisms that cause slippage. The literature is rich with examples of misidentification, rule breaking and torture being used in counter-terrorism campaigns for reasons that have little to do with intelligence gathering. Likewise, the mechanisms that lead to slippage are common features. Stress, error, poor discipline and leadership, the failure to understand or follow rules and tolerance of abuse have all been identified in this book as causes of slippage. This contradicts the claim made by some proponents that there is no evidence of slippage in the use of interrogational torture in counter-terrorism campaigns, and no reason to believe torture could not be controlled within a legal regulatory framework. Even if one were to argue that interrogational torture could be adequately controlled, it leaves the case for torture resting on a claim of effectiveness that is so weak that the intelligence gains allegedly produced by torture are expanded to include infra-structure intelligence. The problem with this approach is that it expands the types of case in which torture could be legitimately used. Indeed, a committed con-sequentialist in favour of legalisation may have to support its use in infrastructure cases because infrastructure disclosures could, at some point in the future, create greater benefit than the cost of torturing a terrorist suspect. This hardly suggests a tightly controlled, rarely used state torture power.

The problem with the expanded-power argument set out in this book is that the reality of legalised interrogational torture may turn out different than is being suggested here. In order to reduce the possibility that the author has overstated the expansive-power argument, this book has critically examined the theoretical underpinnings of the case for legalisation and associated arguments, along with a large body of empirical evidence. However, this approach is not one-directional. Opponents of legalisation also make some weak arguments. For example, the claim that the ticking bomb hypothetical is fiction or a fraud fails when tested with evidence.[1] Instead, a better argument, which is supported by credible evidence, is that the component parts of the hypothetical are interpreted expansively in theory and practice. This is a far more problematic argument for the proponents of legalisation to address because it undermines the way in which they use the component parts of the hypothetical, along with their claim that torture can be effectively controlled.

To erode a high value, absolute right on the basis of theoretical and pragmatic arguments without concern for clear limiting principles, and in the absence of strong empirical data, is not a basis for fundamental legal change. The use of empirical evidence, of course, carries with it a degree of uncertainty. This has led Posner and Vermeule to argue that 'the simplest starting point is to *assume* that law should regulate coercive interrogation within the same type of framework that law uses to regulate similar activities'[2] (emphasis added). This is a far from simple approach and would have major implications for law, state institutions, human rights and society. Given the dangers of legalisation and the high value status of the prohibition it is the proponents of change who shoulder the heavy burden of making a convincing case for creating an exception to the absolute prohibition. In this way, we avoid the creation of a state torture power that would contribute to the 'great evil of adding unnecessarily to [the state's] power'[3] and the many problematic consequences that this would produce.

There is another good reason not to allow the legalisation of interrogational torture. There are certain events that are so unlikely to occur that it would be foolish to legislate on the basis of such a possibility. This is not to fall into the denial-of-reality problem exhibited by many of the critics of the ticking bomb hypothetical discussed in Chapter 2. It is to point out, for example, that the theft or construction of a weapon of mass destruction, such as a credible nuclear device by a terrorist group, while certainly possible, is very unlikely.[4] In making this argument, however, it must be acknowledged, that the consequentialist case for torture does not require such an extreme threat in order for torture to be seen as morally justified. Using the consequentialist arguments discussed in this book, a ticking nuclear weapon could justify torture against innocent family members, children or a hospital ward full of babies if that is what forced the disclosure of intelligence. Even in the case of a much lesser threat, it is difficult to see what harm would not be justified so long as its infliction was seen as outweighed by any benefit. Of course, restrictions could be imposed by law, but as noted in earlier chapters, statutory language would likely grant state officials an expansive power.

As soon as the door to torture is opened, it is clear from the evidence discussed in this book that in theory and practice rules are the subject of expansive interpretation and a desire to achieve consequentialist goals.

The book has also sought to defend the debate and discussion of legalisation on the basis of classical free speech theory. It is perhaps ironic that some scholars who wish to defend human rights and the absolute prohibition have also attacked the right to engage in debate. They have sought through assertion, name-calling or other means to dissuade scholars and others from engaging with this topic. This approach is deeply problematic. The intellectual origins of rationality and liberty were developed in order to create intellectual space for the free exploration of ideas.[5] Despite this rich history and its foundational importance to liberal democracy, Enlightenment values are attacked by both sides of the torture debate. The proponents of legalisation seek a return to a time when torture was legally sanctioned; something leading Enlightenment thinkers sought to challenge in Europe.[6] On the other side, some of the opponents of legalisation are prepared to abandon the defence of free speech and reason offered by Enlightenment thinkers such as Kant and D'Alembert and replace them with attempts to silence dissent and a rejection of the use of rational argument to persuade others.

This book rejects the attempt to silence debate on this topic and suggestions that discussing legalisation opens the door to its legitimisation. Such an approach serves to undermine the case against legalisation by depriving the absolute prohibition of a defence at a time when more speech is needed to develop stronger arguments based on empirical evidence, not enforced silence for fear that discussion is dangerous. Indeed, the words and behaviour of some scholars in the torture debate exhibits the characteristics of what Rauch has described as 'fundamentalism', the 'strong disinclination to take seriously the notion that you might be wrong'.[7] Ultimately, the absolute prohibition should be defended on the basis of rational, evidence-based argument, not on insults and false claims that should not convince anyone of anything. Such an approach gives in to emotion and anger in the same way the proponents, particularly in the aftermath of 9/11, were swept along by a panic and the idea that torture was an answer to a complex problem, without properly considering the weakness of their proposals for eroding the absolute prohibition.

As a result of these concerns, this book has endeavoured to be even-handed to the extent that arguments on both sides of the debate have been critically examined. At times, in the torture debate it would appear any factual claim or related argument will suffice if it can be utilised in favour of a particular viewpoint. In this book, arguments have been critically analysed so as to identify weaknesses so they can either be discarded or refined until they become more persuasive. Of course, this approach may create the risk that it will undermine the absolute prohibition – if that were true, it would not be a reason to stop the debate; it would be reason to reconsider the prohibition. However, this book has strongly argued for the retention of the prohibition while warning of the dangers of relying on arguments that are weak, misleading or untrue. Daniel Patrick Moynihan made the point succinctly: 'Everyone is entitled to their own opinions, but they are not entitled to their own facts.'[8] In this way, this book has criticised arguments made by proponents *and* opponents of legalisation and concluded that the retention of the absolute prohibition is not only justified, but essential.

So what of the future? The phenomenon of democratic torture and the debate over its use and legalisation did not begin with 9/11, nor did it end with the election of President Barack Obama. It would be naïve to think that the argument over legalisation is over. That is a lesson of history. Scholars continue to propose the legalisation of interrogational torture in some form or another,[9] state officials in many countries continue to torture and democratically elected politicians continue to advocate tactics such as waterboarding[10] or explore ways of evading the absolute prohibition.[11] This is a reminder of the importance of responding to these developments with rational, evidence-based argument. As long as states torture, endeavour to evade the absolute prohibition and these actions attract public support, the case against torture must be articulated.

However, what if the *what if* question actually arose and the state was facing a concrete threat of nuclear terrorism, that would lead to the death of many thousands and state officials had little time to discover the ticking bomb? Is there any point at which the interests of the potential victims of terrorism override the interests of a terrorist suspect? As a matter of law, this author maintains that the absolute prohibition must stand. The state has a wide range of lawful powers available to it to investigate crime. If a city faces the prospect of the detonation of a nuclear weapon then we come back to the same problems discussed throughout this text. If conventional policing fails, what to do? What if torture is used and does not work? Is that the end? What if the state tortures a suspect's two-year-old child and that does not work? Is that the end? What if a state official starts shooting his family members one-by-one and that does not work? Is that the end? What if the man's wife is raped? What if … ? Talk of torture, should not blind us to such possibilities. Why would torture of a terrorist suspect be only the end and not the beginning of more desperate and barbarous acts? This is a question that demands an answer from the proponents of legalisation. However, it does not deal directly with the original question.

If police officers or other state officials took the law into their own hands and tortured the suspected nuclear terrorist, then those officials should be subject to criminal prosecution. However, their actions should attract heavy mitigation in sentencing (assuming guilt was established). Mitigation would be very likely in such an extreme case.[12] Indeed, the sentencing of criminal defendants often involves differentiating between defendants in cases involving the deliberate infliction of serious harm. This reflects the fact that there is a moral difference between an interrogator who inflicts pain to save life in an extreme emergency and someone who inflicts pain for the purpose of sadistic pleasure. The sadist has no concern for others and his actions cause harm with no discernible benefit, except to himself. He is not acting in extreme circumstances or endeavouring to minimise harm – in fact, he is doing the exact opposite. It would be perverse for the courts not to take into account these factors in sentencing in order to clearly differentiate between these two cases.

Of course, prosecutors may even decide not to prosecute on the basis that such a case was a 'one-off' or as a result of public and political pressure. However, such an approach would create the danger of endorsing future interrogational torture by state officials. One thing that should not happen however, is that an exception to the absolute prohibition should be created for such an extraordinarily rare event and on the basis of such a limited body of empirical evidence. Even if such an exception were created, there is no reason to believe the state would act with any more restraint or respect for the rule of law than it would under the current law. A democratic state, with a commitment to human rights should not institutionalise the disregard for the very same values that state officials accuse the terrorist of violating.

Notes

1 More often than not, those who claim the hypothetical is a fiction or fraud appear to make no effort to search out supporting or contradictory evidence in order to test their particular factual claims. It is perhaps fortunate that proponents of legalised torture have not been more rigorous in targeting such weaknesses.

2 E.A. Posner and A. Vermeule, *Terror in the Balance: Security, Liberty, and the Courts* (2007) 214.

3 J.S. Mill, *On Liberty and Other Essays* (1998) 122.

4 For a brief discussion of nuclear terrorism, see Chapter 1, nn 67, 70.

5 J. Israel, *A Revolution of the Mind: Radical Enlightenment and the Intellectual Origins of Modern Democracy* (2009) ch. 1.

6 While Enlightenment thinkers are credited with helping to end judicial torture in Europe, Langbein argues that it ended as a result of the erosion of the Roman-canon law of proof and the use of evidential standards that did not require the use of torture to gain convictions: J.H. Langbein, *Torture and the Law of Proof: Europe and England in the Ancien Régime* (2006).

7 J. Rauch, *Kindly Inquisitors: The New Attacks on Free Thought* (1993) 89.

8 This is one of a number of similar quotes attributed to Moynihan which are available online via Wikipedia: http://en.wikiquote.org/wiki/Daniel_Patrick_Moynihan (accessed 1 February 2014).

9 F. Allhoff, 'Torture Warrants, Self-Defence, and Necessity', (2013) 11 *Cardozo Pub. L. Pol'y & Ethics J.* 421.

10 'John McCain Hits GOP Hopefuls over Waterboarding', http://.cbsnews.com 14 November 2012.

11 In 2005, UK Home Secretary, Charles Clarke, in reference to the ECHR, stated: 'in developing these human rights it really is necessary to balance very important rights for individuals against the collective right for security against those who attack us through terrorist violence.' Speech to the European Parliament on 7 September 2005. More recently, Justice Minister, Chris Grayling, and Home Secretary, Theresa May, have made public statements which would suggest a wish to weaken the absolute prohibition in cases involving the removal of foreign terrorist suspects from the UK: C. Hope and T. Ross, 'Abu Qatada: Tories to Fight Next Election on Wholesale Human Rights Reform, Says Chris Grayling', www.telegraph.co.uk 14 July 2013.

12 For an excellent analysis of the *Gäfgen* v. *Germany* case, see: S. Greer, 'Should Police Threats to Torture Suspects Always be Severely Punished? Reflections on the *Gäfgen* Case', (2011) 11 *Human Rights Law Review* 67 (disagreeing with the majority of the *Gäfgen* court who suggested that the police officers threatening a suspect with torture should not be treated leniently).

INDEX

Yaghmour, Jihad 62
Yoo, John 183
Yveton, Fernand 61

Zarqawi, Abu Mousab al 115n91
Zižek, Slavoj 185–6

zombie invasion 63, 76n211
Zubaydah, Abu: intelligence gained
from 97–8, 108; value as detainee
117n142; waterboarding of 26, 94–5,
97–9, 107, 148; and HVD
programme 93